Volume Two

# OF CIVILIZATION

*Seventeenth Century*

*to the Present*

*Prentice-Hall, Inc., Englewood Cliffs, New Jersey*

*Library of Congress Cataloging in Publication Data*

Main entry under title:

A Handbook of civilization.

    CONTENTS: v. 1. Earliest times to the seventeenth
century.—v. 2. Seventeenth century to the present.
    1. Civilization—History.   I. Merrill, George D.
[CB59.H36]      901.9      73-23075
ISBN 0-13-377135-0 (v. 1)
ISBN 0-13-377143-1 (v. 2)

Volume Two

# A HANDBOOK OF CIVILIZATION

Seventeenth Century to the Present

George Merrill
William S. Holley
Donald J. Haley
Nadine Hata
Richard Clark

Printed in the United States of America

10  9  8  7  6  5  4  3  2  1

PRENTICE-HALL INTERNATIONAL, INC., *London*
PRENTICE-HALL OF AUSTRALIA, PTY. LTD., *Sydney*
PRENTICE-HALL OF CANADA, LTD., *Toronto*
PRENTICE-HALL OF INDIA PRIVATE LIMITED, *New Delhi*
PRENTICE-HALL OF JAPAN, INC., *Tokyo*

This book is lovingly dedicated to

      Jan
      Peggie
      Debbie
      Don

# Credits

# Contents

# Preface

It seems to the authors that there has never been a time in history when man has been more in need of both retrospective vision and breadth of vision—the ability to see "far back" to his primal roots as well as the ability to view and appreciate a wide variety of peoples and societies. *A Handbook of Civilization* is neither an outline nor a compendium but is rather a compact, factual, narrative account of the salient features of the history of the world's peoples from their primordial beginnings to the present. It is sufficiently comprehensive for the student and the instructor to depend upon for basic factual coverage, and yet is short enough to leave room for instructional elaboration and interpretation plus the added enrichment of outside reading assignments. It is hoped that the inclusion of individual chapter outlines, chapter overviews and summaries, and subheadings throughout the text will make for more efficient reading and for greater comprehension of substance.

The primary emphasis of this book is on the major civilizations that have emerged from the Eurasian land mass. Only the limitations of space prevented us from more fully exploring the indigenous civilizations of both Africa and the Americas. The reader will note, however, that as these areas of the globe have come to play an increasingly important role in world affairs in modern times, they have been given correspondingly greater attention in the text.

We wish to acknowledge the assistance received in preparing this book. Special appreciation is given to our fellow instructors at El Camino College, particularly Myron L. Kennedy and Robert C. Putzel. We also gratefully recognize the contributions of Marshall F. Johnson. Finally, the authors extend their heartfelt gratitude to Helen Puckett, without whose sympathetic and dedicated aid this work might not have been completed.

Volume Two

# A HANDBOOK OF CIVILIZATION

*Seventeenth Century to the Present*

# 14

# Absolutism—
# Asserted and
# Denied

The Scientific Revolution
   Universe
   The Quest for Scientific Absolutes: Bacon, Descartes, and Newton
Science and Religion
Rise of Absolutists
   Jean Bodin
   Jacques Bossuet
   Thomas Hobbes
   Mercantilism
Absolutism Denied
   John Locke
Summary

European political history from the Peace of Westphalia to approximately 1720 is identified as the Age of Absolutism. Rulers such as Louis XIV of France, Leopold of Austria, Frederick William the Great Elector of Brandenburg–Prussia, and Peter the Great of Russia were increasing their individual powers and the powers of the dynastic state. Hence, political absolutism, at least partially and theoretically, was being asserted in many lands. On the other hand, royalist absolutism for a variety of reasons was not as successful in other nations such as England and Poland. Concurrent with political absolutism were new intellectual currents. The inadvertent thrust of the scientific revolution and the new theories in economics and political science were to heighten the forces for secularization. By 1720, one could indeed recognize that secular authority in European politics and in European thought had steadily increased.

The years from 1648 to approximately 1720 in European history are generally characterized as the Age of Absolutism. During this period, one discerns the rise of the dynastic state under increasingly more powerful monarchs who come to dominate within their own lands and to threaten both their neighbors and the peace of Europe.

In many ways, absolutism is an apt term to describe the political development in such states as France, Russia, or Brandenburg-Prussia. However, in other lands, such as England or Poland, absolutism did not always apply to the political situation. As a matter of caution, one should further bear in mind that even in the most absolutist state no ruler—neither a Peter the Great nor a Louis XIV—could exercise undisputed control; for inadequate means of transportation and communication, coupled with diehard traditionalism or localism, served as checks to thwart and limit the royal will. Absolutism, in other words, indicated more the desires of the ruler than the political realities.

Dividing Europe geographically into West and East, we shall examine countries that show some of the techniques and methods by which the internal might of rulers was increased or decreased. Further, we shall see how internal circumstances increased international tensions and warfare. Later in the chapter, in order to place the politics of this era in its wider environment, the intellectual currents of the Age of Absolutism will be discussed.

### Louis XIV's France

Although Louis XIV probably never made the famous remark ascribed to him by Voltaire—"I am the state" (*l'état, c'est moi*), there was a grain of truth in the phrase. Louis, indeed, took his duties as king quite seriously. God had appointed him as king and Louis, therefore, had to shoulder the awesome burden of state decisions.

The king stood at the head of the government, but men who enjoyed his confidence served on the royal councils (councils of state, dispatches, finances, and the privy council). The councilors at the top and the intendants at the lower level supervised and implemented the royal will. While these bureaucrats exercised a degree of latitude in making decisions, ultimate authority, of course, always rested with the king himself.

### Colbert

Perhaps the most prominent individual in Louis' government was Jean-Baptiste Colbert, minister of finances and internal affairs. It was his task to raise the revenues for Louis' expenses. In constant need of new money, Colbert is credited with devising and implementing the economic philosophy of mercantilism; he also tried to make France a major naval power. However, Colbert was never totally successful in his financial solutions or projects, primarily because of Louis' indifference or unwillingness to give his minister a free hand.

### Court Life

Although Richelieu and Mazarin had removed impediments to royal authority, opposition to the crown was still possible. As a means of asserting his power, Louis chose to conduct himself in such a way as to instill awe in the grandeur of the king's person. Therefore, Louis developed and insisted upon strict court ritual which determined all social intercourse with the king, the royal family, and royal officials. To reinforce his godlike demeanor, the king was determined to be housed in a new, grandiose palace; thus the incredibly beautiful and expensive palace at Versailles was built.

Nobles flocked to Versailles, there to vie for privileges that appear senseless to the modern reader, such as holding the king's britches or shirt. Yet, these empty distinctions served to keep the nobles under the watchful eye of the crown and out of mischief. Furthermore, the proximity of the nobles to the king was an avenue for a royal pension or political and social advancement. For these rewards many were quite willing to play the etiquette game at Versailles.

### Huguenots

Perhaps one of the most controversial internal decisions made by Louis XIV was the revocation of his grandfather's Edict of Nantes in 1685. It should be pointed out that Louis bore the title of "Most Christian Majesty" and he considered himself a devout Catholic. Now

**Figure 14-1.** Louis XIV. Portrait by Rigaud, 1707.

whether this fully explains his actions or not is debatable. Nevertheless, the revocation drove an estimated 200,000 Protestants from France to England, Holland, Prussia, and the New World. In their adopted homelands the Huguenots made many contributions, and in exile became bitter foes of their former homeland.

### The Spanish Hapsburgs

The Hapsburg lands, particularly the Spanish, witnessed a decline in the Age of Absolutism.

Ever since the reign of Charles V, the Hapsburgs had been the most powerful European dynasty. Their domains included Austria, Bohemia, Belgium, Spain, Portugal, Franche-Comté, Sicily, Naples, Milan, and innumerable overseas possessions. By the seventeenth century the Hapsburgs had evolved into two major branches, the Spanish and Austrian, and political contact between the two branches was maintained through constant intermarriage.

During and after the Thirty Years' War the Spanish monarchy was buffeted from within and without. Spanish resources and men failed to suppress the Portuguese revolt from 1637 to 1668. Although it successfully put down the Catalonians (1640–1652), the Neapolitans (1647), and the Sicilians (1675–1676), the Spanish monarchy was in poor straits. In addition, the Treaty of the Pyrenees in 1659 saw France replace Spain as Europe's leading power. This treaty turned over to France land long claimed by Spain, and gave Philip IV's daughter, Marie Thérèse, as bride to Louis XIV.

**Charles II.**    Philip IV died in 1665. His heir was the pitiful Charles II, who to everyone's surprise clung to life for the next thirty-five years despite his physical and mental disabilities. His death brought to an end the Spanish branch of the Hapsburg line. From 1665 onwards the key international question in the West was: Who would acquire the Spanish inheritance when Charles II died?

### England, Encroachments on Royal Power

#### Restoration
In 1660, Charles II, son of the executed Charles I, returned to England. After twenty years, monarchy was again restored; consequently Charles's reign of twenty-five years was known as the Restoration.

In its sentiments, the new Parliament that met was pro-royalist and pro-Anglican. This Cavalier Parliament, destined to sit for a number of years, passed laws reflecting its attitudes. The Clarendon Code, for instance, established the primacy of the Anglican Church and restricted the rights of those who refused to conform to its principles. The Test Act of 1672, further, prevented Catholics and Protestant dissenters from holding political office.

**Treaty of Dover.**    No matter how sympathetic his parliaments were to him, they never provided Charles with enough funds to finance his extravagances. As a result, Charles turned to his former host in exile the king of France. By the secret Treaty of Dover in 1670, Louis XIV agreed to provide Charles with subsidies and, if necessary, troops to ensure the king of England's independence from Parliament.

**Succession.**    However, the chief political concern of Charles's reign revolved around the succession. Despite his many children, not one was legitimate. This meant that the king's brother, James, would become king. James, the Duke of York, was a Roman Catholic. Almost all shades of Protestants, from Anglicans to Calvinists, shuddered at the prospect of a Catholic sitting on the throne. An attempt was made by Parliament to deprive James of his royal rights even before he became ruler. This failed, but Titus Oates aroused the hysteria of the nation by "uncovering" a Popish plot to kill Charles and place James on the throne. However, this political tempest soon passed.

### James II

By the time of Charles' death most Englishmen had reconciled themselves to the inevitability of James becoming their king. This they could accept, for James would be succeeded by his Protestant daughter, Mary—wed to the Calvinist William III of the Dutch Netherlands. But in 1688, James II's second (and Catholic) wife gave birth to a son. Now it appeared as if Anglican England was fated to be ruled by a Catholic dynasty.

### Glorious Revolution

James' son-in-law feared that a Catholic English king would be forever aligned with Catholic and Absolutist France, thereby threatening the peace of Europe. William, with an invitation from influential men in both parties, landed in England with 15,000 troops. It looked as if England would again be plunged into a civil war. Yet, for some inexplicable reason, James II chose to flee with his family to France. This act was interpreted as an abdication and Parliament, conveniently overlooking James's son, named William and Mary as rulers of England. These events are collectively known as the Glorious Revolution of 1688.

### Bill of Rights

The Glorious Revolution was politically important. A series of laws came from Parliament that ultimately altered the future of that island country. The Bill of Rights, passed in December, 1689, protected Englishmen from royalist absolutism such as arbitrary arrest, imprisonment, and cruel punishment. It further included the principle that the monarchy must secure Parliament's consent to levy taxes or suspend laws. Religious toleration was extended to all Christians except for Catholics and Unitarians. This Act of Toleration laid to rest much of the religious controversy that had plagued the land since the reign of Henry VIII.

The significance of these and other enactments was immense. William and Mary, and later Mary's sister Queen Anne, ruled at least partially due to the grace of Parliament. That body was now catapulted to a greater political role. As seen above, it passed laws limiting royal power politically and socially. In 1701, by the Act of Settlement, it even selected the future dynasty of England—the German Hanoverians (1714–1901). Indeed, Parliament was becoming the arbiter of England's destiny.

### Dynastic Wars

It would appear that there were two major considerations in Louis XIV's foreign policy: insurance of Bourbon dynastic rights and the attainment of defensive frontiers (Alps, Pyrenees, the Rhine) for France. And it so happened that these two principles were enmeshed with the Spanish question.

#### Dutch War

The Spanish question was indeed at the center of the wars which disrupted the late seventeenth century. The War of Devolution (1667–1668) was initiated by Louis' dynastic claims to part of the Spanish inheritance after the death of Philip IV in 1665. The Dutch War (1672–1678) may be explained in part by Louis' anger toward the Dutch for allying against him in the Devolution struggle. After the Dutch War, Louis tried a new tack to acquire lands near the Rhine. Courts of Reunion were set up to determine whether France could legitimately lay claim to certain lands. Naturally, these courts backed by French military power justified the vaguest French claims.

#### League of Augsburg

These courts resulted in a decade-long war. The War of the League of Augsburg (1688–1697) saw Spain, Dutch Holland, England, Austria, and numerous Holy Roman states fighting against France both in the Old and New Worlds until 1698.

#### Spanish Succession

Attempts made by Louis XIV and William III to prevent a renewed outbreak of hostilities over the Spanish question failed. When Charles II died in late 1700, his will designated Louis' grandson as heir to all Spanish Hapsburg lands. The War of the Spanish Succession followed. Except for Spain, the sides were the same as in the previous war.

The Treaty of Utrecht, 1712–1713, left France exhausted and economically drained, but a Bourbon sat on the Spanish throne. Although his hopes for territory along the frontier were only partially realized, Louis was successful in insuring his family's rights. In 1714, Louis died and for approximately a generation peace descended upon the West.

### Eastern Europe: States in Decline

In Eastern Europe from 1648 to 1721 three dynastic states became powerful both internally and internationally—Austria, Brandenburg-

Prussia, and Russia. With the ascendancy of these three states, Sweden and Poland, two previously powerful states, fell into decline.

### Sweden

During and following the Thirty Years' War, Gustavus Adolphus and his minister Oxenstierna had built Sweden into a major European power. The Treaty of Westphalia and further military successes awarded Sweden vast territories circling the Baltic. But Sweden possessed lands coveted by her neighbors. The exhaustive Great Northern War, 1700–1721, saw Poland, Russia, Denmark, Hanover, and Brandenburg-Prussia allied against Sweden. Despite the brilliant generalship of Charles XII, the Treaty of Nystad reduced Sweden to a minor power.

### Poland

Poland's fate was even more tragic. The Polish kingdom, which was once one of Europe's largest, gradually and inexorably lost land to its neighbors. For example, White Russia and part of the Ukraine went to Russia by the Treaty of Androssovo in 1667. Even the small state of Brandenburg won Polish recognition of full control over East Prussia in 1660. During the Great Northern War and the Seven Years' War, 1756–1763, Poland was a constant battlefield for foreign armies.

These external problems were compounded by Poland's internal difficulties. Polish kings were elected. Polish nobles dickered for concessions from each prospective candidate for the monarchy. In the Polish Diet each nobleman held veto power over the proceedings. Government was paralyzed. Should a Polish king attempt to impose his will over the nobles, they could appeal to foreign rulers for outside assistance. By the middle of the eighteenth century, the Kingdom of Poland, for all practical purposes, had become an aristocratic republic which survived only by the sufferance of its neighbors. However, once Austria, Brandenburg-Prussia, and Russia agreed to end Poland's existence that nation ceased to be, until its revival at the end of World War I.

### Eastern Europe: Emerging States

#### Imperial Austria

Seemingly, the Treaty of Westphalia had clipped the power of the Austrian Hapsburgs. The title of Holy Roman Emperor held prestige, but little political punch. Westphalia allowed the petty German states to make alliances with powers outside the empire. This, coupled with the presence of French, Swedish, and Danish representatives at the Imperial *Reichstag*, served to preclude any concerted move by the Hapsburg emperor to reassert political power within the empire. Yet, the Austrian

Hapsburgs were destined to fare much better than their Spanish relatives. Thwarted in the north, the Hapsburgs looked in another direction. Under Leopold (1658–1705), the foundations were laid for a multinational Dunubian monarchy that remained under the Hapsburgs until 1918.

**Ottoman Conflict.**    Hapsburg expansion came as a result of the Ottoman menace. The Ottoman Empire reached deeply into Central Europe and included all of the Balkan peninsula and most of the Hungarian plain. A thin slice of Hungary was indeed under Hapsburg control, but the ever-rebellious Magyar nobility tried to play Hapsburg against Ottoman in order to preserve their "liberties." Sooner or later, a showdown had to come.

During the mid-seventeenth century, Austria had to cope with a renewed military threat from the Ottoman Turks. The Köprülü family won the confidence of the Sultans and dreamed of reasserting Turkish power. The high point of Köprülü power came with the siege of Vienna in 1683. But the Turks failed to capture Leopold's capital and from that time on were driven ever southward. By 1699, Leopold signed the Treaty of Karlowitz. The Turks ceded all of Hungary and Transylvania to the Hapsburgs. Nineteen years later the Turks again confirmed Austrian ownership of these lands.

In the meantime, Leopold had asserted his political power inside his domains. The individual governments of his diverse lands were concentrated in Vienna. The rights of the nobles were subordinated to Hapsburg interest. With the removal of the Turkish menace, the Magyar nobles could no longer appeal to an outside power for redress against their sovereign. As a result, the Austrians were ready to play another powerful role in European affairs.

### Brandenburg–Prussia

While the Austrian Hapsburgs were consolidating their power through struggles with the Turks, the small electorate of Brandenburg under the Hohenzollerns was becoming a consideration in Holy Roman and European affairs.

**Frederick William.**    By the end of the Thirty Years' War, Frederick William, the Great Elector (1640–1688), was the Hohenzollern ruler. It was he who laid the basis for his dynasty's later greatness. His domains were in three widely separated parts: centered around Berlin was the core, the electorate of Brandenburg; to the west along the Rhine was the county of Cleves and its dependencies; and to the east on the Baltic, surrounded by Poland, was the duchy of East Prussia. The diversity of these lands made them extremely vulnerable to attack.

**Army.** To protect his inheritance Frederick William found it necessary to build and maintain a large army. Since he lacked the financial resources to do this, the Great Elector came to rely upon the noble (Junker) class as the basis for his military machine. To convince the Junkers to do this willingly, Frederick William made a "deal" with them. In exchange for supporting the construction of a Hohenzollern army, the Junkers were given free reign over their lands and their inhabitants. In other words, the agricultural inhabitants of Hohenzollern lands no longer could appeal to electoral protection and were now at the mercy of their Junker lords.

In his quests for revenues to finance his army, Frederick William came into conflict with the various representative estates in his domains. He did not shrink from using cajolery, threats, bribery, or, at least in one instance, kidnapping to get his way. The upshot was that the estates lost their political powers during his reign.

The Hohenzollern army came to be a major consideration in eastern European politics. At the Battle of Fehrbellin in 1675 it even defeated the Swedish army. This army enabled the Great Elector to add Eastern Pomerania and other territories to his domains. Further, by the Treaty of Oliva (1660) Poland gave up any further claims to East Prussia.

The army aided the Hohenzollerns in other ways. In times of peace, the soldiers could be put to work on the dynasty's farms raising not only crops, but further funds for the ruler's coffers. Its officers could be placed in the state's bureaucracy as loyal servants to the dynasty. Also, since the army was the only institution common to the three separate lands it became a cement to unify the lands under the Hohenzollerns.

Frederick William also concerned himself with domestic matters: agriculture was encouraged, swamps were drained, and canals constructed. Brandenburg began to lose its nickname as the "sandbox" of the Empire. Much of this was due to the influx of some 20,000 immigrants who came mostly from Holland and France. The Great Elector welcomed them and insisted that they be accorded religious toleration.

**Frederick I.** Frederick William's son and heir was Frederick I (1688–1713). Frederick was instrumental in enhancing the Hohenzollerns in other ways. He supervised the remodeling of Berlin and patronized the arts. Although he emulated Louis XIV, some say that he hoped to make the Hohenzollern lands the "Athens of the North."

However, Frederick I's most important contribution occurred in 1701. On that date, at Königsberg, the capital of East Prussia, he was crowned "King in Prussia." This title made the Hohenzollerns now only second to the Hapsburgs in the Empire. Gradually, the name "Prussia," because of the title of kingship that went with it, came to be applied to all Hohenzollern lands.

Despite his interest in the arts, culture, and prestige, Frederick did not ignore the army, which increased from his father's 30,000 to 40,000. He also found the army a convenient source for raising revenue; on occasion, he rented it to his neighbors.

### Peter the Great's Russia

Alexis, the second czar of the Romanov dynasty, died in 1676. He left three sons behind: two by his first wife, Maria Miloslavski, and Peter by his second wife, Natalie Naryshkin. Feodor III's reign ( 1676–1682) was characterized by a struggle between the Miloslavski and Naryshkin factions.

Upon the death of Feodor, his sister Sophia declared herself regent and named her younger brother Ivan, an imbecile, czar. Sophia's allies were the *streltsi* (palace guards) who subjected the Naryshkin faction to a blood bath. However, Sophia did not dare harm young Peter or his mother. Instead, she sent them into exile to the village of Preobranshenskoe on the outskirts of Moscow.

**Young Peter.** This act of Sophia's was highly significant. It meant that Peter would be exposed to influences no future czar had before experienced. Peter grew up fairly unattended, roamed the streets of Moscow at will, and came into contact with all sorts of "undesirable" elements that were very influential on his life and ideas. For example, the foreigners Gordon and Le Fort informed him of technological advances in Western Europe; another, A. Menshikov, a former pie salesman, became a major adviser to him.

Peter gathered dedicated followers around himself and he and his youthful companions played "war games." As a consequence, the Preobranshenskoe regiment dedicated to serving Peter developed. Basing his support on this group and other dissatisfied elements in Russia, in 1689, Peter seized the government. With his half-sister in a convent and the *streltsi* in check, Peter was now czar.

**Westernizing.** Peter spent the first years of his reign consolidating his government. When he felt that matters were firmly in control, he left Russia to tour the Continent. Traveling incognito (although almost everyone recognized the foreign giant with red hair), he visited Western Europe and saw at firsthand the "wonders" of the West. In his absence, the *streltsi* revolted and tried to restore Sophia to power. Peter rushed back home and broke the power of the *streltsi* through public executions.

Under Peter, Russia was altered. He forced the Russians to look more to the European West than to the Asiatic East by breaking many social habit patterns. He introduced Western clothing styles and tried to bring women into social functions. His attempts to make the Russian

**Figure 14-2.** Peter the Great.

males shave their life-time growth of whiskers made him the most famous barber in history.

Peter also tried to control the most powerful groups in his lands. He reclassified the nobles into a Table of Ranks, making all nobles subject to duties to the Crown. He furthermore turned on the Russian Church which he felt was the most reactionary institution in Russia. The office of Patriarch was abolished and replaced by a Holy Synod whose members he appointed.

**Foreign Affairs.** Peter's design in foreign affairs was to strengthen Russia's role internationally. He waged war successfully on the Turks and acquired a foothold on the Black Sea, further whetting Russia's appetite for Constantinople.

In 1700, Russia participated in the Great Northern War against Charles XII's Sweden. Despite his defeat at the Battle of Narva, Peter's victory over the Swedes at Poltava in 1709 broke Charles' military might. The Treaty of Nystad (1721) awarded Peter his coveted "window on the West" where he built the new capital of St. Petersburg.

The thirty-six years of Peter's rule changed the whole course of Russian, if not European, history. Although Peter was not completely successful in all that he attempted, Russia had become an important consideration in international affairs. From his time on, no European could afford to ignore Russia.

## The Scientific Revolution

While "new" political states were being organized during the Age of Absolutism, prominent scientists and theorists were making new discoveries about the nature and operation of man's environment. It is difficult for the modern reader to imagine the shock that a series of scientific revelations had on the European of the sixteenth and seventeenth centuries. It appeared as if everything that he had learned and assumed was no longer valid.

### Universe

Man learned that his and the assumptions of his religion about the universe were incorrect. Not only did Copernicus (1473–1543), Tycho Brahe (1546–1601), and, later, Johannes Kepler (1571–1630) shatter the geocentric theory of man's earth, but Galileo Galilei (1564–1642) proved, by focusing his telescope on the moon, that heavenly bodies were solid and possessed imperfections. The craters on the moon alone showed that God's perfect heavens no longer mocked man's corrupt, imperfect world. Kepler, further, noted the elliptical rotation of the planets around the sun which belied the supposition of perfect circular motion of the heavens which Dante's *Divine Comedy* so aptly described.

Other shocks about his larger environment faced Western man. As Europeans came into contact with non-European societies in Asia and the Americas, they discovered that other cultures were unaware of certain biblical data such as the chronology of the Great Flood or records of the Tower of Babel. This knowledge, of course, eroded the universal historical validity of the Bible for all men at all times and in all places. Although the European was convinced that other societies were pagan and necessarily immoral, he was astounded that a moral society such as the Chinese empire could exist without the underpinnings of Christianity.

Closer than distant planets or continents, amazement lurked in the familiar. It was determined that, hitherto unknown, complex structures and life existed just beyond man's ken. In 1626, William Harvey (1578–1657) confirmed the complexity of man's own body with the discovery of blood circulation. Robert Hooke (1635–1703) further reported that seemingly simple plants were composed of intricate cellular structures. Anton von Leeuwenhoek (1632–1723) was among the first to see amoebi, protozoa, and spermatazoa. Even innocent water teemed with microscopic life!

### The Quest for Scientific Absolutes: Bacon, Descartes, and Newton

Instead of withering before these various assaults on his previous assumptions, Western man sought new means to find new truths and assumptions. Ultimately, Francis Bacon (1561–1626), René Descartes (1596–1650), and Isaac Newton (1642–1727) provided these means.

**Francis Bacon.** The Englishman Francis Bacon was one of the first to propose new ways to arrive at scientific truths. In his work, *The Advancement of Learning,* he suggested that earlier scientists had made too many sweeping generalizations resting on too few facts. Because of this, it was no wonder that earlier scientists had made misjudgments. Bacon's inductive approach to arrive at truth was to experiment and observe as much as possible, then, when enough data had been accumulated, reach a conclusion. This methodology would prevent embarrassing mistakes.

**Descartes.** Across the Channel, René Descartes offered another approach to truth. Descartes found in mathematics a tool by which man might find both scientific facts and God. Since mathematics, particularly geometry, was pure, he argued that it would prevent any imperfect errors from distorting truth and reality.

**Isaac Newton.** It was Sir Isaac Newton whose theories came to have the greatest impact and resulted in a new scientific synthesis on the nature of the universe. Newton's *Principia* demonstrated that the universe operated according to inalterable scientific laws. This he proved to most of his fellow scientists' satisfaction by accumulating his data and logically explaining his views mathematically (and in the process developing modern calculus). As a result, Newton provided new scientific absolutes; namely, the universe was governed by scientific laws that remained valid for all times and places.

Newtonian science had implications for other areas of human endeavor. If reason and science had unlocked the secrets of God's universe, could not these very same tools also be used to explain other human and natural phenomena?

### Science and Religion

Many Europeans were dismayed at what they interpreted as science's attacks on religion. What place, they wondered, did God have in this new scientific order? As evidenced by the summoning of Galileo before an inquisition court, initially the reaction of organized religion was to try and coerce the scientists.

The scientists had not tried to deny God's existence. As a matter of fact, there was a long tradition, reaching back to Albertus Magnus and Roger Bacon, of scientists within the Church. Copernicus, who was one of the founders of the Scientific Revolution and a Catholic priest, was well within this tradition. Descartes felt that mathematics proved God's existence and Newtonians contended that the Englishman's scientific laws were part of His work. Merely because the Scientific Revolution was scientific did not necessarily make it antireligious.

Yet disquieting repercussions from the Scientific Revolution were felt by the religiously devout. Newtonian physics, for example, described the universe as a vast machine governed by scientific laws. Granting that God had created this universal machine, what was God's function now? Newton's theories, therefore, seemed to skirt dangerously close to ungodly theism.

The charge of atheism was often leveled at those who felt that science gave them a new insight into religion. Many cynically saw organized religion as being synonymous with organized superstition used to exploit the naive and gullible. Deists, on the other hand, described God in scientific terms as some sort of Master Engineer who, having created a perfectly operating machine, had perhaps gone elsewhere. The implications of this belief were that prayers served no purpose and that it was foolish to expect divine intervention (miracles) in human affairs. However, Pantheists, such as the philosopher Benedict Spinoza (1632–1677) more positively identified God as the sum total of natural forces.

It should be pointed out, nevertheless, that the seventeenth century was characterized by intensive intellectual debates within organized religions. Jansenists versus Jesuits in France, Puritans versus High Church Anglicans in England, and Nikonian reformers versus "Old Believers" in Russia were but a few outstanding examples of how reason and rationality were issues within the three major areas of Christian theology.

### Rise of Absolutists

Change not only occurred in science, but in political perception as well. Many Europeans had wearied of the incessant internecine strife which characterized the sixteenth century. The logical solution to these internal difficulties was to concentrate authority in one institution or individual.

#### Jean Bodin

Jean Bodin (1530–1596), a French political theorist, wrote *The Six Books Concerning The State,* which laid the ideological foundations for the absolutist state. Bodin stated that the state must possess ultimate authority. Although he recognized that many possible institutions, such as local communities, magistrates, the estates, or the nobility, might possess this authority, Bodin argued that the best and most logical institution to exercise political power was the monarch, whose powers emanated from God and historical tradition.

### Jacques Bossuet
A seventeenth-century French bishop, Jacques Bossuet (1627–1704), took matters a step further. Besides being a bishop, Bossuet was court ideologue for Louis XIV and more fully developed the political philosophy of "divine right." Arguing from the Scriptures, Bossuet wrote that God authorized a monarch to exercise authority. Just as a good Christian obeys God, so too must he obey his monarch. Not to do so is both treasonable and sacrilegious, for the monarch is God's lieutenant on earth. Hence, the authority of the monarch and his dynastic state was rebuttressed by divine sanction.

### Thomas Hobbes
In his work *The Leviathan,* Thomas Hobbes (1588–1679) further justified the increased authority of the state and possibly anticipated modern authoritarianism. However, Hobbes argued from a different perspective than either Bodin or Bossuet, for he was one of the first truly secular political theorists. Hobbes postulated that primitive man had been engaged in perpetual warfare against his fellow man. To prevent this genocidal behavior, man finally surrendered his freedom to wage war by creating government, which Hobbes dubbed "the leviathan." The state, or leviathan, possessed full sovereignty for the purpose of maintaining—to use the modern phraseology—"law and order."

Since he maintained that sovereignty was obtained not from God but from man, Hobbes was one of the first to set forth the "contract-theory" of political power. His view, however was that once the people had surrendered their authority to the leviathan the contract was irrevocable. Henceforth, man's duty was to obey the state and, of course, in this period of European history that usually meant obedience to the monarch.

### Mercantilism
The philosophy of mercantilism was the economic method used to reinforce the absolutist state. Generally speaking, mercantilists had as their goal the concentration and the resultant increase of wealth within their lands. This was to be accomplished by increased state intervention in the economy. State regulation, subsidization, and, in some instances, outright ownership and operation of industries occurred. To prevent wealth from escaping his lands, a monarch tried to discourage foreign imports through tariffs. But, believing he could "capture" his neighbors' wealth, he encouraged exports.

In many ways mercantilism resulted in modernization of the economies of various lands. For instance, Colbert was able to remove most of France's internal tariff barriers and facilitate freer exchange of goods within Louis XIV's domains. In Brandenburg, this was also accomplished by the Great Elector's construction of canals. Mercantilist regulations, further, were often more flexible and realistic than the policies of the guilds which had previously controlled so much of the economy.

Mercantilism, on the other hand, had its negative aspects. If enforced it could be unduly harsh on overseas Europeans. Whether the colonists liked it or not, colonial economies were to be subordinated to the interests of the mother country's economy and industries. Since colonial industry was not to compete but to complement the mother country's industries, prices skyrocketed in the colonies. In addition, the mercantilists' stress on acquiring colonies and promoting trade resulted in increased international friction. Many seventeenth- and eighteenth-century wars may be partially explained by the mercantilist policies of the absolutist political state.

### Absolutism Denied

The apologists for absolutism did not have the field of political theory to themselves; there were critics. One was James Harrington (1611–1677), author of *The Commonwealth of Oceania* who opposed the increased power of the monarchy and proposed the creation of an aristocratic republic with institutions responsive to the non-noble populace. François Fénelon (1651–1715) was another critic. Charging that absolutism set the king above the laws, Fénelon advocated a state that was responsible to the traditional estates and the nobility.

#### John Locke

John Locke (1632–1704) was perhaps the most prominent and influential critic of the absolutist philosophy. Locke's *Two Treatises on Government*, published in 1690, challenged Hobbes's interpretation of the social contract. He argued that in the social contract man did indeed empower the state to rule, but the state was obliged to ensure the peoples' "natural rights" of "life, liberty, and property." As long as the state fulfilled its duties and obligations to man, it possessed the authority and right to rule. However, if the state failed to do so, then the people had the right to alter the state by any means necessary. As the Glorious Revolution of 1688 amply testified, the absolutist state could be overthrown without fear of Hobbesian chaos or the wrath of Bossuet's God. Locke, therefore, secularized the political state and made it answerable to the needs of man.

## Summary

Under Absolutism the dynastic state grew. In order to control more fully their inheritance, the Absolutists found it necessary to subordinate powerful interest groups. To facilitate this, dynastic institutions such as royal bureaucracies and armies emerged and grew important. These once dynastic institutions gradually blurred into state institutions. The dynasts, in other words, laid the foundations for the state to continue without them.

Other developments occurred during the Age of Absolutism that were important to the contemporary world. Naturally, the rise of Russia under Peter the Great foreshadowed its appearance as a first-rate power in the present century. The political struggles between monarchs and Parliament during this period propelled England and, of course, its colonies toward political democracy.

The Scientific Revolution most assuredly has relevance. Europeans during the Age of Absolutism found in science the answers to many of their more perplexing problems. We, too, operate on the assumption that science will provide us with the panaceas for our problems. For that reason one can even argue that the Scientific Revolution continues to the present and has never really stopped. The political events, the scientific knowledge, and the political and economic theories of the Absolutist era still affect us today.

# Despots—

# Benevolent

# or Otherwise

Anti-Mercantilism
  Laissez-Faire
  Adam Smith
The *Philosophes*
  Voltaire
  Montesquieu
  Rousseau
Eighteenth-Century France
  Louis XV
  Louis XVI
Bourbon Spain
  Philip V
Hanoverian England
  George I
  Walpole
  "Prime" Minister
  "Boy Patriots"
  William Pitt
  George III
  Parliamentary Conflict
Austro–Prussian Rivalry
  Charles VI and Frederick William I
  Maria Theresa and Frederick II
  Benevolent Despotism: Frederick II and Joseph II
Russia: From Peter to Catherine
  Elizabeth
  Peter III
  Catherine the Great
Summary

During the two generations which preceded the French Revolution, many Europeans, including intellectuals and rulers, were operating under a new set of standards transmitted to them by the Scientific Revolution. Antimercantilists, such as Quesnay and Smith, and *philosophes,* such as Voltaire, Montesquieu, and Rousseau, challenged many socioeconomic and political practices of the *Ancien Régime.* These critics argued that "natural law" and "reason" ought to be pursued, for then a better and more enlightened Europe would result. Although the usual wars for economic and political gains continued in the eighteenth century, internally the political state took on other dimensions during the reigns of the enlightened or benevolent despots. Various attempts—some major, some minor, some only half-hearted, and some on paper only—were made to implement reforms in such diverse lands as Spain, France, Prussia, Austria, and Russia. However, none of the monarchs succeeded in altering the basic foundations of their rule or their domains. The failure of the monarchs to reform from above opened the way to revolution from below.

During the two generations that preceded the outbreak of the French Revolution, many Europeans were operating under a new set of standards that resulted from the Scientific Revolution and its repercussions on socioeconomic and political behavior and thought. Collectively, these new intellectual currents are designated in European history as the Age of the Enlightenment.

The Age of the Enlightenment saw man in a newer, more positive light. John Locke, so important to political theory, was partially responsible for this new assessment of his fellow man. Locke's *Essay on Human Understanding* stated that each individual is born with a mind that is a *tabula rasa* (a "clean slate"). Anything that an individual learns, therefore, is imposed by his environment. Man, therefore, is not inherently evil and any evil that he subsequently does is a result of the influence of his environment.

Since man is endowed with the ability to reason, it was further assumed that he could better himself and his society. Through the use of reason many could find the remedies for the evils and inequities of social institutions. The individual could not only improve himself but others as well. This meant that progress was feasible. Both man and his environment would become better. Instead of looking over his shoulder at a lost Graeco-Roman "Golden Age," eighteenth-century man optimistically saw ahead a future filled with promises of better conditions. But improvement seemed only possible when those institutions that defied reason were abolished. These assumptions partially explain why the Age of the Enlightenment necessarily became an age of reform in many European lands.

This chapter will first look at some of the more prominent economic, social, and political theorists of the *Ancien Régime,* the French phrase used to describe the "old order" before the French Revolution. Next, the chapter will examine the European body-politic under the rule of various despots—some benevolent reformers, some not.

### Anti-Mercantilism

The Enlightenment assumed that the world was governed by various "natural laws." If there were laws to explain the movement of the heavens, as Newton demonstrated, so too must there be laws that operated in other areas. Economists, for example, came to believe that mercantilism was bad because it impeded the natural laws of economics.

### Laissez-Faire

François Quesnay (1694–1774) was one of the first antimercantilists. His physiocratic school of economics criticized mercantilism as an unnecessary hindrance to the economic development of both the individual and the nation. A nation's economic policy should very simply be no economic policy, which Quesnay described with the phrase *laissez-faire* (let it be).

### Adam Smith

Another prominent antimercantilist was the Scotsman Adam Smith (1723–1790). Two years after Quesnay's death, Smith's *Wealth of Nations* was published. Since mercantilism thwarted man's natural desire to trade and better himself economically, Smith attacked mercantilism, arguing that there was no justification for the state to interfere in the economy. He would limit the state's role to that of a civil policeman protecting the nation as a whole from its external foes. The principles enunciated by Smith incorporated natural law into an economic theory with political implications that has been named *laissez-faire* capitalism.

### The *Philosophes*

By the mid-eighteenth century a group of new social critics had emerged. These new critics (the *philosophes*) criticized many of the institutions, customs, and practices of European society. Yet, in their writings they not only attacked but offered constructive solutions to many of the problems of their age. The *philosophes* also possessed a wide range of interests, from Denis Diderot's attempt to record all knowledge in a set of encyclopedias to Cesar Beccaria's proposals for penal reform. Perhaps the most outstanding of the *philosophes* were François Marie Arouet, better known as Voltaire (1694–1778); Charles de Secondat, Baron de Montesquieu (1689–1755); and Jean-Jacques Rousseau (1712–1778).

### Voltaire

Voltaire was a prolific author and social critic. Although his writings ran the gamut from history and philosophy to novels and biting satire, they shared in common the fact that they drew constant comparisons between traditional beliefs and reason. Invariably, the "old ways" paled before the "new, reasonable" ways. Many of Voltaire's satires were filled with impatience at the persistence of society's ignorance and superstition. His remedy was to apply the standard of reason to these practices and institutions and, if they were found wanting, Voltaire advised man "to destroy the infamous thing."

Politically, Voltaire believed that things could be made better if philosopher-kings reigned on this earth. Rulers, animated by cool intellect and sweet reason, would be able to hold the selfish nobles, the exploitive priests, and ignorant masses in check. In this we see that Voltaire was no political revolutionary, but rather a political traditionalist who accepted his period's political framework of monarchical rule. The major problem, which Voltaire could not resolve, was how to set philosopher-kings on dynastic thrones.

### Montesquieu

Montesquieu was more of a realist than the younger Voltaire. He also used satire in his *Persian Letters,* in which a mythical Persian traveler comments on the foibles and irrational manners of European man. At the more practical level, however, Montesquieu's *Spirit of the Laws* offered a solution to the prevention of royal tyranny. Comparing the French and English governments, he found that a "separation of powers" existed within the English political system which prevented absolutist governments from forming.

### Rousseau

Jean-Jacques Rousseau presented an altogether different analysis of man and society than his peers. He stressed the natural over the rational in man. Since only man was endowed by nature with a sense of pity for his fellow creatures, Rousseau argued that man was inherently good and in precivilized times lived in a happy, harmonious relationship with nature. As institutions of civilization developed, man lost his ties with his natural self and environment which resulted in the development of tyranny, evil, misery, and unhappiness. Hence, Rousseau broke with his fellow *philosophes* on the universal application of reason. His path to truth was not through reason but through the use of spontaneous emotionalism which was more natural. It is for this reason that Rousseau served as an important bridge connecting the eighteenth-century Enlightenment with nineteenth-century Romanticism (see chapter 19).

Like Voltaire and Montesquieu, Rousseau concerned himself with political matters as well. Recognizing that his idyllic state of precivilization could not be restored, Rousseau argued that better government would result if political institutions reflected the "general will" of individuals. Implied within this phrase is the concept of political democracy. For if the "general will" is determined, Rousseau assumed, a better and more just government will result. There was, however, a fundamental ambiguity to the "general will": how is it determined? Although we in the United States assume that the ballot box determines the "general will" of the people, a Hitlerian dictator could argue that he best represents and personifies the "general will" of his people.

### Eighteenth-Century France

The nobles who dominated France after the death of Louis XIV dreamed of turning back the clock to the "good, old days" before Richelieu and Mazarin had brought these over-mighty subjects into line. During Louis XV's minority two noblemen served as regents, the Dukes of Orleans and Bourbon. However, both regencies engaged in such extravagances (the Mississippi Bubble was an example) that many longed for monarchial absolutism as an antidote.

#### Louis XV

Upon reaching his majority, Louis XV returned to the use of a first minister. In 1726, he named his former tutor, Cardinal Fleury, to this post. Fleury's conduct of foreign policy enabled him to present Louis with the duchy of Lorraine.

In 1743, Louis XV assumed personal rule. During the remainder of his reign Louis embroiled France in a series of conflicts with England, Austria, and Prussia. At the end of these wars, France lost much of her overseas empire. The Treaty of Paris, 1763, took away not only parts of India, but Canada as well. The remainder of French America, Louisiana, went to Bourbon Spain. To compensate partially for the loss of land outside Europe, France purchased Corsica from Genoa in 1769—the year of Napoleon's birth.

**Parlement of Paris.**  Domestically, Louis maintained royal absolutism against the demands of at least one privileged group. When the *parlement* (law courts) of Paris insisted that it held veto power over royal decrees, Louis sent its members packing, confiscated their inherited offices, and closed the *parlement*. Nevertheless, when the debacles of his foreign policy resulted in financial difficulties, he failed to push through the *vingtième* (20th) tax proposal after a protest arose from the nobles and clergy.

### Louis XVI

In 1774, hopes were high in France that the new king, twenty-year-old Louis XVI, would introduce reforms sorely desired by many. His restoration of the *parlement* was applauded as was his appointment of Turgot as Minister of Finances. But Turgot's suggested reforms violated the "liberties" of many privileged groups. As a result, pressure was put on Louis who dismissed Turgot as well as his successor, Jacques Necker.

**Finance.** In spite of France's financial circumstances, Louis XVI lent aid to the American Revolution. The satisfaction of seeing England beaten by her former subjects did not balance French monetary accounts. A demand was made for the Estates-General to meet and to discuss the financial crisis. Louis tried to ignore this by summoning an Assembly of Notables in 1787, but the clergy and nobles represented there refused to submit to taxation. Rather, they joined the voices calling for an Estates-General. Louis XVI reluctantly agreed. The road to revolution lay ahead for Bourbon France.

### Bourbon Spain

#### Philip V

The Treaty of Utrecht confirmed Philip V, Louis XIV's grandson, as king of Spain. His reign almost spanned the first half of the eighteenth century. His position inside Spain was in many ways stronger than that of the Hapsburg dynasty. For he, unlike they, effectively solved the Catalonian question. The Catalan support for Philip's enemies during the War of the Spanish Succession justified Philip's abolition of their regional autonomy and privileges. In foreign affairs, Spain was a disruptive force to a war-weary Europe. Philip's willingness to push dynastic interests in Italy for his sons by his second wife, Elizabeth Farnese, threatened the balance of power.

Philip's successors attempted to bring Spain more up-to-date. However, the reforms introduced during the reigns of Ferdinand VI (1746–1759) and Charles III (1759–1788) were rather mild and moderate. Ferdinand's chief minister, Ensenada, improved Spain's military and naval postures. Charles III was most famous for his expulsion of the Jesuits from all Spanish domains.

For all practical purposes, Spain had become a French satellite in foreign relations. This was a result of Spain's declining position as a power and by a series of agreements known as the Family Compacts which tied Bourbon Spain to Bourbon France. So strong was the habit of the French alliance that during the turbulent years of the French Revolution, Charles IV (1788–1808) and his son Ferdinand allied themselves with the Revolutionary successors to Bourbon France.

### Hanoverian England

On September 18, 1714, George, the elector of Hanover, arrived in London as King George I of Great Britain. The Act of Succession had stood the test, for the Catholic descendants of James II had been excluded from the throne and a Hanoverian installed.

#### George I

George I was a fifty-four-year-old Lutheran who spoke little English and never fully understood the customs or culture of his kingdom. His heart remained in his former North German electorate and when Great Britain's interests were weighed against those of Hanover he invariably chose those of the latter.

The Whigs—the party of the Glorious Revolution, anti-Catholic and anti-Stuart—politically entrenched themselves during George I's reign. The fact that some Tories supported the invasion threat of James II's son in 1715 tainted that party with disloyalty. It, furthermore, provided the Whigs with an excuse to make life miserable for the Tories as attested by the Septiennial Act which lengthened the life of the Whig-dominated Parliament for seven years.

#### Walpole

Within the Whig party various factions vied to control the access to the king's ear and patronage. The ultimate winner was Sir Robert Walpole who dominated Parliamentary politics from 1722 to 1742.

#### "Prime" Minister

Walpole had won George's patronage by convincing the king that he supported the king's interests and concern for Hanover. The king not fully comprehending the subtleties of British politics found it more convenient to rely upon Walpole as his "man" in Parliament. Consequently, Robert Walpole's relationship to the king as his first or "prime" minister came to be an accepted political institution during the reigns of the first two Georges.

Walpole dominated politically for other reasons. As a member of the gentry, he was not only socially acceptable but had close ties with this important group. He pushed through Parliament laws such as a reduction in land taxes that benefitted the large landowners. Whig ties with commercial interests were highlighted by his cuts in export duties. Walpole's acute financial management appeared sound in comparison to the wild speculations of the South Sea Bubble of Lord Stanhope, his Whig rival.

Walpole was also able to convince George II (1727–1760) that he could serve the new king faithfully. George II was suspicious, since the king had despised his father and all he had represented. But George II was persuaded by his wife's subtle advice that Walpole was the man to continue running Britain smoothly.

### "Boy Patriots"

Walpole's fall came about as a result of a struggle within his own party. A new generation of Whigs appeared, eager for a taste of power and glory. These so-called "Boy Patriots" asserted that Walpole was not pushing English commercial interests strongly enough against the Spanish Empire. Under William Pitt, the "Boy Patriots" maneuvered Parliament into declaring war on Spain (the War of Jenkin's Ear) in 1739. This conflict merged with the War of the Austrian Succession in 1740. Two years later, the more pacifically inclined Walpole left office.

### William Pitt

Throughout the next twenty years, Britain was engaged in the wars revolving around the Prussian-Austrian conflicts. William Pitt came into power when England's fortunes were at their lowest point, in the Seven Years' War. Pitt's policies of committing Britain to all-out victory in the colonial areas proved successful. The Treaty of Paris, 1763, saw Britain emerge as Europe's most powerful nation. Britain possessed a mighty empire in the New World and in India.

### George III

When George II died he was succeeded by his twenty-two-year-old grandson. George III (1760–1820) stood in contrast to his predecessors. His interests and heart did not lie in distant Hanover but rather in England. His tutor, Lord Bute, had instilled patriotic pride in the young George and instructed him in the virtues of ruling as a wise and "patriotic king."

George III intended to set things aright, to restore the old political balance in which the king was also a consideration in English politics. To the Whigs, of course, this smacked of "royal tyranny"; for they no longer could dip into the royal treasury and use the crown for their interests.

### Parliamentary Conflict
Therefore, during George's reign a contest developed to see who would dominate Parliament. Did the king have the right to name his own men to Parliamentary and governmental offices, or was Parliament's consent necessary? Both sides cloaked their arguments in the highest terms. The king and his supporters stated that only the king would rise above the petty politics and corruption within Parliament. The Whigs, on the other hand, argued that it was a question of Parliament and the people arrayed against the potential absolutism of the crown. Ultimately, the debate turned into an English Civil War, more commonly known as the American Revolution (1775–1783). The American triumph discredited the followers of George III. And, although great powers continued to reside with the crown, Parliament was the victor.

## Austro-Prussian Rivalry

### Charles VI and Frederick William I
In 1711, Charles VI, Leopold's second son, ascended the Hapsburg throne. The greater part of his reign was spent trying to ensure that his daughter and only heir, Maria Theresa, would inherit intact all Hapsburg lands. This he hoped to guarantee through negotiations with the major European nations. Charles and his diplomats agreed to almost any concession in order to acquire signatures for the Pragmatic Sanction.

Contemporaneous to Charles VI's reign was that of Frederick William I, who became king of Prussia in 1713. Prussia underwent an overhaul during his twenty-seven-year reign. Instead of the Athens, Prussia became the Sparta of the North.

Frederick William found his nation in dire economic straits. After giving his father an expensive funeral, he introduced rigid economies into his kingdom. Two-thirds of all government employees were fired, and those who were fortunate enough to remain found their wages lowered with heavier workloads. So demanding was Frederick William of his subjects that in French the expression "to work for the king of Prussia" was a synonym for slave labor. The result, however, was that the Prussian state became more efficient and solvent. Upon his death, his heir inherited increased state revenues and a war-chest of approximately eight million thalers.

Frederick William I merited his nickname, the "Sergeant-King," for he was noted for his militarism. He had a passionate interest in the Prussian army which he increased to a force of 83,000. Constantly in uniform, Frederick William spent much of his time with the army. He subjected his troops to long, frequent, and precise military drills and maneuvers.

Therefore, it was not the size of the Prussian army that made it so formidable, but its unthinking responsiveness to commands which destined Prussia for great military successes under the son of Frederick William I.

### Maria Theresa and Frederick II

It would be difficult to imagine two more dissimilar individuals than Maria Theresa and Frederick II, both of whom came to power in 1740. Maria Theresa's portraits conjure up the image of a peasant Hausfrau—stolid and colorless. Frederick, on the other hand, was a highly sophisticated wit and cynic. Urbane and talented, he wrote prose, poetry, and musical compositions which he played on his flute. Whereas Maria Theresa was religiously devout and devoted to her husband and children, Frederick was an agnostic who treated his wife with icy indifference, vastly preferring the company of his pet dogs over his fellow man. Yet, these two personalities were destined to be intertwined in a duel for the domination of the Germanies.

**Austrian Succession.** The rivalry between Frederick and Maria Theresa plunged Europe into two major wars. As soon as Maria Theresa came to power, Frederick demanded that Prussia be given the rich Hapsburg province of Silesia as his price for abiding by the Pragmatic Sanction. When Maria Theresa refused, the Prussians moved into Silesia. The Prussian victory at Mollwitz served as a signal for other nations to enter the conflict and try to despoil Hapsburg lands. During this War of the Austrian Succession (1740–1748), Austria and Britain fought against France, Spain, Bavaria, and Prussia. Frederick, who had triggered the events, was in and out of this war on two occasions. The only victor at the Peace of Aix-la-Chapelle was Frederick, who obtained recognition for Prussian ownership of Silesia.

**Hapsburg Alliance.** After Aix-la-Chapelle, a reservoir of resentment formed toward Prussia and Frederick. While Maria Theresa was unwilling to accept the loss of Silesia, other countries viewed Prussia as an upstart. In the meantime, Frederick's acid barbs about his fellow monarchs' personalities and habits deepened the antagonisms toward both him and his land. Capitalizing on this, Count Kaunitz, Hapsburg foreign minister, arranged the "Diplomatic Revolution." After centuries of French-Austrian enmity, France and its satellite Spain agreed to an alliance with Austria. Russia also reached an accord with Austria. Once Prussia and Britain arranged the Treaty of Westminster, the ground had been laid for the Seven Years' War.

**Seven Years' War.** Frederick decided to strike before his enemies moved in on him. He, therefore, ordered his army into neighboring

Saxony, occupying the whole country and subordinating its treasury and soldiers to Prussia's needs. From 1756 to 1763, Frederick was forced to fight against the overwhelming might of his enemies. He dazzled Europe with his military campaigns and successes, but it seemed merely a matter of time before Prussia would be overrun.

However, in 1762, at the lowest point in Frederick's fortunes, Elizabeth of Russia died. As an avid admirer of Frederick, the new czar immediately negotiated a settlement and offered to place the Russian army at Frederick's disposal. This "miracle of the House of Hohenzollern," coupled with British victories overseas, convinced France to drop out of the war. Left alone, Austria had no recourse but to go along with events. The Treaty of Paris, 1763, again confirmed Prussian control of Silesia. Besides winning this province, Frederick II also gained a place in history as Frederick the Great.

For the rest of his reign, Frederick was satisfied with the great-power status his nation had achieved. Frederick had good reason to be content; for not only had he added a million Silesians to his domain, but in 1772, with the First Partition, the 600,000 inhabitants of Polish West

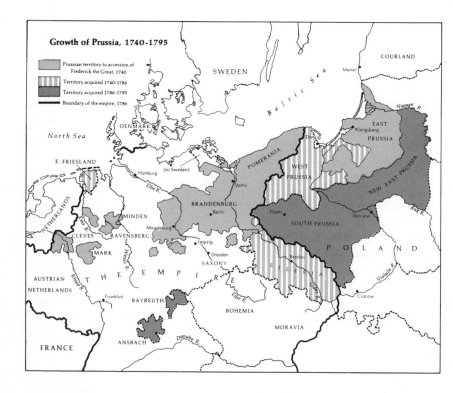

**Figure 15-1.**

Prussia further augmented his kingdom. Although he had had his fill of warfare, Frederick fought the Potato War against Austria in 1778 to 1779. This brief war, if it can be named such, was really a show of force to prevent the Hapsburgs from acquiring Bavaria.

### Benevolent Despotism: Frederick II and Joseph II

Frederick prided himself on the long hours he devoted to governmental affairs. From early morning to late night, he sat at his desk poring over accounts, reading reports, and writing correspondence. According to natural law, these were his duties as ruler. Frederick felt obligated to be the "First Servant of the State."

**Frederick's Reforms.** As an enlightened despot, Frederick tried to introduce reforms. Rationalism was incorporated into the laws of Prussia, as seen by new legal codes and the ending of most uses of torture. Besides patronizing culture, he introduced the latest scientific methods of agriculture. However, when the interests of the Prussian state conflicted with "reason," it was Prussia that prevailed. This was exemplified by his continuation of mercantilist economic policies and by his commitment to the social status-quo—Junkers still dominated serfs.

Probably a better example of an enlightened despot was Joseph II, who succeeded his mother, Maria Theresa, in 1780. Joseph desired to create a more efficient, unified empire. To centralize the Hapsburg lands, Joseph tried to reorganize the various governmental agencies in Vienna, dissolve the provincial estates, and to make German the sole official language. Of course, one may argue that these were merely the old goals of the Absolutists.

**Joseph's Failure.** However, Joseph II tried to introduce the most up-to-date and farsighted reforms possible. For example, he abolished special legal privileges for various social groups. He also ended all torture and made moves to do the same with capital punishment. Moreover, he tried to introduce full religious toleration. His was the only Roman Catholic land to attempt this. Joseph even attempted to dismantle the power base of the nobility by abolishing serfdom in Austria and Bohemia.

Unfortunately for him, Joseph's reforms stirred up a hornets' nest of resistance. The most powerful vested groups, such as the clergy and nobility, were incensed. Hungary, the Austrian Netherlands, and Lombardy offered armed resistance to the emperor. Consequently, Joseph's reforms failed to take root and died, as he did, in 1790.

### Russia: From Peter to Catherine

For the first sixteen years after the death of Peter the Great, Russia suffered from instability. During this period there were four separate rulers: two czars (Peter II and Ivan VI) and two czarinas (Catherine I and Anna). In 1741, things finally stabilized when Peter's youngest daughter, Elizabeth, seized the throne with the aid of the palace guards.

### Elizabeth

Elizabeth proved to be a worthy daughter of a great father. She furthered the process of Westernization by patronizing such cultural endeavors as universities, the state theater, and the academies of science. Russia's international position was enhanced by Elizabeth's defeat of the Swedes in 1742 and participation in the Seven Years' War.

Elizabeth's chief concern, however, was the question of the succession. She lacked an heir and feared that another Romanov might destroy all that she and her father had accomplished for Russia. As a consequence, she brought her sister's son from the Danish duchy of Holstein-Gottorp to be her adopted heir. The strong-willed Elizabeth easily dominated her nephew Peter, and she wanted an equally pliable wife for him. To this end, she selected as Peter's bride a princess from an inconsequential principality. This Sophia Augusta Fredericka of Anhalt-Zerbst is better known by her Russian name as Catherine the Great.

### Peter III

As far as most Russians were concerned, Peter III's six-month rule was a debacle. He succeeded in alienating many influential groups. The fact that he snatched defeat from the jaws of victory in the Seven Years' War appeared insane to the Russian military and nobility. Peter's slavish imitation of Prussia and his desire to wage war on Denmark for Holstein-Gottorp's interests wounded Russian national pride. Since he was of foreign origin, Peter's confiscation of church lands smacked of blasphemy, besides threatening the clergy. These policies, along with his erratic public behavior and threats to his wife, resulted in a *coup*. Peter was arrested, placed in "protective custody" by the palace guards, and his death was announced one week later. His wife was proclaimed Empress Catherine II by the grace of God and the palace guards.

### Catherine the Great

Usually cited as an enlightened despot, Catherine the Great was more despotic than enlightened. To be sure, she corresponded with leading literary figures, spoke of giving Russia a more humane legal system, and dreamed of establishing a public school system. Yet, a closer examination of her acts reveal only that the crown was increasing its authority in many areas. Her governmental reforms, for instance, merely created greater control for the crown over local and provincial political units.

Particularly in social policies, Catherine might be labeled reactionary. Her Charter of the Nobility negated Peter the Great's Table of

**Figure 15-2.** Catherine the Great.

Ranks. By this decree, nobles no longer had responsibilities to the crown. Catherine even accorded the nobles more privileges, such as tax-exemption and trial by their peers, than they had previously possessed. Further, she confirmed noble control over the serfs and the number of serfs increased. When freemen who found themselves threatened with enserfment resisted, as during the Pugachev Revolt of 1772 to 1774, Catherine treated them harshly. In many ways, therefore, her reign was the golden age of the Russian nobility.

**Expansion.** Catherine expanded Russian territory to the south and to the west. She waged two wars with the Turks (1768–1772 and

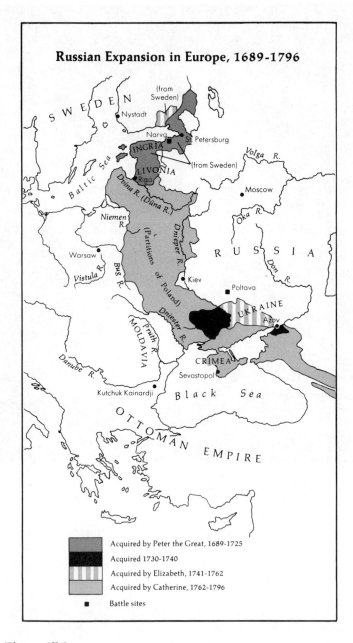

**Figure 15-3.**

1787–1792), by which Russia acquired more land on the Black Sea. These wars also recognized Russian interests over the Balkans and in the Christian subjects of the Sultan, thereby justifying future czars' interference in Turkish internal affairs. To the west, the three Polish Partitions (1772–1773, 1793, and 1795) added huge slices of that country to Catherine's domains. If under Peter the Great Russia had become an important consideration in European affairs, under Catherine the Great Russia was now a first-rate power in both Europe and the Near East. This was how she warranted the title of "great" to the Russian people.

### Summary

The legacy that we in the twentieth century have inherited from the intellectual currents of the eighteenth century is great. As we look at the assumptions of the Enlightenment, for example, we discover that these are very similar to the assumptions we use. Indeed, we believe in progress and in the improvement of life—we Americans often elect politicians who promise us progress is possible. We, in addition, accept the environmentalism of Locke and operate institutions (the public schools) to improve the individual.

As for the political and economic questions of the eighteenth century, the debates then are similar to those today. What economic philosophy should the state adopt—interference or noninterference? What obligation does the state have toward us and we toward it? These questions were not fully resolved then, nor are they today.

Yet, the state took on another dimension during the reigns of the enlightened or benevolent despots. During the last generation of this age there was a flurry of attempted reforms. To many, it was tacitly recognized that the ruler and the state were obliged to improve political, social, and economic conditions. As a result, the despots made various attempts to bring their domains more up-to-date and to impose reason or rationality upon their institutions, traditions, and customs.

However, most eighteenth-century monarchs did not succeed in altering the foundations of their societies. The basic explanation for this was inherent within the monarchical reformers themselves. The despots did not dare push reform and reason too far against tradition and privilege. For, after all, the monarchs were the most privileged of the privileged and rule based on the accident of birth was also a defiance of reason. The half-hearted reforms from above consequently failed and revolution from below followed.

# The Last Stand

# of

# Tradition

During the seventeenth and eighteenth centuries, the traditional civilizations of India, China, and Japan were challenged by Westerners who came in search of trade and commerce. In India, the British East India Company established footholds that gradually expanded to include much of the subcontinent. While Company rule had some beneficial aspects, it came to an end in 1858 when the British Crown took over. During this same period, China was defeated and occupied by a non-Chinese people, the Manchu. The real challenge to the Middle Kingdom came, however, from Westerners. Until their defeat during the first Anglo-Chinese War, the Chinese held the upper hand. After 1842, Imperial China retreated in the face of increasing Western encroachments upon her sovereignty. The Japanese response to Western pressures was to close their doors to outside contacts in 1639. The long decades of peace and isolation, which were not broken until Commodore Perry arrived in 1853, created a unique societal and political structure which would be a major factor in the emergence of Japan as a world power by the turn of the century.

## Europeans in Asia: The Old Imperialism

From the seventeenth through the first half of the nineteenth century the traditional societies of Asia were visited by ever increasing numbers of Westerners who came in search of trade and commerce. In general, this early or "old" imperialism was characterized by the activities of private commercial companies which were rooted in northern European countries bordering the Atlantic Ocean. Unlike the later phase of imperialism of the late nineteenth century, this was not an era of *colonial* empires. Instead, the relationships between European nations and their overseas possessions were based on trade, because of demands for commodities such as spices to preserve and season foods, chinaware, silk, and tea. The establishment of colonies was further hampered by the lack of clear-cut governmental policies supporting such a move. Moreover, scientific inventions and technological innovations had not reached the stage where they could overcome such difficulties as the vast distance between Europe and Asia and the enormous size of the Asian land mass. The early European outposts were usually planted in coastal areas that were easily accessible by sea. Western political domination and annexation of Asian lands did not materialize until the nineteenth century.

Those nations that were preeminent during this phase of imperialistic ventures were maritime powers with navies capable of defending their distant overseas commercial interests. Thus the English, French, and Dutch took the lead. By the mid-nineteenth century the position of private companies had deteriorated and government intervention and support became necessary to maintain and expand existing activities.

Europe was on the verge of a new and vigorous era of overseas expansion in Asia.

During the seventeenth through nineteenth centuries, India and the East Indies were too disorganized to resist the Western onslaught. In comparison, Japan—and to a lesser extent, China—were able to deal with the foreigners on their own terms. In each of the above situations, however, traditional cultures were making their last stand.

### British India: Era of Company Rule

In 1600, Elizabeth I granted a charter to the London East India Company, enabling it to build factories and forts on Indian soil. Like their contemporaries, the English depended on spices, cotton cloth, and luxuries such as silks for most of their profits. During the seventeenth century the Company acquired three ports which were to form the backbone of their Indian empire. First came Madras in the southeast in 1639. Then Bombay was added when Charles II married a Portuguese princess in 1661. And in 1690 Aurangzeb gave the British permission to settle near the mouth of the Ganges, a settlement later known as Calcutta. During

**Figure 16-1.** Private army of the British East India Company drilling on Bombay Green.

this early period, the British in India wore Indian clothes, ate Indian food, married Indian women, and enjoyed Indian forms of entertainment. They would not insist upon remaining separate from the local populace until later.

### Eighteenth-Century India: Emergence of Company Rule

The death of the Mughal emperor Aurangzeb in 1707 marked the end of the first and primarily commercial phase of British interest in India. Mughal control began to disintegrate as independent, competing states were created, raiders plundered the northern regions, and the British were forced to take a strong defensive posture in order to protect their investments.

**Early Presidencies.** The three major centers of British influence in India during the eighteenth century were Bombay, Madras, and Calcutta. Each had fortress walls for protection. Garrison troops were needed to man these outposts of empire, and native inhabitants were trained and equipped by the British to supplement their regular troops. And thus emerged the sepoys, Indian troops under British officers.

Each of the three centers was known as a "presidency" and each had a president or governor who was elected from among the senior British merchant residents. The governors were in charge of their local areas, but all major decisions were made by the directors of the East India Company in London.

**Anglo-French Rivalry.** England was not the only European power interested in expanding her holdings in India. France, too, was eager to make inroads in South Asia. The Anglo-French rivalry in the subcontinent was a clear reflection of their competition in Europe. For example, during this period England and France were on opposing sides in European struggles such as the War of the Austrian Succession (1740–1748) and the Seven Years' War (1756–1763). Moreover the two powers were also embroiled in other parts of the non-European world such as North America (French and Indian War, 1756–1763).

**Robert Clive.** Despite some early French successes in India, the British emerged victorious. In 1751, a British Company clerk by the name of Robert Clive (1725–1774) captured the city of Arcot. By holding the city in the face of a fifty-day siege by French-supported Indian troops, Clive broke the French hold on the state of Hyderabad and became a national hero in England.

Clive further established English control of the subcontinent in 1757 at the Battle of Plassey. In that engagement he defeated the pro-French governor or *nawab* of Bengal, and thereby enabled the British

East India Company to assume virtual control of the rich Ganges Valley. The British military triumph was acknowledged by the Treaty of Paris (1763) which concluded the Seven Years' War and resulted in the total French withdrawal from Bengal. Thereafter, England was the preeminent European influence in the subcontinent.

After a series of campaigns against other independent Indian rulers, the British finally consolidated their control over all of India. Delhi was annexed in 1805 and by 1818 powerful holdouts such as the Hindu Maratha empire had been defeated. England and the East Indian Company were now the most important power in India. By this time, the British in India began to separate themselves socially from the Indians. It was no longer fashionable to wear Indian clothes, eat Indian foods, or live in Indian-style homes.

**Company Rule.**   Under the guidance of the joint stock venture, called the East India Company, the subcontinent was divided into two distinctly different states: those under direct British rule and others ruled by native princes who swore allegiance to the Crown. Although the Company permitted the Indian princes varying degrees of local autonomy over their domestic affairs, the Indians had no voice whatsoever in the conduct of foreign relations. This system of princely states and British provinces was continued when the Crown took over in 1858. It completely ignored natural boundaries such as those created by cultural, linguistic, or racial ties. This has been one of the causes of continued crises in India—notably in 1947 at the time of Partition and in the continuing Kashmir conflict between present-day India and Pakistan.

While Company rule resulted in the economic exploitation of India for the benefit of its stockholders, certain changes occurred—some of which were beneficial. Governor-generals such as Lord William Bentinck abolished *sati*, introduced Western education which emphasized English, allowed Indian participation in judicial and company administrative posts on the lower levels, eliminated corruption among Company officials, and began work on transportation, communication, and public works projects. Famine relief, Western medicine, and sanitation techniques benefitted Indian and European alike. On the other hand, these improvements gave rise to a problem that still faces India today—overpopulation.

By 1858 the East India Company's dominant role in India was taken over by the Crown. In part this was a reflection of Parliament's concern over Company corruption, especially when officials such as Clive returned to England with personal fortunes. It was also a growing response to expanding Russian moves in the direction of India, as well as to the Evangelical Movement in England which pressured the government to "save India." Legislation such as the Regulating Act of

1773, the India Act of 1784, and the Charter Act of 1813 deprived the Company of its trading monopoly. Moreover, the Company surrendered its political control over the three presidencies and its own representatives.

"Great Mutiny."   1857 was the year of the "Great Mutiny" in India. Numerous fears led to the violence and chaos that wracked the entire subcontinent: there were those who resented the growing Westernization of Indian society; rumor had it that the caste system would be discarded; some feared that Christianity would replace the orthodox Hindu and Muslim faiths; the elite feared their loss of influence. The year-long turmoil was touched off by a relatively minor incident. The sepoys, both Hindu and Muslim, rejected a new issue of cartridges for their Enfield rifles because they were greased with fat—the fat of cows and pigs. And since the cartridges had to be bitten before they could be used, the Hindu and Muslim troops interpreted the new greased ammunition as a calculated affront to their religious convictions. The Sepoy Mutiny soon spread beyond the confines of the barracks and became a national confrontation between indigenous traditions and Westernization. This was a turning point in Anglo-Indian relations.

The impact of the "Great Sepoy Mutiny" was widely felt. The British government was shaken. London developed a cautious attitude toward Westernization and focused on public works projects rather than reforms that would impose Western values. In 1858, Parliament created a Secretary of State for India who had cabinet rank and who had direct responsibility for the subcontinent. The era of East Indian Company rule was over, and the Mughal empire was also formally dissolved.

## The Ch'ing: A Non-Chinese Dynasty in the Autumn of Traditional China

### Manchu Conquest and Occupation
In 1644, a Manchu army from north of the Great Wall (Manchuria) helped a Ming general subdue a Chinese rebel army that had seized Peking. After the rebels were defeated the Manchus refused to relinquish the city and gradually extended their control over all of China. By the middle of the eighteenth century the Manchus dominated China proper and incorporated Mongolia, Chinese Turkestan, and Tibet into their empire. Once again China was governed by non-Chinese "barbarians" and they called themselves the Ch'ing or "clear" dynasty.

The Manchus in China comprised a mere two percent of a total population of over a hundred million in the mid-seventeenth century. They were faced with two formidable tasks: how to govern the vastness of China and how to maintain their separate identity. Military superiority was essential and this was achieved by stationing regular Manchu garrison armies in all major cities. Local police matters were assigned to "Army of the Green Standard" units which were recruited from the Chinese populace and commanded by Manchu officers.

**Administration.**   The Ming administrative structure was retained by the Ch'ing. The only significant modification was the inclusion of Manchu officials in major positions at Peking and in the provinces. Thus a joint Manchu-Chinese dyarchy was created with equal numbers of both groups in key posts. Even the Board of Censors included equal numbers of Chinese and Manchus. Talent was recruited as before—through the traditional Confucian examination system.

Manchu emperors such as K'ang-hsi (who ruled from 1662 to 1722), Yung-cheng (1723–1735), and Ch'ien-lung (1736–1796) were astute administrators and capable warriors who shrewdly secured the loyalty of the Chinese scholar-bureaucracy. Under their sponsorship, Chinese scholars produced dictionaries, encyclopedias, dynastic histories, and various other publications. The Ch'ien-lung emperor also ordered the compilation of a manuscript library, the *Complete Library of the Four Treasures,* which included nearly 3,500 complete works that had been written in earlier centuries. The Ch'ing period also witnessed the development of long vernacular novels such as the much celebrated eighteenth-century work, *The Dream of the Red Chamber (Hung-lou meng)* by Ts'ao Hsueh-ch'i.

**Segregation.**   The Ch'ing were not unaware of the strong attraction of Chinese customs and the inexorable acculturation process that had overcome earlier non-Chinese invaders such as the Mongols. Thus they made a conscious effort from the outset of their control to preserve their identity as Manchus. Official decrees forbade Manchus from intermarriage with Chinese, the wearing of Chinese style clothing was banned, and Manchus were cautioned about adopting certain Chinese customs such as footbinding. After the mid-seventeenth century the Manchus even tried to keep their homeland free of Chinese influence by closing Manchuria to Chinese immigrants. In an effort to impose Manchu cultural characteristics on the Chinese they forced them to wear their hair in queues. The queue persisted as a reminder of the Manchu period, but little else. As years passed, the Manchu minority learned the Chinese language, and the use of the Manchu language declined. China was ruled by foreigners, but once again the strength and superiority of Chinese tradition absorbed the outsiders.

**Decline.**   The decline of the Ch'ing political structure became increasingly evident after the death of the emperor Ch'ien-lung in 1799. Decay had already set in before his death, for officials throughout the bureaucracy had become complacent and corrupt. As the ability of the government to rule deteriorated, problems of every sort began to erode the foundation of Ch'ing control. Natural disasters such as floods and droughts created famine and discontent, for the government granaries were empty. Communications between the capital and the far reaches of the empire broke down as roads and canals fell into disrepair. And as rebellions began to flare up, the Ch'ing discovered that their garrison armies had lost their will to fight. The peace and stability that had characterized the earlier period of the dynasty also worked against the Ch'ing, for peace had caused a dramatic increase in population. Official Ch'ing estimates in 1741 counted 142 million persons in China; by 1851 the total had risen to 432 million. But the problem of more mouths to feed and declining resources with which to meet the needs of the masses were not the only problems confronting the Ch'ing. In addition to the deteriorating domestic situation China was faced with a new threat from outside the Middle Kingdom.

The foreign peril that would ultimately destroy the Ch'ing dynasty and confront traditional Chinese civilization with its greatest challenge was seemingly innocuous at first. It began with the arrival of seagoing vessels, manned by white men in search of trade. From bases in south and southeast Asia the tiny ships unfurled their sails and headed north. Their destination: Canton and the port cities of southern China.

### The Canton System: China Trades with the West

Canton has long been an important trading center because its location along China's southern coast makes it easily accessible to traders arriving by both land and by sea. In Canton early Hindu and Muslim traders, and later the Portuguese as well, exchanged their wares for Chinese goods. During the Ch'ing period Canton became the center of European commercial activities in China. Eventually it was the British East India Company that cornered the largest share.

**Co-hong.** The first English ship arrived in Canton in 1637 but it was not until 1699 that the British finally received permission to establish a trading factory there. By 1700 other countries, including the French, the Dutch, and the Spanish, had joined the British in Canton. By 1760, the Western-Chinese commercial contacts evolved into what has been called the "Canton System." Thereafter, all Western trade was restricted to Canton and had to pass through the hands of the Co-hong or licensed guild of Chinese merchants. The Co-hong held a tight monopoly of all foreign trade with China, and the Co-hong was in turn directly responsible to the *hoppo*, the superintendent of customs who was directly responsible to Peking.

The Co-hong controlled all contacts between Chinese and Westerners in the port. They closely supervised individual merchant activities

**Figure 16-2.**   The Canton waterfront.

such as the payment of duties, sale of cargo, and purchase of necessary supplies. The Western merchants were confined to their factories and were subject to Chinese criminal law. Wives and foreign women were not allowed.

It is important to note that at this stage in Chinese-Western contacts, the Chinese were in control. As long as Peking could force the Westerners to accept Canton as the only port open to trade and commerce, the Westerners could be kept at bay. But this situation could not continue for long. And once the basic assumption of Chinese control was successfully challenged, the internal weakness of the Ch'ing and their inability to resist the military and maritime superiority of the Westerners would be revealed in full.

**British Diplomacy.**   The British in particular searched for ways to eliminate their restriction to Canton. In an effort to circumvent the *hoppo,* they sent a diplomatic mission headed by Lord Macartney to negotiate directly with the emperor. With official credentials from the Crown (but funded by the East India Company), Macartney reached the court of the Ch'ien-lung emperor in 1793. This first official contact was a failure, but it was not without a certain element of tragi-comedy.

The Chinese saw the delegation as a tribute mission (as they had traditionally viewed all non-Chinese diplomatic delegations) and demanded that Macartney demonstrate his inferior status by performing the *k'ou t'ou* (kowtow) ceremony. The *k'ou t'ou* required that the person seeking an audience with the emperor kneel and touch his head to the floor. Imagine the indignation that filled Macartney. He adamantly refused to perform the act, which he interpreted as grossly humiliating. The Chinese saw his refusal as a rejection of basic protocol, and the audience was cancelled. The *k'ou t'ou* would remain a major obstacle in establishing diplomatic contacts between China and the West, for subsequent Western delegations could not overcome their distaste for this act which the Chinese expected as a matter of course.

**End of the Canton System.**   The Canton system continued until 1839. The Ch'ing remained convinced that the "foreign devils" from the West could be handled as other "barbarians" had been dealt with before—as tributary nations. Unfortunately for the Chinese, the British were growing increasingly frustrated over their diplomatic and legal inferiority, numerous Co-hong abuses, and an unfavorable balance of trade. After the defeat of China during the first Anglo-Chinese War (1839–1842), the shoe was on the other foot. It was the beginning of "unequal treaties" and the last stand of imperial China.

### Tokugawa Japan: Isolation and Peace

Following on the heels of Oda Nobunaga (1534–1582) and Toyotomi Hideyoshi (1536–1598) who unified Japan after a century of civil war, Tokugawa Ieyasu (1514–1616) created a stable military government that was to endure from 1600 to 1868. The Tokugawa *bakufu* was officially established in 1603 when Ieyasu was given the title of shogun.

### Consolidation and Control

In order to maintain peace and stability within Japan and to ensure the longevity of the Tokugawa house, the new shogun and his descendants adopted a number of shrewd policies. For one, Ieyasu did not enter into long and costly wars to annihilate those who had opposed him at the Battle of Sekigahara in 1600. His former enemies as well as the neutral *daimyo* were treated generously; many suffered only some loss of territory. Furthermore, he categorized the *daimyo* into classes: *shimpan*, or clans directly related to the Tokugawa who could not assume the title of shogun; *fudai*, or "hereditary" *daimyo* who acknowledged Ieyasu's leadership in 1600; and *tozama*, or "outside" *daimyo* who were Ieyasu's equal—friend or foe—in 1600. In order to prevent *tozama daimyo* from conspiring against the Tokugawa, *fudai daimyo* were given fiefs located next to or near *tozama* fiefs. In this fashion the Tokugawa could easily monitor activities in the *tozama* domains.

**Regulation of Daimyo.** The *daimyo* were largely autonomous in their own domains, but in order to prevent anti-Tokugawa conspiracies or rebellions, the shogunate issued a number of edicts that severely reduced the possibility of successful uprisings. The alternate residence requirement, which required *daimyo* to spend part of the year in the capital at Edo (Tokyo), was actually a hostage system for when the *daimyo* left for his *han* (fief) he had to leave members of his immediate family (wives and children) in Edo. Checkpoints were set up at frequent intervals on the major roads, and travelers had to carry identification showing their departure points and destinations. When the *daimyo* traveled to and from Edo they were accompanied by numerous vassals, and when they arrived in their *han* they could not expand or repair their castles without official approval. Their children could not marry into another *daimyo* family unless the Tokugawa gave their permission, and marriage between different classes in society was forbidden in order to prevent social upward mobility. The enormous time, energy, and expenses involved in the alternate residence requirement alone was sufficient to keep the *daimyo* off-balance and unable to mount a potential rebellion. In addition the Tokugawa maintained a widespread network of spies and professional assassins.

**Seclusion Edict.** In 1639, soon after the Tokugawa came to power, the shogunate eliminated outside influences from interfering with their consolidation of total control. This was in the form of the *sakoku* or Seclusion Edict which banned all foreigners (except Dutch and Chinese in Nagasaki) from entering Japan and forbade all Japanese to leave. Violations were punishable by execution. One of the major factors that influenced this drastic policy was the Tokugawa fear of Christian missionary activity as a prelude to a Western invasion. The very success of the missionaries in converting thousands of Japanese to Christianity was in itself viewed by the Tokugawa as frightening evidence of how Christianity was a subversive element. Moreover, the fierce competition for converts led to fighting among the various missionary groups, and the spectacle of Japanese fighting Japanese under alien religious banners was a direct threat to Tokugawa control. In 1637 a peasant uprising against high taxes quickly took on the appearance of a Christian rebellion. The Tokugawa mustered a force of 100,000 troops to annihilate the 20,000 rebels (including women and children) who were trapped at Shimabara, and two years later Japan entered into a period of isolation from the outside world which would not end until 1853.

**Neo-Confucianism.** Confucianism, in particular Neo-Confucianism, provided the philosophical foundations for the Tokugawa shogunate. It appealed to the *bakufu* because of its emphasis on social harmony, class distinctions, and a ruling elite. The samurai class was identified with the Confucian scholar-bureaucrat and a rigid social structure was established with the samurai on top, then the farmers, artisans, and merchants in descending order. Coupled with Confucianism was the samurai's own ethical system, *Bushido* or "the Way of the Warrior." The values that the warrior upheld as virtuous—discipline, honor, duty, and loyalty to one's lord before one's family—gradually filtered down to the lower classes as well. Later, these values would play a major role in the creation of a modern Japanese state.

There were those, however, who opposed Neo-Confucianism. These anti-Confucian, pro-Shinto nationalists were known as the "National Learning" school. In addition, there was also a school of Dutch learning (*Rangaku*) which flourished during the eighteenth century and contributed to Japanese knowledge of Western science, medicine, and political events.

### Tokugawa Society

**Economic Growth.** The stability of the Tokugawa period led to significant economic growth. Agricultural productivity increased and farmers turned to commercial farming and cash crops such as cotton, tobacco, and sugar cane. Village industries such as sake-brewing (Japanese rice wine) prospered. All of this activity was due to the increased demands of an expanding population and numerous towns and cities. Merchant associations established monopolies over commodities such as textiles.

***Chonin* Culture.** The focal point of Tokugawa cultural activity was the city, especially the amusement quarters. Here the artists created for the *chonin* or townspeople who had both money and leisure time. Kabuki plays and the Bunraku puppet theater provided action, drama, and beautiful costumes. Men such as Chikamatsu (1653–1724) wrote plays that are still popular today. Novelists such as Saikaku (1642–1693) began to describe the merchants and amusement quarters. The poet Basho (1644–1694) established a reputation as a master of *haiku*, the seventeen-syllable poem. Paintings and woodblock prints known as *ukiyo-e* or "pictures of the floating world" depicted the carefree existence of the *chonin*, actors, and *geisha* or courtesan. Other artists including Hiroshige are known for their landscape prints. It was an era of conspicuous consumption, and in order to pay for it many of the samurai fell victim to the evils of a growing money and credit economy.

**Decline of Feudal Institutions.** The arrival of Matthew Perry and his black ships in 1853 seriously undermined an already obsolescent feudal political structure. While the merchants prospered, the samurai and even the *bakufu* faced financial difficulties. Two hundred years of peace, commercial growth, and urban comforts had taken their toll of the feudal land-based warrior class. For the increasingly impoverished samurai, one way out of indebtedness was to marry the merchant's daughter. This meant that the old class distinctions grew blurred and financial wealth competed with social status. There was also peasant discontent and rioting due to the demands made by a rising population on limited resources and higher taxes. Efforts at reform were unsuccessful and by 1853, Tokugawa Japan was but a thin feudal façade. In many ways, however, the social and economic changes caused by the long isolation enabled Japan to meet the nineteenth-century Western impact with far more resilience than China.

## Summary

During the seventeenth and eighteenth centuries the traditional civilizations of India and China and their spheres of cultural influence were confronted by the growing military and technological superiority of the West. The balance of power between East and West shifted in favor of Europe as Westerners discovered that India and China were faced with internal problems that forced them to ignore the growing Western domination of peripheral areas.

By the mid-nineteenth century the Indian subcontinent succumbed totally to the British, and Indians did not rule themselves again for nearly a century. By 1800 the traditional Chinese hegemony over neighboring areas such as Korea, Japan, and central and southeastern Asia was more façade than reality. The very spirit of adventure and curiosity that had driven Westerners to embark on their earlier "reconnaissance" of the world beyond Europe reflected the stark contrast between a complacent and stagnant China looking to past glories and a dynamic Europe in search of change and "progress." Unlike India, the mid-nineteenth century saw the survival of the traditional order in China. But the Middle Kingdom was now a mere shadow of its earlier power.

Japan, on the other hand, had been unaffected by outside pressures, as Westerners focused on China and southern Asia. Her long isolation had led to a unique societal and political structure which contained and perpetuated elements of Confucian tradition from China, while providing for the evolution of an economy similar in many ways to Western capitalism. When the Western impact reached Japan in the mid-nineteenth century, Europeans and Americans found a strange mixture of the traditional and modern, a synthesis that enabled the Japanese to emerge as the preeminent Asian nation in both Asia and the world.

# On the High Road

# to

# Revolution

The years from 1789 to 1815 were extremely important for Western Civilization. These 26 years encompassed a series of incidents which historians have labeled as either the French Revolution or as a part of the Age of Democratic or Atlantic Revolutions. This chapter shows that many of the vital political questions, which men argued about and even killed for during the French Revolution, had been raised earlier than 1789 and continued to be raised after 1815. Political events within France moved at a staggering pace: at the outbreak of the Revolution, France was an Absolutist, dynastic state, only to become in a few years a constitutional, nationalist monarchy which, in turn, became first a Jacobin then a plutocratic, conservative republic. By 1804, France had come full cycle when Napoleon was proclaimed emperor. In the meantime, France was engaged in almost continuous wars with its neighbors until Napoleon had mastered most of the mainland. However, great stresses and strains lurked beneath the surface of Napoleonic Europe, for he had not only antagonized Britain and Russia but other lands as well. Napoleon's debacle in Russia served as a signal for much of Europe to rise up against French overlordship. By 1815, Napoleon had met his final defeat and was sent into permanent exile. Although many had hoped to restore Europe to the days before the French Revolution, the ideals and ideas unleashed between 1789 and 1815 were not laid to rest by the Battle of Waterloo.

On July 14, 1789, the Bastille, that hated symbol of royal authority, fell to the people of Paris. This has been the traditional introduction to the outbreak of the Age of the French Revolution, 1789–1815. In more recent times, however, a great historical controversy has arisen concerning the exact nature of the French Revolution. The most fundamental question has been whether the Revolution was solely an isolated French affair or merely an incident in a broader "age of revolutions."

**Nature of Revolution**

The arguments in favor of a purely French Revolution find that circumstances peculiar to that nation brought about this great upheaval. The powers of the absolutist Bourbon kings had become too great and abusive. The privileged orders, with royal approval, rode roughshod over the middle and lower classes. Social, political, and economic oppression and inequities existed throughout the nation and had become intolerable. Suffering from these abuses, the French people rose up in a fury and destroyed the *Ancien Régime* and its institutions. Under the slogan of "Liberty, Equality, and Fraternity," the Revolution spread into other lands. First the revolutionaries and then Napoleon imposed a harsh, exploitive rule upon their unwilling and defeated enemies.

Others see the French Revolution as merely one—not even the first —in a series of revolutions in the larger context of an Age of Democratic or Atlantic Revolutions. This view holds that Western civilization possessed a common heritage of culture and institutions. Consequently, any stresses or strains felt in one country would be reflected in other countries. The *Ancien Régime's* foes, using similar tools and methods to analyze and criticize, were located throughout the Atlantic world. Although the revolution in France attracted the most attention, there were upheavals in other lands, both large and small. One, therefore should not let the French Revolution overshadow these facts. For, indeed, the period must be described as an "age of revolutions."

The controversy continues to rage. As is usually the case, both sides have their strong and weak points. Nevertheless, let us turn to the broader background of the outbreak of the French Revolution.

## Preparation for the Revolution

### Earlier Revolutions

In many ways, the English Civil War of 1642–1649, the Glorious Revolution of 1688, the American Revolution, and the Dutch uprisings of the 1780s were previews or forerunners of what was to occur later in France. It, therefore, would be beneficial to take a closer look at these events.

In seventeenth-century England many of the crucial constitutional and political questions that later appeared in Revolutionary France presented themselves. The problem of the authority, responsibilities, and limits of the institution of kingship was there partially resolved.

As attested by the English Civil War, a monarch could not ignore and violate traditions or public opinion. Indeed, the execution of Charles I vividly showed that a king was answerable to his subjects. Later, in 1688, the Glorious Revolution resulted in one of the first attempts to rationalize the political removal of a ruler. The political theorist John Locke spoke of all rulers as being empowered by an unwritten and inviolable pact between them and their subjects. The right to rule rested upon the consent of those governed. A ruler failing to fulfill his obligations to his subjects could be removed by them or by their institutions. Thus Parliament could legitimately declare the English throne vacated by James II and place William III and Mary II in his place.

The English colonists in the New World could also cloak their rebellion in constitutional arguments. Relying heavily on Locke, American Revolutionaries held that England and George III no longer deserved their loyalties. By failing to honor the colonists' rights and privileges as Englishmen, the mother country and its king had broken the bonds binding a people and their rulers. Revolution, in an instance such as this, was not only justifiable, but obligatory. Along with other "unalienable" rights, man's right to alter his government was incorporated into Thomas Jefferson's Declaration of Independence.

Following the American Revolution, the equivalent of a "democratic revolution" in miniature occurred in the Dutch Republic. A group of citizens, known as the Patriots, challenged the political and economic domination of their nation by the Amsterdam patriciate and the Orange dynasty. Groups of Patriots clashed with the supporters of the Patriciate-Orangists in the streets of Amsterdam. In 1787, an assault on the queen by Patriots resulted in Prussian and English forces entering the country. The power of the Patriots was broken by the invaders and the Patriciate and Orangists were firmly reestablished. However, the political ideas of the Patriots left an impression and continued to circulate in the land.

### Enlightenment

One speaks of the generation before the outbreak of the French Revolution as the Age of Enlightenment. During this time there were numerous critics of the status quo; these so-called *philosophes* insisted on applying rationality and reason to analyze the existing institutions. They usually found the *Ancient Régime* lacking. Yet, the *philosophes* did not merely criticize, they also offered solutions and alternatives. Some, such as Voltaire, called for philosopher-kings to set things right again. Baron de Montesquieu wanted countries to imitate his interpretation of the English constitution, as the framers of the U.S. Constitution did. Jean-Jacques Rousseau, on the other hand, insisted on an end to the decadence of civilization, advocating a return to a simpler, more reasonable society. Although his concept of the "General Will" was rather imprecise, it seemed to imply the principles of democracy.

The works of these men and other *philosophes* circulated widely. All too often readers found in the *philosophes'* critiques heavy ammunition with which to attack the existing society. A commonality of rhetoric and ideas developed which was generally used by potential reformers throughout the Atlantic world. It is for this reason that the Age of Enlightenment is adjudged by some to be the "cemetery of the *Ancien Régime*," with the *philosophes* serving as the gravediggers.

### Outbreak in France

The European world saw France as one of the great powers. The nation exerted profound cultural influences. The French monarchy, even under the successors of Louis XIV, appeared to be undisputed master of its domains and was a model many other rulers hoped to emulate. But beneath the veneer of theoretical power and absolutism lurked social strains and stresses within Louis XVI's France.

### Monarchy

The monarchy did not rule unchallenged. To be sure, Henry IV, Richelieu, Mazarin, and Louis XIV had streamlined and enhanced the powers of the monarchy. Nevertheless, there was a difference between theoretical and actual powers. Tradition, localism, and inadequate methods of communication served as checks upon the monarch's powers. In addition, powerful interest groups such as the nobility wished to reassert their former powers at the expense of the crown.

### Nobility

There were two classifications of nobles: the nobility of the sword and the nobility of the robe. The former were nobles in the traditional sense; they were descendants of the "great families" of France and held their rank on the basis of birth and inheritance. The nobility of the sword longed to restore their political power which had been lost over the past few centuries. The nobility of the robe, in contrast, were usually descendants of bourgeois lawyers or judges who had been ennobled either by the crown or by purchase. As the crown had expected, there was, at first, mutual distrust and suspicion between the two groups. However, gradually the two had reconciled their differences, intermarried, shared similar desires and aspirations, and had solidified against the monarchy above and the "third estate" below.

### Third Estate

There were degrees of discontent among the diverse groups that formed the third estate also. The economically powerful commercial and manufacturing classes, for example, resented their lack of social and political status within an increasingly petrified system. It was very difficult for them to move upwards socially into the nobility. Other business elements were frustrated by lingering medieval and mercantilist economic practices and, at the same time, feared the restless proletariat, who were subject to insecurities themselves. Since both Church and State opposed trade-unionism, workers found it almost impossible to protect themselves economically. It seemed as if workers' wages would never catch up with the cost of living. In the sixty years before the Revolution, for instance, wages rose only one-third in relation to the increased price of grain.

The rural situation was also filled with social antagonisms. Although serfdom had practically disappeared, noble and bourgeois landowners were trying to establish a "new feudalism." In lieu of payment in kind, cash was demanded from the small farmers and peasantry. Half-forgotten feudal dues were squeezed from them in order to provide the landowner with a monetary profit. The *corvée*, by which the landowner received so many days of free labor, was deeply resented. Invariably, the *corvée* was evoked during the harvest, when the peasant could least afford the loss of time. Most assuredly, the majority engaged in agriculture desired social change.

### Financial Crisis
Concurrent with these social tensions, France faced a financial crisis. A series of misjudgments in foreign affairs coupled with domestic extravagance placed the nation in dire financial straits.

An outmoded system of raising and collecting revenues controlled the economy. The wealthiest groups paid little or nothing. Nobles were exempted from the *taille,* the property tax, as was the Church. To make matters worse, this tax was collected by tax-farmers, private individuals who had paid the ever-hungry state a lump sum to gather taxes in a given area. The tax-farmers, seeking a profit from their investment, gouged the commoners. This meant that the tax burden rested disproportionately on those least able to afford it.

Nor was the *taille* the only financial inequity. The bourgeoisie was hindered by economic barriers, such as road and bridge tolls and internal tariffs, erected throughout the nation. Commoners also had to pay the hated *gabelle,* a tax on one of life's necessities—salt. The amount of the *gabelle* differed from province to province and place to place. Naturally, many felt that the present tax structure could not continue and that something had to be done. It was against this backdrop that the Estates-General was summoned.

### Estates-General
The summoning of the Estates-General, which had not met for 175 years, created great excitement in France. Different groups and individuals hoped to use this body for their own ends. The election of delegates to the estates resulted in numerous debates and an intensification of political activity in some areas and regions. Armed with *cahiers* ("notebooks") crammed with grievances, special demands, and suggestions for improvements and reforms, the elected delegates convened at Versailles on May 5, 1789.

However, even before the Estates-General convened, fundamental political questions arose. Were the delegates representatives of the estates (clergy, nobility, and commoners), or did they represent the nation collectively? Should the vote be tallied by estates, meaning one vote per estate, or by the individual? The crown and more conservative elements insisted on following the traditional method of representation by estates and vote by estates. But the commoners in alliance with some clergymen and nobles, notably Lafayette and Count Mirabeau, demanded the opposite.

The king, following an irresolute and vacillating policy, had the decision taken out of his hands. The third estate along with its allies declared itself to be the "National Assembly" of France which would continue to meet wherever necessary in order to provide the nation with a constitution. Louis XVI did not want this to happen, but he shrank from using his soldiers to enforce his will. He reluctantly accepted the *fait accompli* and, for one of the first times in history, the king of France had been defied.

**Bastille.**   Political agitation, in the meantime, had not been confined to Versailles; for it had spilled into the streets and fields of France. A mob of Parisians stormed the Bastille, a symbol of royal authority, privilege, and oppression. And on July 14, 1789, this building was razed, to the jubilation of many. Throughout that month the countryside was swept by a phenomenon known as the "great fear." Peasants and small farmers felt threatened and vented their fears on local manors and the estates of the nobility. Buildings were set afire and fields were burnt; the fears of the dispossessed were transferred to the privileged.

**Declaration of Rights.**   On the historic night of August 4th, only three months after the convening of the Estates-General, nobles and clergymen stood up and renounced their privileges. The renunciation of privilege was formally incorporated into a document known as the Declaration of Rights of Man and Citizen on August 27, 1789. Thus was "privilege" destroyed and equality, at least theoretical, established in Revolutionary France.

### The Revolution Quickens

Following the Declaration of the Rights of Man and Citizen, the Revolution temporarily abated. To be sure, the masses took matters into their hands when in October, 1789, a group of Parisians forced Louis XVI and his family to settle in the Tuileries Palace in Paris. The National Assembly, too, moved to Paris, where the more politically charged atmosphere was destined to dictate almost every future government of France. Nevertheless, in the capital the work on a written constitution was completed in 1791.

#### Constitutional Monarchy

This constitution made France a constitutional monarchy. The "king of the French" had his powers limited to the areas of diplomacy and military matters. He was also given the power to delay all legislation, except financial, for up to four years. Ministers from the Legislative Assembly advised him. The assembly was elected in two separate stages by male citizens meeting a property qualification.

There was a great deal of dissatisfaction with the Constitution of 1791. The failure to extend the suffrage to all males drove a wedge into the ranks of the third estate. Increasingly, the "passive" citizens, those not accorded the vote, turned to the more radical political clubs of Paris and read Jean Marat's newspaper, *The Friend of the People*. The clubs and Marat portrayed the new government as a reassertion of privilege in a new guise. In addition, the rural populace was disappointed by the government's failure to give them expropriated Church lands, while urban workers resented the laws continuing to restrict trade unions.

It was not these elements alone that disliked the Constitution, for monarchists did too. Fearing further revolutionary excesses and losing hope of altering events favorably, Louis XVI was convinced to flee France. This he tried to do in June, 1791. Not until he had almost reached the border at Varennes was Louis recognized and returned to Paris, a virtual prisoner.

**Coalitions.** While the Revolution raged within France, foreigners looked on with interest. At first, France's neighbors found a great deal of satisfaction from the events. Nations long menaced by the French monarchy's quest for glory could not help but smile at that institution's difficulties at home. However, as French noblemen (*émigrés*) fled their homeland, it dawned on noblemen and rulers elsewhere that the venerable institutions of privilege and monarchy were being fundamentally challenged and altered in France. If it could happen there, then why not in their own domains?

The *émigrés,* who were now joined by Louis XVI's brothers, hammered away at this point. German nobles who had lost their feudal privileges in Alsace by the Revolution seconded the arguments of the *émigrés* and demanded intervention in the events in France. Eyes turned to the Austrian Hapsburgs, the family to which Marie Antoinette belonged, to spearhead the drive against France. Fearful of these foreign intrigues, France declared war on Austria and Prussia in April, 1792.

**Brunswick Manifesto.** The Duke of Brunswick, commander of the Austro-Prussian troops, issued a declaration of purpose. The "Brunswick Manifesto" threatened that if any harm befell the king or his family Paris would be leveled. Within France, resentment was great. Disliking foreign interference, feeling that even the most modest gains of the Revolution were endangered, and suspecting Louis of being in collusion with the *émigrés* and foreigners, the French rallied to the defense of their besieged

**Figure 17-1.** The execution of Louis XVI.

homeland. By the middle of 1794, the invaders had been repelled and the war taken into their lands.

### Death of Louis XVI

Louis' behavior in attempting to escape, coupled with the foreign threat, saw an increase in revolutionary zeal. A vengeful mob in June and August, 1792, attacked the Tuileries and slew a number of the king's guards. The king was forced to seek refuge with the assembly. In the next month, the prisons of Paris were broken into and over 1,000 prisoners were summarily executed. The Jacobin clubs, popular with the city masses, increased their power and demanded the king's trial. Parisians descended on the assembly to provide the Jacobin delegates with physical support. Louis XVI was ultimately tried, found guilty, and executed, to be followed less than nine months later by his wife, Marie Antoinette.

### First Republic

Prior to the execution of the king and queen, France was declared a republic on September 20, 1792. A National Convention, elected to write a new constitution, initially held political power. However, within this body a political struggle occurred between the Jacobins and the Girondists, who tended to represent the countryside. The Jacobins emerged victorious and purged the convention. Jacobin reforms followed: price controls for the city-dwellers, land reform for the peasantry, and the extension of democracy by the abolition of all titles of privilege.

**Reign of Terror.** The convention selected an executive, known as the Committee of Public Safety. This body, coming under the leadership of Maximilien Robespierre, inaugurated the Reign of Terror, which lasted from September, 1793, to July, 1794. During this period an attempt was made to cleanse France of suspected "impurities" and establish thereby a republic of the virtuous. To this end, the guillotine was used, and neighbor spied on neighbor. Robespierre, a believer in reason, tried to introduce the worship of the Supreme Being. This, and the earlier calendar reforms, which provided a new reckoning of time on the basis of revolutionary events, a renaming and rationalizing of months, and the denial of the Sabbath led many to believe that Christian traditions were under attack. The feeling was reinforced by the closing of Paris' churches. These events alienated many. And, in the meantime, an internal struggle among the Jacobins, along with increased disaffection among their power base, resulted in the fall of Robespierre. The Reign of Terror was at an end. Another explanation for Robespierre's decline was the temporary halt to the external threat to France.

**Thermidorean Reaction.** Fearing that the Terror would engulf them, Robespierre's erstwhile allies removed him and his lieutenants. This is known as the Thermidorean Reaction which resulted in a new government for France and a new phase of the French Revolution.

The men of the Thermidorean Reaction provided France with a new government and constitution. The Constitution of the Year III (1795) is generally characterized as a conservative, even reactionary, document. Political participation and suffrage were again restricted to the propertied classes. If under the Terror the Parisian masses and their political clubs held a disproportionate amount of power, the Thermidoreans set out to abolish this influence. The political clubs were suppressed; and the independent city government of Paris, the Commune, was also restricted. Roving bands of "golden youth" (*jeunesse dorée*) physically intimidated and stilled the opposition of the urban supporters, the *sans-culottes*, of the Jacobins and the Terror.

According to the new constitution, the executive branch was nominated and elected by the upper legislative chamber. There were to be five executives, collectively known as the Directory. This form of government lasted for only four years, from 1795 to 1799. Generally, these years were marked by political and economic corruption.

The Directory was attacked from both the political left and right. In April and May of 1795, Jacobin sympathizers marched on the legislature demanding economic relief for the dispossessed. These uprisings were quickly quelled, as was Gracchus Babeuf's "Conspiracy of Equals" in 1796. Royalist attempts to control the government were halted in October, 1795, and September, 1797. In order to remain in power, the Directory came to rely heavily on the military. It therefore, came as no great surprise that the Directory was replaced by a military man—General Napoleon Bonaparte who seized power in the *coup* of the 18th Brumaire (November 9, 1799).

**Rise of Napoleon.**   At the time of the 18th Brumaire Napoleon was thirty years old. He had been born on Corsica in 1769, one year after France had acquired this island from Genoa. The Bonapartes belonged to the island's native nobility. As part of France's policy of assimilation, Napoleon was granted a military scholarship on the mainland. Because of his thick Italian accent and foreign manners, Napoleon had to endure the jeers and taunts of his classmates. Nevertheless, he graduated and obtained the rank of Lieutenant in the artillery. Had it not been for the outbreak of the Revolution, Napoleon, no doubt, would have remained frozen in the lower echelons of the royalist army.

Of course, fate ruled otherwise. Since numerous noble officers left France during the early course of the Revolution, opportunities to advance opened for Napoleon and others. Thus, Napoleon must truly be described as a "child of the Revolution."

The Revolution did provide Napoleon with ample opportunities. Fighting in the south of France, he became captain and, in 1793, brigadier general. Because of his earlier flirtations with Jacobinism, he fell into temporary disfavor with the Thermidoreans. But he soon saw his fortune on the rise. During the royalist uprising in October, 1795, Napoleon was in charge of the artillery that fired into a royalist crowd. As a result of this deed and his influential contacts with the Director Barras and Josephine Beauharnais, a widow, and arbiter of Parisian society, Napoleon was placed in command of the French forces in Italy.

Napoleon was everywhere victorious in the Italian campaign. By the middle of 1791, Italy was cleared of France's enemies. And in October, Napoleon dictated the Treaty of Campoformio, by which Austria recognized France's conquests to the west of the Rhine and in Italy.

Flushed with these successes Napoleon led an army into Egypt in 1798. In a skirmish with the Egyptians by the pyramids Napoleon claimed a great victory and occupied Cairo. In early 1799, his forces marched into Syria but returned to Egypt in May. Hearing of the growing discontent in France, Napoleon left his army in Egypt and returned home to intrigue with the Directors Siéyès and Ducos. After the 18th Brumaire, even greater battles—both military and political—lay ahead of him.

## Spread of the Revolution to Other Lands

### Sympathizers

As the French fought against their neighbors, the ideals of the French Revolution went with them. In almost every nation in the Atlantic world there were potential allies and sympathizers of the French Revolution. Public opinion concerning the Revolution was everywhere divided. Many vehemently opposed it. But many also approved of it and its goals and possibly hoped to install French Revolutionary institutions and principles in their own native lands.

Even before the spread of the Revolution, foreigners had flocked to France (as some did to America during the Revolutionary War) to breathe the air of Revolution. Thomas Paine, that revolutionary of two continents, came, as did many Dutchmen, Italians, Swiss, Germans, and others. When the French armies marched, volunteer foreign legions accompanied them, for many foreigners saw the Revolution as part of their own struggle.

To the French this was only right. They, too, saw their Revolution as part of a world-wide battle to liberate all mankind. For example, at the end of the Italian campaign, Napoleon had inscribed on his banners the various peoples freed by his army. Others, such as the Girondist Jacques Brissot, injected an ideological note into the struggle by arguing for a peoples' war against kings, particularly those of the Bourbon family. By implication there could never be peace for humanity as long as kings sat on their thrones.

Although sympathizers and potential collaborators abounded in most European countries, their reasons for this were not as uniform. They might not totally agree with all of the Revolution, but could find some aspect of it that was desirable. Artisans and small shopkeepers approved of the political participation of the masses during Jacobin rule. Serfs and peasants, like their French counterparts, wanted land reform and abolition of feudal privileges. Anticlerics, particularly in Catholic lands, hoped to subordinate the Church in political and economic affairs. The bourgeoisie wanted an end to privilege and lingering feudal economic practices. Finally, reformers coming out of the *philosophe* tradition saw the Revolution as the culmination of the Enlightenment and wanted to impose reason on their own societies.

Therefore, as the French entered foreign lands, willing collaborators were easily found: Dutch Patriots; Belgian followers of Jan Vonck; adherents of *Josephismus* in Austria; Italian, German, and Polish nationalists, and followers of the Enlightenment in Spain and the Holy Roman Empire. Admiration often turns into slavish imitation. And in those "liberated" lands, the establishment of "little Frances," such as the Batavian, Helvetic, and Cisalpine Republics, followed. It should be recognized that these internal elements were not powerful enough by themselves to revolutionize their lands. Their opportunity came only through the victories of the French armies.

### The Wars

It will be recalled that the French Revolutionaries first entered into war in April, 1792, against Austria and Prussia. In 1793, Spain, Holland, Great Britain, and various Italian states were also at war with France.

The powers that composed this First Coalition anticipated an easy campaign against the Revolutionary rabble. But the Revolution had unleashed a heretofore unknown military factor: the determination of a people to resist collectively. The population was totally mobilized. This was known as the *levée en masse,* in which all elements within society—old men, young men, women, and children—had their assigned tasks to perform for the nation. The French army swelled to over three-quarters of a million by 1794. Enthusiasm and large numbers alone did not account for the victories; able, innovative military leaders, such as Napoleon, Dumouriez, and Jourdan, also provided an explanation. At any rate, the French surprised their enemies by their will to resist.

The First Coalition collapsed; but by 1798, a Second Coalition, composed of Russia, Austria, and Britain, was formed. Russia withdrew after being defeated in Switzerland. Napoleon's victory at Marengo in 1800 forced the Austrians to sue for peace in 1801. And the Peace of Amiens in 1801, ended the Anglo-French conflict.

After ten years of fighting against the combined resources of the most powerful European nations, France was not only victorious, but even more powerful than before. Revolutionary France had obtained the goal of royalist France: the natural frontiers of the Rhine, Pyrenees, the Alps, and the Juras. Besides the territories annexed, France was also surrounded by faithful, trustworthy satellites. This was the legacy destined for Napoleon Bonaparte.

### Napoleon in Power

After the 18th Brumaire, the government of France was again reorganized. The Constitution of the Year VIII provided for a tricameral legislature and for three executives, called Consuls. An elaborate constitutional system of checking and diffusing political power was established. How-

**Figure 17-2.**   Napoleon at bridge of Arcole over the Adige River on Nov. 16–17, 1796. Italian Campaign. Painting by Gros.

ever, it was Napoleon Bonaparte, serving as First Consul, to whom the majority of the nation looked for leadership. He seemed to offer stability and order. And, being a product of the Revolution himself, he posed no threat of restoring the *Ancien Régime* or the Bourbons.

### Consulate

As First Consul, Napoleon did provide stability and, as has already been indicated, peace, in the Treaties of Lunéville with Austria and Amiens with Britain. Napoleon's political course was charted for the Imperial throne. In early 1802, his term as First Consul was lengthened by ten years, but in August the voters by a landslide approved of extending it to life. The outbreak of hostilities with Britain, fear of *émigrés'* plots, and threats (both real and manufactured) on Napoleon's life were used to transform the Consulate into the Grand Empire. By another overwhelming majority, the voters approved of Napoleon becoming Emperor of the French. While the Pope looked on, Napoleon crowned himself and his wife Josephine in Notre Dame Cathedral on December 2, 1804. The French Revolution had come full cycle—from monarchy to monarchy.

### Empire

Under both the Consulate and the Empire, the machinery of the state operated to ensure Napoleon's undisputed control of the French. Opposition was simply not tolerated, and means by which to prevent it were introduced. Theaters, literature, newspapers, and bookstores were subject to state censorship. Great powers were accorded the police. Joseph Fouché, the Minister of Police, maintained strict surveillance over the nation through a vast network of secret agents, informers, *agent provocateurs,* and postal censors. Political interference with the judiciary occurred. Enemies of the state faced imprisonment for political beliefs. Harsh punishments, such as branding or the wearing of an iron collar, were allowed. And, at least on two occasions, opponents of the regime were charged with lunacy. Indeed, the methods of operating the state and controlling the citizen in Napoleonic France smacked of modern totalitarianism.

**Reforms.**    Despite the harshness of his methods, Napoleon was responsible for giving France many important reforms. Perhaps Napoleon's most famous contribution was the code of laws, collectively called the Code Napoleon. For the first time, all of France was governed by a uniform series of laws, enabling the citizen to know at all times how he stood in relation to the law. The Code Napoleon, considered so logical and so superior to previous laws, has spread from France to numerous lands the world over.

Napoleon also deserves credit for ending the rift between Church and state. His Concordat of 1801 with Pope Pius VII was one of the first definitions of the role of the Church in a modern state. By this agreement, Napoleon recognized Catholicism as the dominant faith of France, but separate from the state, which would not use its powers to impose Catholicism upon the citizenry. The Pope was guaranteed his possessions in Italy; however, clerical lands confiscated by the Revolution were not to be restored. Church rites and processions were allowed, although subject to public regulations. High ecclesiastical officials would be nominated by the government, and, in turn, the Pope would appoint them. In lieu of the tithe, clergymen were salaried by the state. Unquestionably, Napoleon won a great political victory by the Concordat. He endeared himself to his more conservative subjects and placed French clergymen in his camp, while at the same time giving very little to the Pope.

A system of secular education was also promoted by Napoleon. Community controlled primary schools were supplemented by the *lycées.* The *lycées,* secondary schools to train the future leaders of the nation, were Napoleon's creation. Those who attended received state scholarships. It was only natural that Napoleon with his military interests also built new military schools.

One final example of Napoleonic reforms was in economics. France was placed on a sounder financial base by replacing paper currency with precious metal. To facilitate credit, the Bank of France was established in February, 1800. Tax farming was abolished to be replaced by more orderly and rational state collection. These reforms along with the strong, authoritarian nature of Napoleon's government created a sound financial atmosphere for the nation.

**Quest for Legitimacy.** Despite his record of reform, Napoleon used his powers to aggrandize himself. But he was not totally content. In order for his work to endure, the Napoleonic System had to be ensured of continuing. An Imperial Hierarchy, replete with rituals, titles, and honors, was created. Still, Napoleon was dissatisfied; he knew that he was seen as an upstart, a "child of the Revolution." This he hoped to erase by legitimatizing himself. To this end, his relatives, merely for being of his blood, were uplifted: three brothers and a brother-in-law became kings, while a stepson was named an Italian viceroy. Napoleon himself divorced Josephine in 1810, and married Marie Louise, the nineteen-year-old Hapsburg Archduchess and grandniece of Marie Antoinette. She bore him a son entitled the "king of the Romans." But no matter how many honors Napoleon bestowed on himself or his family, he held power through his military prowess. This is what the European dynasts respected —not titles.

Not only was France under Napoleon's rule, but most of Europe, too. Holland, Belgium, much of Italy, and the distant Illyrian Provinces on the Adriatic were annexed outright to France. For all practical purposes, Spain, Switzerland, the Grand Duchy of Warsaw, the German principalities in the Confederation of the Rhine, and the Kingdoms of Italy and Naples were French satellites. By 1810, the nations of Denmark, Sweden, Prussia, Austria, and Russia were allies of Napoleonic France. However, the catalog of nations owing allegiance to Napoleon was deceptive, for few of these nations were willingly allied and subordinated to France. The majority of these lands and their populace were merely biding their time, waiting for the opportune moment to expel the French and the Napoleonic System.

## The Fall of Napoleon

### English Resistance

The most persistent enemy of Revolutionary and Napoleonic France was Great Britain. This nation's geographical location and navy repeat-

**Figure 17-3.**

edly defied military conquest. The Battle of Trafalgar in 1805 proved that the French navy, even in combination with the Spanish, could not break Britain's sea power. Britain, further, was always more than willing to finance resistance against the French. This country, disdainfully called "a nation of shopkeepers," was already in the beginning stages of an industrial revolution; her commercial power was a constant thorn to Napoleon.

Recognizing that he was in a duel to the death with the British, Napoleon decided to strike at that nation's most vulnerable spot: its economy. Britain absolutely had to export its manufactured goods in exchange for food and money. If Britain lost its markets on the Continent, then the British would be immensely weakened and have to beg Napoleon for peace or face a possible internal revolution. Consequently, Napoleon decided on economic warfare. He issued the Berlin and Milan Decrees which closed the Continent to British trade.

**Continental System.** These decrees, however, boomeranged. Not only did Britain need the Continent, but the Continent needed and depended on British goods and trade. An economic slump hit the major ports of Europe. Import duties, which otherwise would have been channelled into French pockets, were lost. To make matters worse, Britain was not badly hurt by the decrees; for smuggling of British goods at higher prices became commonplace. And, since France lacked the necessary naval power, nothing could be done by Napoleon to prevent British goods from entering Europe. Napoleon refused to admit the futility of his economic blockade, and ignored the pleas of his allies to revoke the Berlin and Milan Decrees. In December, 1811, Alexander announced that his nation would resume trading with Britain. This was an open violation of Napoleon's "Continental System" which he could not afford to ignore. Napoleon, therefore, prepared the Grand Army to punish the Russians.

The relations between Napoleon and Alexander had always been rather stormy. Along with Britain and Austria, in 1805, Russia entered the Third Coalition against France. Toward the end of the year, the Austro-Russian troops suffered defeat at Austerlitz. Austria signed another peace. Prussia soon took Austria's place in the war. The Prussian Army, which had been so glorious under Frederick the Great, was defeated at the Battle of Jena. Russia's turn was next. The Battle of Friedland made Alexander seek accommodations with Napoleon.

Alexander and Napoleon met at Tilsit in 1807 to negotiate a settlement. Since the two met alone on a raft in the middle of the Niemen River, it is difficult to know precisely what the terms at Tilsit were. It is generally agreed that the two decided to divide Europe into Russian and French spheres. Russia was to honor the blockade against Britain and to recognize and respect French interests in Western Europe. France, on the other hand, was to help Russia acquire Finland from Sweden and Constantinople from the Ottoman Empire.

However, suspicion soon developed between Napoleon and Alexander. Alexander did not favor Napoleon establishing the Polish Duchy of Warsaw in proximity to Russian Poland. Nor did he approve of Napoleon being in contact with the Ottoman Sultan or dabbling in German affairs close to his border. When Austria again rose up against France in 1809, the czar refused to send aid to Napoleon. Alexander's failure to abide by the blockade of British goods was the last straw.

### Russian Campaign

In order to punish Russia and crush the independence of Alexander, Napoleon with an army of over a half-million entered Russia in June of 1812. Battles were fought with Napoleon usually besting the Russians. Yet, Alexander's forces remained intact. Plunging deeper and deeper into Russia, Napoleon reached Moscow in September. The city mysteriously caught fire and the French had no recourse save retreat. During the withdrawal from Russia, the French suffered tremendous disasters. They not only had to contend with the harsh Russian weather and a lack of supplies in a countryside laid to waste, but with Russian guerrillas. A mere one-fifth of those who crossed into Russia returned.

The news of this disaster electrified Europe. Perhaps, at long last, the time had come for another attempt to crush Napoleon. Indeed, it had. Before discussing the threat to Napoleon after the Russian fiasco, it should be pointed out that other nations within Napoleonic Europe were resisting French encroachment and undermining Napoleon's power.

### Continental Resistance

Prussia, humiliated by the Peace of Tilsit which left that nation only a rump of its previous territory, went through a process of "regeneration." The philosopher Johann Fichte delivered a series of addresses that instilled in the Prussians a patriotic pride of being German. Baron von Stein reformed the more glaring abuses within the Prussian state. As the result of the work of these men and others, Prussia was prepared to spearhead a German "War of Liberation."

A similar situation developed in Spain. The Spanish masses, seemingly impervious to French Revolutionary propaganda, fought tooth and claw for their beloved deposed ruler Ferdinand VII, their Catholic religions, and their *fueros* (traditional corporate "rights"). A genuine peoples' crusade was waged against the French and their Spanish collaborators, the *afrancesados*. The Spanish resistance was aided by the British, who landed a force commanded by the future Duke of Wellington in July, 1808, in the peninsula. From that time on, Spain was a running sore to the French. The Spanish, Portuguese, and British moved inexorably toward the Pyrenees.

Opposition to the French existed elsewhere in Europe. But only in Britain, Spain, and Sicily did the exponents of reaction have a genuine popular following. To be sure, there were opponents to the French and to Napoleonic rule. This did not necessarily mean hostility to the French Revolution. The tragedy was that most people had to choose between Napoleonic despotism and reaction—not between the Revolution and reaction. In the final analysis, the overwhelming majority, without enthusiasm, opted for the defeat of Napoleon and the reaction that inevitably had to follow.

### Napoleon's Defeat

Even before his army had left Russia, Napoleon was back in France in order to raise a new army to protect his conquests and empire. In the meantime, most of his allies had deserted him. The last and most formidable coalition (Britain, Prussia, Russia, Austria, and Sweden) was formed to defeat him. In October, 1813, outside Leipzig, Saxony, 160,000 French clashed with double that number of allied troops. This "Battle of All-Nations" was another defeat for Napoleon who now had no hope of preventing an invasion of France.

Napoleon again returned to France to take charge of defenses. There was not to be another *levée en masse* as had previously occurred.

The French had wearied of Napoleon's wars. Besides, why should they fight for an authoritarian state dedicated to the glory of one individual? Without allies, resources, revenues, or reserves, Napoleon abdicated in favor of his son on April 6, 1814. On the 20th, he was sent to the small island of Elba to remain, it was hoped, in exile.

The allies had absolutely no intention of allowing another Bonaparte, even if only a child, to sit on the throne of France. The victors had already agreed to restore the Bourbon dynasty. Louis XVI's younger brother was to be king of France. Louis XVIII was greeted rather unenthusiastically by the French people. Too much had happened since they had last had a Bourbon king. Although Louis XVIII promised a charter with some civil liberties and protection of individual rights, his régime was looked upon with suspicion particularly since he was surrounded by diehard *émigré* nobles and clergymen. In retrospect, Napoleon began to look better to the people of France.

### Hundred Days

Napoleon had kept abreast of events on the mainland. He received reports of the discontent within France and the squabbles among the victors at Vienna. As a consequence, he decided to risk seizing control of France once more.

The Hundred Days began when Napoleon landed in the south of France on March 1, 1815. His landing party was augmented by thousands of veterans who flocked to his standards on the way to Paris. On March 14, Marshal Ney, a Napoleonic veteran who commanded the Bourbon forces, went over to Napoleon with his total army. After this, Louis XVIII and the *émigrés* had no recourse but to flee. France was again in Napoleon's hands. He vowed that his empire now represented peace and that he had no further territorial or personal ambitions. Of course, the allies did not believe him. Both they and he knew that the future of Napoleon had to be decided on the battlefield.

A French army marched toward Brussels, but along the road near the little village of Waterloo an English force under the Duke of Wellington with the Prussians under Marshal Bluecher awaited it. Napoleon's final defeat and abdication followed. On July 15, 1815, he sailed from France forever. The Hundred Days had come to an end.

Napoleon's final days were spent on the small island of St. Helena in the South Atlantic. On May 5, 1821, he died of stomach cancer. However, even before his death, he had become a living legend whose name brought tears to the eyes of many and struck fear into the hearts of others. The magic of his name enabled a nephew to gain control of France twenty-seven years later. As recently as 1969, celebrations were held in France to commemorate the bicentennial of Napoleon's birth. Most assuredly, the name of Napoleon Bonaparte has been indelibly written on the pages of Western man's history.

## Summary

Although there is disagreement concerning what the Age of the French Revolution exactly represented, it is beyond dispute that the age marked a watershed in the history of Western Civilization. But what sort of watershed? Was the Revolution an end, the last gasp of the *Ancien Régime,* or a beginning of something new and different? Was mankind worse or better off because of the Revolution? Did it leave a legacy of good, evil, or a combination of both? These are merely a few of the fundamental questions raised in assessing such an important span of twenty-six years. However, it is usually agreed that the French Revolution left Western man with a legacy that was often contradictory and at cross-purposes.

One of the traditions to come out of the Revolution was the belief that a country can be ruled best by a written document that fully delineates and specifies the rights, duties, and obligations of the citizen and his rulers. The Americans and, more importantly to Europe, the French perpetuated and spread constitutionalism very widely. Almost all nations —Great Britain is the most outstanding exception—have come to agree with the absolute necessity of being ruled by written constitutions. For the century following the French Revolution, one of the major political demands throughout the Continent was constitutionalism.

Nationalism, also, was a crucial element brought about by the Age of the French Revolution. The ideal was to abolish privilege and castes based on birth and to level all individuals politically to "citizens." Under the Constitution of 1791, for example, Louis XVI's title was king of the French, not of France. New symbols to replace those of the dynasty arose: the motto "Liberty, Equality, and Fraternity"; the tricolor, a national flag; and national hymns such as the *Marseillaise.* These served as the new cement to provide the people with a national identity. For those who refused to accept the national identity, such as Alsatians, Bretons, or Normans, the force of the national state was brought to bear.

The French inadvertently fostered nationalism among other Europeans. Napoleon himself abolished the centuries-old Holy Roman Empire and merged dozens of German principalities into larger blocs. This, coupled with the patriotic fervor of the "War of the Liberation" headed by the Prussians, helped to sow the seeds of German nationalism. The same was done for the Italians, who saw "Italy" appear on maps for the first time in history during the Revolution. Spanish identity was more firmly forged by the struggle against the French. And the creation of the Duchy of Warsaw reawakened the slumbering Poles. So the list goes, down to the very present, as nationalism continues to be a potent political force.

Political democracy was another outstanding legacy of the Revolution. Theoretical civil equality was introduced after the adoption of the Declaration of the Rights of Man and Citizen. "Liberty, Equality, and Fraternity" for all, regardless of birth or economic status, is a fundament of democracy. Citizen participation in and approval of governmental decisions were introduced. Suffrage, although restricted at times, was established as a citizen's right. Even a despot like Napoleon recognized this.

From political democracy to social democracy was not too great a step. It came to be argued that political equality was not possible unless socioeconomic equality also existed. Thus, the French Revolution served as the wellspring for socialism. Indeed, there was much in the Revolution, particularly during the Terror, for socialists to admire: price controls for food, direct participation by the masses in government policy, and the introduction of the *levée en masse*. Finally, socialists and communists alike came to consider Babeuf and his "Conspiracy of Equals" as one of their earliest pioneers.

Tremendous social changes were also brought about by the Revolution. The masses had participated in the great events. The peasants formed the backbone of the armies. The urban poor not only served in the army, but also made their influence felt on the government. The masses had earned a new dignity. Classified as citizens, they were no longer passive bystanders to the events around them.

As it spread, the Revolution delivered a deathblow to feudalism and mercantilism. The removal of these political and socioeconomic barriers enabled the bourgeoisie to come into its own. Now it, like the masses, was an important element that governments increasingly had to respect. As the bourgeoisie rose in importance, the traditional nobles declined. Those *émigrés* who returned to France and other lands long under French domination found that they could not truly restore the previous system. In some lands the nobles reluctantly entered into alliance with the bourgeoisie and survived. Where the nobles insisted on the old ways they ceased to be an important or influential group.

There is a negative side to the legacy of the French Revolution. The Revolution swept away tradition that had served as a barrier to the encroaching powers of the state. After all, it was in the interest of privileged groups such as noble and clergymen to prevent the state from increasing its powers. As a consequence, these elements had formed a natural buffer between the state and individuals. With their removal the state increased in power. In their reforming zeal, Revolutionaries created a superstate that could in the name of nationalism or logic ride roughshod over the individual. Is this not a form of totalitarianism? It is very difficult for the single citizen to stand up against the mighty nation that was first created by the French Revolution.

# On the Low Road

# to

# Revolution

Following over a hundred years of almost continual warfare, the leaders of 1815 were determined to have peace. Inasmuch as they blamed liberalism and nationalism for the latter stages of the war, they were also determined to suppress these. The Congress System was created to accomplish this. The decades of the 1820s, '30s, and '40s were periods of revolution, when the people attempted to acquire what they considered to be their rights.

Peace! Following twenty-three years of almost constant warfare there was peace in Europe. If one includes the four wars for world domination (1689–1763) and the War of the American Revolution (1775–1783), there was peace after a century and a quarter of war. The difference between 1815 and the earlier years was the determination of the leaders to keep the peace. But maintaining the peace within the old framework was not easy, challenged as it was by powerful forces of nationalism and sovereignty.

Nationalism as both a concept and problem was not new; Charlemagne, Alfred the Great, and others had recognized it and had attempted to deal with it. The French Revolution changed the concept of nationalism drastically. The definition before the Revolution was the loyalty one felt toward a certain ruler or overlord. Following the Revolution it was a feeling that held a group of individuals together. Included in this "feeling" was common language, geographical location, and cultural traditions (such as history and folk heros). With the tune of the *Marseillaise* in their hearts, Napoleon's armies marched across Europe spreading this new nationalism. The new nationalism gave rise to two problems: people of the same nationality separated by political boundaries, such as the Germans and also the Italians, wanted to be unified; and, people of one nationality who were ruled by another, such as Czechs, Irish, Poles, and Greeks, wanted to form their own nations. However, the leaders of Europe in 1815 chose to ignore or suppress nationalism.

As for sovereignty, with whom does it rest? Kings chosen by God? Rulers controlled by the middle classes? Or leaders selected by the masses? To the monarchs of 1815 democracy and mob rule were the same and only legitimate rulers were fit to lead.

Four terms that were used extensively during the nineteenth century are still popular today: radical, liberal, conservative, and reactionary. In 1815 the use of the terms usually depended on one's outlook toward nationalism and sovereignty, and in 1815 the conservatives and reactionaries were in command.

### Congress of Vienna

To implement a lasting peace, the largest gathering of diplomats ever seen in the Western World met in Vienna. There were representatives from every soverign nation in Europe except Turkey. In order to entertain the dozen heads of state and their attendants, there were constant presentations of plays, operas, balls, and banquets, leaving outside observers with the conclusion that the Congress of Vienna was one continuous party. But behind this façade, the representatives of five nations made decisions that deeply affected Europe.

### Big Five

One man dominated not only the Congress but Europe in the decades to follow: Prince Klemens von Metternich. Metternich, as foreign minister of Austria, represented the strongest nation of central Europe and was dedicated to restoring Europe as it had been before 1789. Alexander I of Russia oscillated between liberalism and conservatism but he was determined to strengthen Russia. Frederick William III of Prussia was ready to endorse Alexander's ambitions, if Prussia's influence in Germany increased. Great Britain's representative, Lord Castlereagh, was practical and not interested in territorial gains on the Continent. Favoring the balance of power he pushed for a nonpunitive treatment of France. Under a secret agreement (spring, 1814) the big four powers decided they would draft the settlement at Vienna and submit it to the smaller states for approval. Acting as spokesman for the excluded little countries a fifth representative worked his way into the inner circle. Surprisingly, it was the French representative and even more surprisingly, it was the wily Talleyrand—formerly serving the Republic, the Empire, and now Louis XVIII.

The major issues facing the Congress of Vienna included what to do with France, how to redraw the boundaries of Europe, and how to guarantee a lasting settlement.

### French Settlement

Following the exile of Napoleon and restoration of Louis XVIII, the Treaty of Paris (May, 1814) was very lenient toward France. She was permitted to retain her boundaries as of November 1, 1792, including the Austrian Netherlands and parts of Savoy and Germany, and did not have to pay an indemnity. A second treaty was imposed on France following Napoleon's Hundred Days. This treaty reduced the boundaries of France (still larger than in 1789) and an indemnity was paid.

**Figure 18-1.** Contemporary French cartoon satirizing the Congress of Vienna. From left to right: Tallyrand stands by waiting to see how matters develop, Castlereagh hesitates, Metternich leads the dancing, the king of Saxony clutches his crown in fear, and Genoa tries to enter into the spirit of the occasion.

### Redrawing Europe

The geographic-political settlement of Europe was based on legitimacy, encirclement of France, and compensation—which were not always in harmony.

**Legitimacy and Encirclement.** The Congress was dedicated to restoring legitimate rulers to their thrones. Although it did so in France, Spain, Holland, Naples, and Piedmont-Sardinia, the determination to strengthen the nations bordering France minimized the return to *status quo antebellum.*

The best examples of this was the decision to retain Napoleon's Confederation of the Rhine as the German Confederation, which meant potentially stronger German states bordering France and over two hundred legitimate rulers not returned to their thrones. Further strengthening of states near France took place when the Netherlands received the Austrian Netherlands, Piedmont-Sardinia was given territory bordering southern France, and Prussia acquired possessions along the Rhine River.

**Compensations.** There were compensations and exchanges of territories: Austria received Lombardy and Venetia in exchange for the

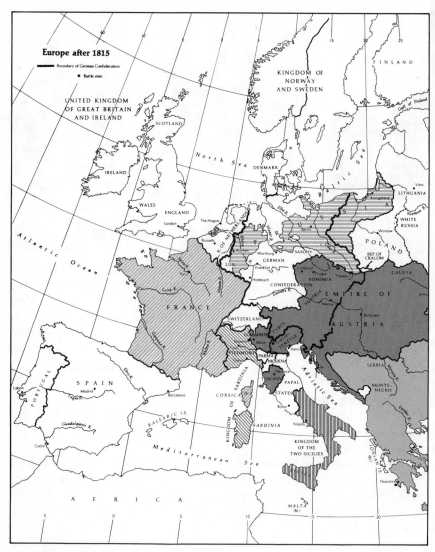

**Figure 18-2.**

Austrian Netherlands; Sweden was given Norway in exchange for Finland; Prussia acquired forty percent of Saxony in exchange for relinquishing her share of Poland; Great Britain retained Ceylon and Cape Colony; and, Russia received Finland and Poland. The question of the disposition of Poland caused the most frustrating disagreement between the big five, but Talleyrand's proposal of further territorial compensation for both

Austria and Prussia stopped a threatened dissolution of the Congress.

Even before the final settlements were decided, the leaders of Europe had created the machinery to guarantee the settlements would last by the formation of the Congress System.

## 1820s: Congress System and Revolution

### Congress System

Along with the Second Treaty of Paris, the Big Four—Great Britain, Russia, Prussia, and Austria—also signed a secret agreement called the Quadruple Alliance which declared each would contribute troops in case there was another attempted Napoleonic return. The Alliance also stated that they would meet every few years to discuss problems of "common interests" and take measures for the "maintenance of peace in Europe."

Two months prior to the formation of the Quadruple Alliance, Alexander I of Russia, under the influence of the German mystic Baroness Barbara von Krudener, proposed that the monarchs of Europe as Christian rulers make an alliance with God to renounce war. The reactions to this Holy Alliance were interesting. Metternich called it a "loud sounding nothing," and Castlereagh said it was "mysticism and nonsense." But since Alexander was serious, and Metternich said nothing harmful about it, the monarchs of Europe agreed to the Alliance except the Ottoman Sultan, because he was not Christian; the Pope, because he was above such agreements; and, the future George IV of Great Britain who claimed an alliance with God was contrary to the British Constitution.

Inasmuch as there were two alliances, confusion has been caused among both students and historians as to the relationship of the Congress to each of them. The Congress System originated from the secret Quadruple Alliance, but when Metternich needed some sort of legal basis for repressive measures against revolutionaries, he referred to the very Holy Alliance which he originally had considered a joke.

### Congresses of Aix-la-Chapelle and Troppau

In 1818, the members of the Quadruple Alliance met at Aix-la-Chapelle and except for the addition of France as a member, making it the Quintuple Alliance, there was nothing of significance settled at the gathering, but two years later at Troppau conditions were different. In 1820, revolutions were beginning in many parts of Europe: Spain, Sardinia, Naples, and Portugal. Despite the official protest of Great Britain and lukewarm support of France, the three Eastern European powers prepared the Troppau Protocol which stated that the right existed to interfere in the internal affairs of a nation if strife within that nation threatened the peace of the "European Alliance." To further endorse this theory, Austria was authorized to aid Ferdinand I, King of Naples, in putting down the Neapolitan revolution in January, 1821.

### Congress of Verona

The final meeting of the Quintuple Alliance was in Verona in 1822. The revolutions were continuing: the king of Spain was in the hands of revolutionaries; the liberals of Portugal desired the return of King John from exile in Brazil; and, the Greek subjects of the Ottoman Empire were in revolt. There was one change in the structure of the allies: the French government under the control of the ultras (conservatives) now favored the Troppau Protocol. Great Britain, standing alone, was unable or unwilling to do anything about the French army sent to return Ferdinand VII to power in Spain. Spanish America was a different matter.

### Latin American Independence

During the Bonaparte domination of Spain, *juntas* were formed in the Spanish colonies in the name of Ferdinand to resist the French. Once Ferdinand was restored and had demonstrated his repressive rule in Spain, the Spanish American colonies declared their independence. Simon Bolivar, San Martin, and other leaders created new states by the time the Alliance reinstated Ferdinand in control of Spain.

The question in 1823 was, would the Alliance now help restore her American colonies to Spain? Great Britain was determined to stop any such restoration, not for political or cultural reasons, but economic. The end of the Napoleonic Wars had brought a depression to industrialized England, but Spanish America free from mercantile restrictions had become a ready market for British goods. If the former colonies were returned to Spain, Great Britain would lose a major area for exports. Great Britain also realized that if it came to a war over the Americas an ally was needed, and there was only one major power in the Western Hemisphere—the United States.

**Monroe Doctrine.** George Canning, Foreign Minister of Great Britain, proposed an alliance to John Quincy Adams, Secretary of State of the United States. At subsequent cabinet meetings, President Monroe and most of the cabinet favored such an alliance, but Adams had a different proposal. He argued that the alliance would place the United States second to Great Britain. If, on the other hand, the United States initiated unilateral action against the Quadruple Alliance, Great Britain would have to go along. Thus the Monroe Doctrine came into existence on December 2, 1823, as part of the President's State of the Union message. It stated that the Western Hemisphere was no longer open for European colonization; any attempt of European powers to expand their influence would be considered a threat to the United States; the United States would not interfere with existing colonies; and, the United States would stay out of strictly European matters. The first part was aimed at the Quadruple Alliance and the second, at Russian advances along the west coast of North America. Canning's first response was anger, but he later boasted, "I called the New World into existence to redress the balance of the Old." Although the stand of the United States and Great Britain stopped the Quadruple Alliance for the first time, there was another revolution in the 1820s that completely disrupted the concert of Europe.

### Greek Revolution

The revolt of the Greeks was different from any of the others: it was Christian Greeks versus Moslem Turks; there was a philhellenic movement in Europe expressed in art, literature, and architecture; and, Russia wanted to increase her holdings in the Balkans.

The revolt, which started in 1821, had little popular support outside of Greece, until the Turks began numerous brutalities, including hanging the Greek Patriarch of Constantinople in 1821 and massacring almost a hundred thousand Greeks on the Island of Chios in 1822. Volunteers, funds, and goods went to Greece from throughout Europe. The death of Lord Byron in 1824 while fighting for Greek independence brought even further aid. In 1825, Sultan Mahud II, unable to contain the revolution, persuaded his vassal Mehemet Ali, pasha of Egypt, to intercede. The Egyptian military and naval actions began to turn the tide against the Greeks.

Actual intervention by any European power had been blocked by Metternich and the concept of the Congress System. But in 1827, Great Britain, Russia, and France signed the Treaty of London, under which they agreed to secure an armistice in Greece. As a combined British and French fleet moved into Greek waters, a Russian army marched into the Balkans.

At Navarino the British-French armada met the Egyptian fleet, and in "defending" itself, destroyed the Egyptian. French troops then landed and drove out the Turkish-Egyptian forces. Lord Wellington, the new Foreign Minister, apologized to Turkey for the "accident." Meanwhile, Russian forces were fighting their way across Rumania and Bulgaria. With these troops nearing Constantinople, the Sultan asked for peace. Under the Treaty of Adrianople in 1829 Greece was recognized as an independent kingdom; and, Serbia and Rumania were made autonomous states.

The 1820s were over and so was the Congress System. Although it had been able to stop revolutions in Spain and Naples, when national aspirations became more important than the international status quo, this first modern attempt at organized cooperation ended. The Congress System was finished, but the revolutions were not.

## 1830s: Reaction, Revolution, and Reform

### Restoration France

Louis XVIII (1814–1824), in many ways, was an excellent restoration ruler. He was not a liberal, nor a reactionary, nor ambitious, nor a great intellect. He issued a charter guaranteeing parliamentary government, yet with restrictive enough suffrage that only the aristocrats and wealthy middle class were able to vote. He was well served by various ministers in both internal and external affairs. Industrial growth brought prosperity and France's participation in foreign affairs made her an equal partner in the Congress System by 1818.

Although there was some resistance to Louis from all factions—Bonapartists, republicans, workers, and the middle class—it was the attempt to push France back to pre–1789 by ultra-royalists in the legislature under the leadership of Louis' brother which frustrated the moderate Restoration government. At Louis' death it was this leader of the ultras who became Charles X (1824–1830).

**Charles X.**   Charles was determined to rule as an absolute monarch and in attempting to do so, managed to turn most factions against him. He made it a capital offense to destroy church property, which alienated even moderate clerics. His desire to compensate *émigrés* for losses from the Revolution, cost him the support of the peasantry, who feared the loss of their lands. His disbanding of the National Guard because it was "the army of the people," isolated the middle and lower classes, and his dismissal of non-ultra army leaders irritated the military.

**July Revolution.**   When the elections of 1830 placed a large anti-ultra majority in the Chamber of Deputies, Charles issued the Ordinances of St. Cloud on July 26 which dismissed the new legislature, authorized censorship of the press, and changed the electoral system, leaving only the aristocracy with the vote. The answer in Paris was barricades in the streets. And, when troops sent to Paris joined the resurrected National Guard under Lafayette, Charles X fled to England on July 29.

The Assembly which Charles had ordered disbanded was the only governmental body that existed in France. Although anti-ultra, it was royalist in nature, favoring neither a republic nor Bonaparte restoration. The Assembly, therefore, offered the throne to Louis Philippe, Duke of Orleans.

**July Monarchy.** Louis Philippe, was an acceptable choice to most, except possibly radical republicans. As a direct descendant of Louis XIII he had a legitimate claim to the throne. Both he and his father had sided with the Revolution until the reign of terror. Since the restoration he had been the leader of the middle-class opposition to the Bourbons. For dramatics, once he was appointed by the Assembly he and Lafayette appeared before the masses of Paris with the tricolors of the Revolution draped over both of them. He accepted the title of "King of the French People" not of France; he reissued the Charter of 1814, so liberalized as to extend suffrage to all the upper middle class; he dressed like a member of the middle class; and, he dedicated himself to expanding industrialization.

The reaction of the conservatives to this first successful overthrow of a legitimate monarch was predictable. Metternich stated that his life's work was destroyed and numerous rulers became uneasy. To many liberals and nationalists the revolt was a signal for action. Although revolutions began all over Europe, only the one bordering France was really successful.

### Belgian Revolution

The present area of Belgium has had a thousand-year history of conflict: Viking raids, Hundred Years' War, Hapsburg possession, and Napoleonic conquest. When made part of the Netherlands, the Belgians (Flemings and Walloons) due to their different religion, language, and cultural backgrounds were dissatisfied. Following the July Revolution, the Belgians declared their independence. The army sent to quell the uprising was defeated and William I of the Netherlands turned to the major powers for assistance, but none was available: Prussia was occupied in Germany; Austria, in Italy; and Russia, in Poland. The reaction from the governments of Great Britain and France was the opposite from what the Netherlands wanted. France's new minister to Great Britain—Talleyrand—informed the British that France endorsed an independent Belgium. Britain, not wanting an independent Belgium dominated by France, also backed the Revolution. With the French army and British navy behind the Belgians, the Netherlands soon relinquished her claims.

Because of Belgium's strategic position, the Treaty of London (1839) specified that the signatories of the treaty (Great Britain, Prussia, Russia, France, and Austria) would guarantee the independence and borders of Belgium.

### German Confederation

Although the German Confederation was no longer part of a Hapsburg controlled Holy Roman Empire, Metternich soon was able to make it a weapon against liberal movements. The only organ of government was the unicameral diet which represented the rulers of the Confederation. The only significant nationalistic movement was among the young intellectuals at the German universities. At Wartburg in 1817 thousands of students, mostly members of the *Burschenschaften,* gathered to dedicate themselves to the cause of "union and freedom." A year and a half later, Karl Sand, a mentally unbalanced member of the *Burschenschaften,* assassinated the reactionary dramatist August von Kotzebue. Metternich used this as an excuse to act against the nationalists. He prepared the Carlsbad Decrees which the Confederation Diet adopted in 1819. These decrees abolished student nationalist groups, placed censorship on newspapers and surveillance on universities. The Carlsbad decrees effectively restricted the activities of liberals and nationalists during most of the 1820s, but by the latter part of the decade, these groups commenced to meet again secretly.

The July Revolution touched off a series of revolutions in Germany. In three states (Brunswick, Saxony, and Hesse-Cassel) the rulers were forced to abdicate and their replacements issued constitutions. When these and other demonstrations occurred, Metternich once more convinced the diet to pass restrictive measures against organized political groups, which held down any significant liberal movement until the 1840s.

### Young Italy

The last group stimulated by the July Revolution was the Italian Carbonari, a secret society favoring unification and independence for Italy. Its members started rebellions in Modena, Tuscany, and the Papal States. Hapsburg troops quickly put down the revolutions and the Carbonari was destroyed. However, one of the leaders founded a new revolutionary group, *Giovine Italia* (Young Italy). Giuseppe Mazzini was a fiery and intelligent revolutionary who attracted many dedicated Italian nationalists, including Giuseppe Garibaldi, who became one of the most respected Italian patriots. Their activities eventually led to exile; Mazzini to London where his prolific pen sent broadsides back to Italy; and, Garibaldi to Latin America where he became a fighter for freedom.

### Imperial Russia

Alexander I, who gave Poland a constitution and convinced Louis XVIII to give one to the French, died in 1825 without accomplishing any significant reform for Russia. Although the heir to Alexander's throne was his liberal brother Constantine, Constantine abdicated his claim to a third brother Nicholas. In the confusion, revolts occurred in various parts of Russia, usually under the slogan of "Constantine and Constitution." They were poorly led, failed to gather any popular support, and were easily crushed. The only result of the so-called Decembrist Revolt was to convince Nicholas I that Westernized liberal ideas were not good for Russia.

**Nicholas I.** Nicholas ruled Russia for the next three decades under the slogan of "Autocracy, Orthodoxy, and Nationalism," meaning one ruler, the Czar; one religion, Russian Orthodox; and, one Russia, Russification. Foreign visitors were limited, and no non-Russian publications were allowed. Only undesirable Russians were allowed to migrate. The secret police became very well organized and kept an eye on schools, churches, books, newspapers, and music.

**Polish Revolt.** Although they were the recipients of a liberal constitution from Alexander, which Nicholas honored, the Poles wanted complete independence. Inspired by the French revolution of 1830 and the absent Russian governor, Constantine, the Poles revolted in November, 1830, driving out the Russian garrison. With independence within their grasp the leaders broke into factions, which allowed their reconquest. Nicholas repealed the constitution, closed the universities, harassed the Catholic Church, and put Russian officials in charge of Polish internal affairs, all of which reduced Poland to a mere province.

### Peaceful Britain

The Tories, soon to be called the Conservatives, controlled the government of Great Britain until 1830. Although representing the conservative aristocracy, men such as George Canning, William Huskinsson, and Sir Robert Peel helped bring about a series of reforms during the 1820s. In 1824 the Combination Acts which prohibited labor unions were repealed. An emancipation bill removed restrictions against Catholics and allowed them to be members of Parliament and hold most public offices. Finally, Peel instituted reforms in criminal justice, including abolishing the death penalty for almost two hundred offences such as sheep stealing. He also created the London Metropolitan Police, whose nickname of "Bobbie" is in Sir Robert Peel's honor.

**Reform Bill of 1832.** The death of George IV in 1830, by tradition, meant parliamentary elections, and the Whigs gained control of the Parliament. Earl Grey, Prime Minister, 1830–1834, favored sharing political power, monopolized by the landed aristocracy, with the middle class. The Reform Bill failed to pass Commons the first time, the House of Lords the second, and only William IV's threat to create new peers pressured the Lords to pass the Bill on the third attempt. The Reform Bill shifted representation from sparsely populated rural areas to more highly populated industrialized centers, abolishing what were called "rotten boroughs"— for example, Old Sarum no longer existed as a town, yet still had two representatives in Parliament, while Manchester had none. It also lowered property requirements for voting, which extended suffrage fifty percent. Although it stands as one of the major political reforms in Britain, the Reform Bill gave the vote to neither city workers nor farm workers.

The revolutions of the 1830s, if measured by gains and losses, stood roughly two wins, four losses, and numerous non-contests. In all, the 1830s were the preliminaries for the revolutions of the 1840s.

### 1840s: Revolution and Counter-Revolution

The first half of the nineteenth century was a period of Romanticism which stimulated a growing nationalism. The works of writers, poets, artists, and composers tended to glorify the past history of a nation. Politically, the continued frustration of the middle class desired a voice in government and the growing consciousness of the working classes came to a head by midcentury. Economically, times were bad, for crop failures caused a food shortage, and a business recession created unemployment.

### The Preliminaries

**Great Britain.** In Great Britain, the middle class had gained in 1832 what their counterparts elsewhere still desired. As the first nation to have a large laboring class it was logical that British workers were the first to push for their rights. And inasmuch as the middle class had used peaceful means to gain its ends, so did the working class. The Chartist movement, by gathering hundreds of thousands of signatures on petitions to Parliament, presented six demands: universal suffrage, secret ballot, no property qualifications for Parliament, payment of members of Parliament, annual elections, and equal electoral districts. Starting in 1839 these petitions were delivered to Parliament only to be ignored. The Chartists continued to present new petitions throughout the 1840s, but then the movement declined.

One of the major reasons for the Chartist movement's loss of support was the effort to repeal the Corn Laws. The Corn Laws placed a tariff on wheat imported to England. Since the farmers were unable to grow enough wheat to feed the nation and it had to be imported, the large landowners made huge profits and the people paid high prices for bread and liquor. The repeal of the Corn Laws (1846) expanded free trade, favored by the manufacturers, lowered the price of bread, and helped create a more content labor force. And in 1848 there was no revolution in Great Britain.

**Switzerland.** It was not a standard revolution in Switzerland, but a capsule form of the religious and political contest that had beset the Holy Roman Empire: Catholic versus Protestant and weak central government versus strong central government. Fearing that the Protestant majority would force changes upon them, the seven Catholic Cantons seceded from the Confederation to form the *Sonderbund*. In November, 1847, the *Sunderbund* forces were defeated, but a liberal peace allowed the secessionists to return. Two years later a new constitution was adopted which was modeled after that of the United States.

### France Under the July Monarchy

France under Louis Philippe had become second only to England as an industrial nation, but by the 1840s problems were developing. The government, practicing a *laissez-faire* attitude, did nothing about the evils associated with industrialization, and there was no attempt to extend voting rights to the lower middle and working classes. This in turn led to the growth of socialism under Louis Blanc. And France was dull. French writers and historians began to write about the glories of the Napoleonic era, which led to a Bonaparte revival, capped by the reinterment of Napoleon's remains in Paris.

**February Revolution.** As the demands for more rights grew, so did the repressive measures of Louis Philippe's government. Newspapers and books were censored, and political activities were restricted, including public meetings. To circumvent these restrictions, opponents of the government inaugurated banquets where the after-dinner speakers criticized Louis Philippe. To add drama to their cause, the dissidents formed torch parades on the way to the banquets. After seventy such meetings during the winter of 1847–1848, on February 22, a large banquet was planned as a final protest. On the day of the banquet the government ordered a ban, which started the revolution. The minor skirmishes of the 22nd became an uprising on the 23rd, and by the 24th Paris was in the hands of the Revolutionaries, Louis Philippe abdicated and fled to Great Britain, and the Second French Republic was proclaimed on February 25th.

**Provisional Government and the June Days.** The provisional government, under the poet Lamartine, consisted of moderates and radicals, including Louis Blanc. Blanc proposed and had adopted the National

Workshops to put to work the mass of unemployed workers. Blanc and the socialists hoped to use this as the start toward socialism, but the National Workshops were placed under Alexander Marie, an avowed antisocialist, which guaranteed their failure.

The provisional government called for elections in April for a National Assembly to prepare a constitution. The nine-hundred-member assembly elected by universal suffrage consisted of five hundred moderate republicans, three hundred monarchists, and one hundred radicals.

The radicals in Paris, observing that they were losing control of the government, used the announcement of the disbanding of the National Workshops as an excuse for another revolution in June. This time it failed. General Louis Cavaignac, a virtual dictator, put down the uprising, killing about ten thousand people. He followed this by arresting and exiling to Algeria eleven thousand suspected insurrectionists.

**Elections of 1848.**    The constitution adopted in November reflected the moderate-to-conservative attitudes. It provided for a legislature and executive elected by universal manhood suffrage and for separation of powers; also the chief executive, the president, was empowered to act against future internal dangers.

On December 10, 1848, presidential elections were held and Louis Napoleon Bonaparte with no organization, no extensive financial backing, few public appearances, and little publicity was elected president by 5,500,000 votes to Cavaignac's 1,500,000 and Lamartine's 200,000. Louis's opponents had considered him a joke, the masses had voted for a name, and this nephew of Napoleon looked upon himself as the one to fulfill his uncle's destiny.

### Revolutions Continued
*Italy.*    It was not a revolution in Italy, rather it was a series of revolutions. The first was in Naples in January, 1848, against Ferdinand II, who granted a constitution. Next, the Grand Duke of Tuscany was forced to follow suit. King Charles Albert of Sardinia and Pope Pius IX of the Papal State issued constitutions without coercion. The Austrian possessions of Lombardy and Venice declared their indepedence.

Charles Albert was convinced by his advisers that the time was right for a united Italy under Sardinia. Calling for support from the other Italian States he invaded Lombardy in March.

The last phase of the Italian revolutions grew out of dissatisfaction in the Papal States. After Pius' premier, Count Rossi, mishandled the government (which led to the assassination of Rossi by a fanatic in November, 1848, a Republic of Rome was proclaimed and Mazzini was invited to become the ruler.

## THE GREAT SEA SERPENT OF 1848.

**Figure 18-3.** Political cartoon with Liberty as the sea serpent and the dingy "L'Ancien Régime."

**Austria.** The causes of the revolution or revolutions in Austria were different from the causes in Italy. Whereas in Italy there was the spark of separated peoples looking toward unification, in Austria it was Hungarians, Croats, Czechs, and Rumanians looking toward separation.

In Hungary, a nationalistic feeling under the leadership of Louis Kossuth had been building. The news of a successful revolution in France was Kossuth's signal to propose that Hungary be given a constitution which would make it a commonwealth, somewhat similar to Canada's present status.

Students in Vienna who were preparing a list of grievances against Emperor Ferdinand, also demanded a constitution. Joined by workers, the students demonstrated for their demands. Troops were used, and the clash caused loss of life on both sides. Fearing further loss of life, Ferdinand consented to the demands of March 13. That day Metternich resigned and fled to England, according to rumor, dressed in his mistress's skirts.

With the revolution spreading, the Hungarian diet passed the March Laws which turned its demands into reality. Ferdinand accepted the March Laws, Lombardy and Venetia declared their independence,

Bohemia revolted for the same rights as Hungary, and the Croats and Rumanians demanded autonomy. Ferdinand's advisers finally convinced the feeble-minded emperor to abdicate in favor of his nephew Franz Joseph.

**Germany.** The revolutions in the German Confederation were similar to those in Italy. Students, middle-class bourgeois, and workers agitated for their rights in most of the states. Many rulers capitulated before violence occurred by replacing conservative ministers with liberal ones or promising liberal constitutions.

Frederick William IV of Prussia, for example, could not believe that demonstrations were aimed at him and gave orders for soldiers not to fire on the crowds, but while dispersing one group, shots were fired from an unknown source and street fighting followed. The king agreed to withdraw the troops from Berlin which left him a prisoner of the people, and Frederick William agreed to a constitutional assembly elected by universal suffrage to work on a constitution during the summer and fall of 1848.

*Frankfurt Assembly.* Meanwhile, a gathering of liberals at Heidelberg dreaming of unification, conceived the idea of a national parliament with representatives elected from every German state. Meeting at Frankfurt, more than eight hundred delegates debated both the form and size of the New Germany. The constitution finally adopted was liberal for mid-nineteenth-century Europe, including even guarantees of free public education. The question of what to include in the New Germany had been the biggest stumbling block. The decision was to include all German states if they gave up their non-German territory, which amounted to an exclusion of Austria. The Frankfurt Assembly then voted to make the King of Prussia the Emperor of Germany.

The year 1848 appeared to bring success to the ambitions of the liberals and nationalists, but within twelve months most of the successes were replaced by failure.

### Counter Revolution

*France.* The French had their own peculiar counter revolution. Here Louis Napoleon was constitutionally limited to a single four-year term as president. Not wishing to step down from power, and having the support of the peasants, clerics, most of the monarchists, and the army, he dissolved the Assembly on December 2, 1851. A plebiscite held eighteen days later overwhelmingly reelected him president for ten years. Within a year, a second plebiscite proclaimed the Second French Empire, finishing the Second Republic.

**Italy.** Inasmuch as Italy had experienced numerous revolutions, there were many counter revolutions. Charles Albert failed to invade Venice after his success in Lombardy, which allowed the Austrian General Radetzky to regroup his forces. Radetzky defeated him at the Battles of Custozza and Novara. In order to save Piedmont from invasion, Charles Albert abdicated and entered a monastery.

Radetzky easily put down the minor resistance in Lombardy and then turned on Venice. Because of its natural defenses he was forced to besiege the city of Venice, and was successful only after a cholera epidemic swept the city. Ferdinand II of Naples was supported by the army and revoked the constitution he had issued during the uprisings of 1848. Pope Pius IX requested aid to regain the Papal State, and Louis Napoleon, seeking Catholic support in France, sent French troops to aid the Pope. Under the command of Garibaldi a small army of volunteers resisted the French attack from April to July, 1849, before Rome was retaken. The last two escapees from Rome were Mazzini and Garibaldi.

**Austria.** In Bohemia the Czechs and Sudetens quarreled giving the Austrians the opportunity to regain control (June, 1848). In September, troops put down demonstrations in Vienna and the constitutional assembly was dismissed. Hungary's demise started with her failure to recognize the rights of minorities she had demanded from Austria. The boundaries of Hungary traditionally included Croatia, and when Croatia requested her independence, Hungary refused. When Franz Joseph revoked his uncle's promise for Hungarian autonomy, the Austrians enlisted a Croatian army to invade Hungary. The Hungarians, who then declared their independence with Kossuth as regent, held out against both the Croatians and Austrians, until a Russian army placed at the Austrian's disposal invaded from the north, Serbians revolted in the south, and the Rumanians rebelled in the east. The Hungarians were defeated, and Kossuth became an exile in the United States where he espoused Hungarian independence.

**Germany.** When the throne of a united Germany was offered Frederick William of Prussia, who wanted to rule Germany, he refused for two reasons: as an advocate of divine right, he could not "pick up a crown from the gutter," and he feared Austrian reaction. With neither Prussia nor Austria willing to endorse a united Germany, the Frankfurt Assembly came to an inglorious end.

At a conference at Olmütz (1850), Nicholas I and Franz Joseph, who knew Frederick William still wanted to be the ruler of a united Germany, made him promise to restore and support the settlement of 1815. This "Humiliation of Olmütz" convinced many German nationalists that Austria could never be part of a united Germany.

## Conclusions

Although it is easy to reject the antidemocratic and antinationalistic objectives of Metternich's Congress System, any evaluation of the system must be positive. Its main objective was Peace, and there were no wars between major powers in the Age of Metternich; the next global war was not until 1914, one hundred years after the Congress of Vienna.

Another objective of the Congress System was international cooperation. It was the first organized attempt at an international organization, and became the prototype for both the League of Nations and United Nations, particularly their security councils.

As an instrument against democracy and nationalism, the results are demonstrated by this chapter. The Age of Metternich as an Age of Revolution is quantitative not qualitative. There were approximately thirty major revolutions between 1820 and 1850, with less than a half dozen succeeding.

Yet, in the midst of the failing revolutions, there were achievements: the last vestiges of feudalism were abolished in central Europe; every German state acquired elected diets; some states retained their liberal constitutions, most significantly Piedmont-Sardinia; and, Great Britain demonstrated reform was possible without revolution. Furthermore, the successes of the second half of the nineteenth century were built on the failures of the first half.

## Summary

Most of the revolutions of the first half of the nineteenth century were failures, that is, they did not gain their proposed objectives. The Congress System ceased to exist, following the 1820s, because of conflicting objectives, particularly in the Greek Revolution; but loyal armies were usually able to put down the uprisings. Yet progress was made. Many nations gained elected legislatures and more liberal constitutions, and Great Britain demonstrated that change was possible without revolution.

Culture in the Nineteenth
Century

# 19

# Mass Production
# and
# the Masses

Chapter 19 deals with the social, economic, and cultural transformation of Europe during the 99 years from the Battle of Waterloo to the outbreak of World War I. Although the immediate post-Napoleonic period has been characterized as being socially and culturally reactionary, great forces for change were straining to push through the veneer which the Congress of Vienna had imposed upon Europe. Perhaps the most notable force for change was industrialization. Indeed, the Industrial Revolution, operating contemporaneously with an agricultural revolution, a growth of urbanism, and a population explosion, had tremendous effects upon Western society both then and now. Even today the arguments raised by proponents and critics of industrial societies are still being debated. By the turn of the century, a renewed optimism was apparent. For not only was *laissez-faire* capitalism on the defensive, but the transportation and communications revolutions, coupled with medical advances and various socioeconomic reform movements, seemed to augur a Golden Age of peace, harmony, and understanding for Western society and culture. However, the fact that many of these hopes were dashed by World War I did not alter the great socioeconomic and cultural heritage that nineteenth-century man transmitted to the twentieth century.

With the possible exception of this century, no other hundred-year period in European history experienced such vast and rapid changes as the nineteenth century. Changes occurred in almost all areas and at almost all levels. Some noteworthy examples of these are the transition of an overwhelmingly agrarian economy into one of industrialization, the growth of small towns into huge metropolises, and the challenge of the recently emerged bourgeois attitudes and values by the proletariat. Indeed, mass production and the masses were molding the political, social, economic, and cultural institutions of the time. This chapter will examine the transformation of European society within the century from Waterloo to Sarajevo.

### Post-Waterloo Intellectual Currents

Following the Napoleonic Wars, an intellectual reaction against the French Revolution's dominant beliefs was apparent. These wars had caused many Europeans to shrink back in horror from the blood shed in the name of liberty, natural rights, and reason. A desire arose to re-bottle the evil jinni which many felt had brought revolutionary events to pass.

## New Conservatism

Consequently, a "new conservatism" emerged. Arguing that society could only prevent further revolutions fought in the name of reason by restoring previous social and political patterns, individuals such as Prince Metternich incorporated these goals into the settlement at Vienna (chapter 18). Intellectual support for Metternich's political action was provided by those philosophers who also reacted against the reason and rationality of the Enlightenment and the *philosophes*. Two such philosophers were Edmund Burke (1729–1797) and Friedrich von Gentz (1764–1832), Metternich's secretary. Both felt that it was wrong to try and impose reason on human behavior and institutions.

As a stabilizer and as an antirevolutionary force, organized religion was encouraged. With the clergy teaching submission, the team of "throne and altar" was hopefully to enforce old social and political patterns. When the Congress of Vienna restored the Pope to his temporal domains, he reestablished the Jesuit order, the inquisition, and the Index as bulwarks against political and religious dissidents.

## Romantic Age

Since the spirit of reason that epitomized the Enlightenment was suspected and tainted with the French Revolution, the so-called Romantic movement, with its praise for the emotional and irrational, dominated in this age. Of course, the origins for Romanticism could be traced back to the writings and thoughts of the *philosophe* Rousseau (chapter 15), who was atypical of Enlightenment thinkers.

The artistic reaction against the formalism of Classicism, which seemed to have peaked during the First Empire, was widespread. Even before the Revolution, emotionalism was quite apparent in the German *Sturm und Drang* (storm and stress) literary school which included two of Germany's most eminent writers: J. Schiller (1759–1805) and J. Goethe (1749–1832). The Gothic revival was another indication of the revolt against eighteenth-century reason. While Sir Walter Scott (1771–1832) wrote sympathetic accounts of the Middle Ages, the irrational and ominous were incorporated into the works of Mary Shelley (1797–1851), Charlotte Brontë (1816–1855), and Emily Brontë (1818–1848), to mention but a few of this literary genre. Ominousness and forebodence were also conveyed by the smoky, cloudy, and hazy landscapes of Joseph Turner (1775–1851) which contrasted greatly with the sharp brilliance of seventeenth and eighteenth-century oil painting.

In seeking new sources for inspiration many artists reached back further than the Middle Ages and discovered the myths and legends of the common folk. This was particularly evident in the works of Jacob Grimm (1785–1863) and his brother Wilhelm (1786–1863), both of whom diligently recorded and published the folk and fairy tales of the German people. Richard Wagner (1813–1883) combined the legends of the pre-Christian Germans with music and rendered some of the most exciting operas of all times. The Italian composer Giuseppe Verdi (1813–1901) made a comparable contribution.

This discovery of the wisdom and lore of the common folk could also serve as a vehicle for nationalism. Both Wagner and Verdi, as the Czech, B. Smetana (1824–1884), and the Finn, Jan Sibelius (1865–1957), later on, aroused national consciousness within their audiences. The Romantic movement, consequently, was not necessarily antagonistic to the forces for democracy and nationalism, which many post-Waterloo intellectuals had tried to halt.

### The Industrial Revolution

Romanticism and "new conservatism" were not the only new forces at work in the nineteenth century; for of much greater importance was the Industrial Revolution, which may be defined as the transformation of production from reliance on muscle and erratic natural forces, such as water or wind, to more reliable mechanical devices. The Industrial Revolution created a new society with new standards and relationships which made the restoration of the *Ancien Régime* impossible.

#### British Origins

Despite speculations about Britain's geographic location, its socio-economic and political institutions, its history, or its natural resources, we cannot definitively explain why Britain led in industrialization. The Industrial Revolution very simply began and had its earliest impact there.

It is perhaps easiest to see the process of industrialization in the manufacturing of British textiles. Traditionally, many a British yeoman or peasant supplemented his living through textiles. Prior to the French Revolution some ninety percent of British textile workers spun and wove in private homes. Yet, by the mid-nineteenth century ninety percent of Britain's spinners and weavers worked in factories. This principally came about through a series of inventions in the textile industry. James Hargreaves' Spinning Jenny, Richard Arkwright's Water Frame, Samuel Crompton's "Mule," and Edmund Cartwright's Power Loom increased textile production while using fewer workers. These developments enabled Britain to become the leading textile producer (in 1830 alone Britain exported 445 million yards of cloth).

Inventions alone did not explain the increased production. For to operate these new inventions a cheap and dependable source of power

was sought and finally found in steam. As early as 1712, Thomas New-
comen (1663–1729) developed a steam pump for use in mines. Later in
the century, James Watt (1736–1819) devised a method by which New-
comen's pump could be used to turn a shaft and operate machinery.

Concurrent with these developments, innovations in the iron industry resulted in stronger and better metals for the production of
machinery. Henry Cort (1740–1800) was the leader in the British iron
industry. Cort's rolling mills and puddling techniques produced a
cheaper and more durable metal. Others emulated him until British
iron production rose from 60,000 tons in 1788 to 250,000 in 1806. However, it was not until 1856 that Henry Bessemer (1813–1898) developed
his famous process which enabled low-cost production of steel.

### Spread

Emulating and often improving upon British inventions, principles,
and techniques, industrialization spread elsewhere. The economic warfare against Britain waged by Napoleon and his allies encouraged industrialization; consequently, after the Congress of Vienna an incipient
Industrial Revolution had begun on the European mainland. In France,
for example, approximately 2,000 steam engines were being used by
1830. French textile manufacturing was also being modernized, as attested by some 2,000 power looms operating in the province of Alsace
alone. Coal production, another index of industrialization, was up in
both Belgium and France, where output more than doubled between
1815 and 1830. Foundaries for machinery were emerging in France and
the Rhineland. Indeed, a strong basis for a continental-wide industrial
economy had been laid by mid-century, and by the twentieth century
industrialization had reached eastward to Russia and westward to the
United States of America.

### Population and Urbanization

During the age of the Industrial Revolution there was a rapid increase in the number of Europeans. Despite wars, revolutions, and large-
scale emigration, from the mid-eighteenth century on, the Continent's
population increased at a staggering pace. The statistics speak for themselves: in 1750, there were an estimated 140 million on the Continent,
in 1800, 180 million; in 1850, 266 million; in 1900, 401 million; and on
the eve of World War I, 460 million.

Increased urbanization also occurred during the nineteenth century. City growth seemed to accompany industrialization. British industrial centers provide an example: Glasgow, from 1750 to 1850, in-

creased tenfold in population, whereas Manchester in the same period grew from 12,000 to 400,000. Urbanization was apparent elsewhere: In five brief years (1841–1846) the number of Parisians rose by 120,000, and to cite another example, Berlin's 18,000 in 1815 reached around 1,122,000 by 1881.

A higher birth rate did not explain this urban explosion, for the bulk of it came from internal migration—from farming communities to factories or from declining towns to growing towns. Significant population shifts, as the growth of the English Midlands testified, consequently occurred in European lands.

The tremendous growth of cities placed innumerable stresses and strains on city governments. They had to cope with the headaches of providing adequate housing, and sanitation, checking for potential diseases and epidemics, preventing crime and fires, protecting property, providing transportation, lighting, and recreation. In other words, the problems of today's American cities, which we find so elusive to combat and resolve, were evident then.

## Triumph of the Middle Class

It was in the nineteenth century that the European middle class, or bourgeoisie, finally emerged. Many European states found it increasingly necessary to reckon with this socioeconomic group. Throughout this period, the middle class came to share in political power, and a king of France (Louis Philippe) even aped the dress and habits of his bourgeois subjects! Because of their association with commerce and manufacturing, the middle class, particularly in Western Europe, formed a new and monied aristocracy.

### Classical Economists

The middle class was inextricably linked with capitalism. In Britain, which was the home of modern industrialization, the leading spokesmen for Classical or Capitalist Economics appeared: Adam Smith, David Ricardo (1772–1823), and Thomas Malthus (1766–1834), who provided the rationale for *laissez-faire* capitalism.

Since Smith's ideas have already (chapter 15) been discussed, we need only to examine briefly the views of Richardo and Malthus. Ricardo devised the "iron law of wages," which justified workers' receiving minimal pay. In his *Essay on the Principle of Population*, Malthus showed how population increases geometrically (1·2·4·8), while food production increases arithmetically (1·2·3·4). Hence, both men justified according to scientific laws the economic deprivation of the working classes on the grounds that any attempt at improvement would enlarge the population and threaten all of mankind with famine, epidemics, and so on. In their works, we also find further reinforcement for *laissez-faire* governmental policies.

### Utilitarianism

Another generation of English philosophers, however, tempered the earlier Classical Economists. Jeremy Bentham (1748–1832) called for the adoption of utilitarianism, which he simply defined as the greatest good for the greatest number. The implication of utilitarianism was that government had a responsibility to promote the general welfare by alleviating the sufferings of its citizens. *Laissez-faire* was undermined also by John Stuart Mill (1806–1873), who advocated governmental regulation in areas other than commerce. These arguments convinced many prominent men, who formed the Manchester School to enact Bentham's and Mill's ideas.

### The Worker

Industrialization necessarily created a new, large social group—factory workers. The factory system altered the very nature of the laboring classes, who found their circumstances at times nearly intolerable. Before industrialization one could be an artisan, an individual who possessed a skill or craft. But afterwards this changed, and one became a proletarian, a wage/time slave desired for unthinking responsiveness and raw muscle.

The employee, furthermore, was inferior to his employer. After industrialization, it was practically impossible to maintain close employee-employer relations. The worker was often seen as only a time-clock number or as another raw material to be paid as cheaply as possible. Since machines did not discriminate sexually or chronologically, why should the employer? The cheapest and most tractable of human labor—women and children—was consequently used, to be consumed by the factory system. Human inferiority to the factory was compounded by the long, monotonous, and often hazardous conditions of employment.

### Remedies for the Workers' Plight

Many Europeans developed concern for the plight of the factory workers and the other "evils" of industrialization and urbanization. Challenges arose to the concepts of industrial capitalism. The potential remedies ran from a call for increased state regulation of the economy to the establishment of the political and economic foundations of society on a socialistic basis.

Figure 19-1.   "Hurrying Coal." A girl drawing a loaded wagon of coal
weighing between 200 and 500 pounds in an underground
Yorkshire mine.

**Socialism.**   Socialism is a rather difficult word to define precisely.
Although there are as many interpretations of socialism as there are
brands of soup, it can be said to offer a solution to competitive capitalism
by replacing human competition with human cooperation and redistribution of the wealth by controlling the means of economic production.
There are three basic categories of socialism: Christian, Utopian, and
Scientific (or Marxian).

Christian socialism's roots, of course, reach back to Christ's precepts,
such as the parable of the camel passing through the eye of a needle.
The concept of economic equality was seen in the teachings of Peter
Waldo (chapter 11) and the ditty chanted during Wat Tyler's thirteenth-
century revolt:

> When Adam delved/
> And Even span,/
> Where then was the gentleman?

However, in the nineteenth century Christian Socialists deplored the
materialism and stress on competition inherent within *laissez-faire* capitalism. Appealing to Christian consciences, many clergymen tried to
implement the concepts of brotherly love and Christian charity in capitalist societies. In Protestant lands, institutions such as the YMCA and
YWCA or the Salvation Army of William Booth (1829–1912) reflected
this attitude. Popes Pius IX (1846–1878) and Leo XIII (1878–1903),
particularly in his *Rerum Novarum*, showed Catholic concerns.

**Utopians.**   English Utopian Socialists also appealed to the consciences of their fellow men. Hoping that his example would alter the
hearts of his fellow capitalists, the textile manufacturer Robert Owen

(1771–1858) made his mills at New Lanark a model of solicitude for the factory workers and their families. The basic principle that cooperation would usher in a new social and economic world was also shown in the retail cooperative movement, begun in the 1820s by Dr. William F. King (1786–1865) and the Rochdale Pioneers in 1844.

French Utopians inherited principles from the Enlightenment. Claude-Henri, Comte de Saint-Simon (1760–1825), advocated an industrial state operated for the benefit of the masses by a small elite of *savants*, (by the formula of "from each according to his capacity, to each according to his need"). François Fourier (1772–1837) wanted industrial society to be rationally organized into self-sufficient communities with equal distribution of the wealth within each "phalanx."

Louis Blanc (1811–1882) brought French socialism down to earth. The worker, Blanc stated, must capture the state, which is the supreme regulator and can guarantee the worker his right to work. Blanc went on to argue that if it were necessary the state should create "national work-shops," as was done temporarily after the French Revolution of 1848.

**Karl Marx.** In his two famous works, *The Communist Manifesto* and the three volumes of *Das Kapital*, Karl Marx (1818–1883) provided the fundamental analyses and arguments for Scientific Socialism. Marx showed how capitalism was inevitably doomed since under capitalism wealth would be increasingly concentrated in the hands of a few. Further, Marx "proved" that society is determined by economic forces (the "materialistic conception of history") and that the exploited have replaced their exploiters. Hence in the coming revolution the oppressed of the industrial world—the proletarians—will throw off their capitalistic shackles and a classless society will follow.

Ably aided by his close friend and collaborator Frederick Engels (1820–1895), Marx made immense contributions to socialism, which have lasted to the present day. Marxism provided a "scientific" and "historically" justified alternative to the abuses of capitalism. It showed, moreover, how a better and brighter future lay ahead for all workers. The workers' plight, in other words, was not permanent, as Malthus and Ricardo gloomily predicted, but soon to end through the proletarian revolution that would usher in a politically and economically just world society.

**Anarchism.** Other philosophical solutions to capitalistic society were offered by anarchism and syndicalism. Anarchists desired the complete abolition of the political state, arguing that governments intrinsically exploit and restrict the rights of mankind. Some anarchists accepted the view that violence was justifiable against the state, a violent institution itself. This resulted in a wave of anarchistic assassinations from the 1880s to the eve of World War I. Syndicalism placed its hopes in organizations of workers, which would use sabotage, slowdowns, and ultimately the "general strike" to end capitalism and the capitalist state. Upon the ruins of capitalism, syndicalists foresaw the reorganization of society with the workers' unions as the fundamental political units. Syndicalism was quite strong in the major trade-union organization (the CGT) of France and in the American Industrial Workers of the World (the IWW).

**Unionism.** While others bantered about philosophical panaceas, the workers themselves took more practical steps by finding a means of presenting a united front to their employers. The idea that there is strength in a union stimulated trade-unionism. As seen by the anti-union bias of England's Combination Acts of 1799 and 1800, and France's La Chapelier Law of 1791, nascent trade-unionism suffered under legal restrictions. Despite their illegality, trade-unions persisted and had won legal recognition throughout most of Europe by World War I.

Workers and intellectuals combined to form organizations dedicated to serving the working class, its goals and interests. The First International (1862–1876), however, collapsed largely from the incessant feuds between Marxists and the anarchistic followers of Michael Bakunin (1814–1876). With the disintegration of the First International, Marxists concentrated on forming political parties within their respective nations. The lead was taken in Germany, where due to the labors of Ferdinand Lassalle (1825–1864) a Marxist Social Democratic party (the SPD) was organized in 1875. With trade-unionists as its backbone, the SPD was the largest party in the *Reichstag* by 1912. The SPD of Germany was copied elsewhere on the Continent until by World War I there were parties committed to some form of Marxian socialism in almost every European country.

There were enough socialist parties by 1889 to form the Second International. But the Second, like the First, was riven by arguments: Marxists accused other Marxists of violating "pure" Marxism, national Marxists bickered with internationalists, and others charged their comrades with accepting bourgeois reformism. As a consequence, although the International was dedicated to ending the fighting of workers against fellow-workers, it was not surprising that it failed to serve as a check on the outbreak of World War I.

### The State's Response to the Worker

For different reasons, in different countries governments modified their views on *laissez-faire* industrialization. Whether they came from novelists such as Charles Dickens (1813–1870), Émile Zola (1840–1902), and Leo Tolstoi (1828–1910) or from noblemen who resented the increased wealth and power of the bourgeoisie or from opportunist politicians, the voices demanding reform of capitalistic abuses were raised.

Laws were subsequently passed which increased the state's power to intervene in many economic and social matters. In Britain, beginning in 1802 with a law regulating the hours of child labor, a series of factory acts were legislated to place the factory and its conditions under the supervision of Parliament. Louis Napoleon and the Third Republic passed comparable legislation. But Bismarckian Germany, with its state health, accident, old-age, and unemployment insurance plans of the 1880s and 1890s, introduced the most comprehensive laws to protect the industrial worker. Before World War I, the Liberals under Herbert Asquith (1852–1928) and David Lloyd George (1863–1945) enacted similar schemes for Great Britain. Hence this period witnessed the foundations being laid for the modern "welfare state."

## The Rural Situation

Concurrent with the Industrial Revolution was an Agricultural Revolution, which was the result of a number of improvements and innovations introduced into the countryside. Curiously enough, Britain was the home for this revolution too. While Jethro Tull (1674–1741) introduced mechanization, "Turnip" Townshend (1674–1738) and Robert Bakewell (1729–1795) improved crops and animal breeding respectively. Through his writings, another Englishman, Arthur Young (1741–1820) popularized agricultural "modernization."

Despite the dwindling numbers of rural workers (whose release from agriculture swelled the factories and cities), food production increased in the nineteenth century. This was not merely because of the eighteenth-century improvements mentioned above; rather it was a consequence of industrialization. The growing industry in agricultural machinery, complemented by advancing chemical knowledge such as the fertilizers of Justus von Liebeg (1803–1873), largely explained the rising crop yields.

## Transportation and Communications Revolution

The nineteenth century also saw improved methods of transportation and communications appear. A flurry of road and canal construction, particularly in Britain at first, occurred. Primarily because of the innovations of John McAdam (1756–1836), whose name has contributed "macadamization" to our language, British roads were no longer hazardous. The result was that regular and reliable communications and transportation then connected various communities. Regular mail coach services operated and, in 1840, Britain introduced the penny-post.

### Steam Power

If steam could run factory machinery, maybe it could also drive a vehicle. In 1804, Richard Trevithick (1771–1833) experimented with steam locomotives, which found their principal use in hauling coal. George Stephenson (1781–1848) improved upon Trevithick's locomotives and by 1830 his *Rocket* traveled regularly between Manchester and Liverpool carrying passengers at the outrageous speed of 30 mph. The "railroad age" had began and countries throughout the world rapidly built and encouraged railroads. By the end of the century, railroads linked every European capital and vast transcontinental railroads stretched across the Siberian wastes and the U.S. and Canadian prairies.

Steam was also applied to water vessels. The American Robert Fulton (1765–1815) popularized the steamboat by going up the Hudson River in 1809. If a steamboat could operate in fresh water, why not in salt water? In 1832, two steamships crossed the Atlantic, and, from 1840 onwards, regular trans-Atlantic voyages were made.

### Electricity

Besides steam, other forms of motive power were discovered. Although Michael Faraday (1791–1867) developed the principle of the dynamo in 1831, it did not find practical application until toward the end of the century. Increased knowledge of geology and chemistry enabled the practical application of oil and gasoline. Perhaps Rudolf Diesel (1858–1913) was the most famous name associated with fuels and fuel-operated machinery.

In communications, the innovations were equally staggering. The construction of large international canals (for examples, the Suez, Kiel, and Panama Canals) facilitated the flow of goods and knowledge to distant shores. The telegraph, normally credited to Samuel Morse (1791–1872), made instantaneous communications possible. Communications were further improved by the laying of transoceanic cables, the telephone of Alexander Bell (1847–1922) in 1876, the "wireless" of M. G. Marconi (1874–1937) in 1896, and the phonograph and movie projector of Thomas Edison (1847–1931).

### Humanitarianism

While many Europeans and Americans tinkered with machinery and technical apparatuses, others devoted themselves to improving the lot of their fellow man. A strand of humanitarianism, a holdover from both the Enlightenment and Romanticism, could be found in the century before the First World War. Whether it was through the efforts of a nation to improve its citizenry, or the collective efforts of small groups of people, or the acts of isolated individuals, humanitarianism could and did take many forms.

## Education
Perhaps in recognition of the increased intellectual demands of the Industrial Revolution upon Europeans, many nations made moves to educate their citizens. Early in the century, a number of Mechanics Institutes and popular scientific societies sprang up on the continent to offer courses and lectures in numerous fields of learning. As the century progressed, national school systems were established. This did not occur without difficulties. Although in Protestant lands there was no great difficulty in creating public-school systems, it was otherwise in Catholic lands. As France evidenced, the question of disassociating the Church from education was a thorny problem. Nevertheless, by the outbreak of World War I respectable public educational systems, at least through the primary grades, existed throughout most of Western and Central Europe.

## Emancipation
Further instances of humanitarianism abounded. Spearheaded by Britain's example in 1833, the abolition of black slavery had come about by the twentieth century. Demands were also made for better treatment of women and greater participation by them in all levels of society. Emmeline Pankhurst (1858–1928) of Britain and Rosa Luxembourg (1870–1919) of Germany were but two of many individuals concerned with the struggle to liberate European women. While various suffragette movements were active, individual women such as Florence Nightingale (1820–1910) turned to welfare work and nursing to alleviate the sufferings of the more unfortunate found in the slums, hospitals, and battlefields of Europe.

Women and men alike channelled their energies into international humanitarian movements, like the Red Cross or Universal Peace Congresses. Politicians and rulers, on the other hand, met in disarmament conferences in 1899 and 1907 at The Hague, where a World Court was established. Collectively, these activities offered solutions for many possible areas of international friction.

## Medicine
Medical developments might also be considered part of the humanitarian impulse. Medical and scientific discoveries by Crawford Long (1815–1878) in the use of anesthetics, Joseph Lister (1827–1912) in introducing hygiene practices, Louis Pasteur (1822–1895) in showing the relationship of germs and bacteria to disease, and Wilhelm Roentgen (1845–1923) in the discovery of X-rays were but some of the examples of how medical science filled Europeans with promises of better, healthier, and longer lives.

### Late Nineteenth-Century Cultural Developments

By mid-nineteenth century the driving force of Romanticism in the arts had been fairly well spent. A younger generation of artists wished to find and explore newer methods and avenues of expression. This expression took many forms, which critics conveniently lumped into various categories such as social criticism, realism, naturalism, impressionism, or expressionism.

The arts came to mirror increasingly the harsh and often brutal struggle for existence in industrialized societies. The writings of Charles Dickens, Honoré Balzac (1799–1850), Victor Hugo (1802–1885), Eugene Sue (1804–1857), Henrik Ibsen (1828–1906), Gerhart Hauptmann (1862–1946), and Maxim Gorki (1868–1936) provided scathing criticism of industrialized societies' institutions, customs, and practices. As the drawings of Honoré Daumier (1808–1879) showed, social criticism was also found in the graphics.

**Figure 19-2.**  Van Gogh, *Starry Night,* 1889. The swirling meteors emit an unearthly glow above cypress trees. Museum of Modern Art, New York. Acquired through the Lillie P. Bliss Request.

Other artists directed their attention inwardly in order to try and tap their own reactions and emotions to their surroundings. Edouard Manet (1832–1883) and Claude Monet (1840–1926) attempted to record on canvas their immediate visual impressions. Evocative tonal impressions were elicted by composers such as Claude Debussy (1862–1918). Personal emotions were vividly seen in the oils of Vincent Van Gogh (1853–1890) and heard in the sounds of Igor Stravinsky (1882–1971).

As subjectivity was pursued, others experimented with more mechanistic approaches. Examples of this were the pointillism of Georges Seurat (1859–1891) and the cubist paintings of Georges Braque (1882–1963) and Pablo Picasso (1881–1973). Mechanization was only one of many themes handled in the writings of Jules Verne (1828–1905) and H. G. Wells (1866–1946).

These artists and artistic movements provide but a few indications of the great cultural ferment at work in Europe from the mid-nineteenth century to World War I. The post-war generations inherited from these cultural forces a rich, innovative, imaginative, and varied heritage.

## Summary

It seems rather superfluous to point out the legacy transmitted to us from the civilization and culture of nineteenth-century Europe. Almost any aspect of the period from 1815 to 1914 seems to touch or have some relevance to our present lives.

Without even going into the obvious importance of such things as socialism, other -isms, trade-unions, women's rights, or public education, let us take as examples two fundamental problems that arose in the nineteenth century: industrialization and urbanization. Are we not seeking solutions to the headaches these two forces have presented? What kind of industrialization and industrial society do we wish—one committed to meeting the needs of the people at large or one serving the interests of the industrial operators? As the nineteenth century grappled with the difficulties presented by towns becoming metropolises, we must deal with megalopolises. Much like the nineteenth century, our cities are beset with disease, pollution, and crime. Can we reconstruct or renew our cities in order to make them fit for human habitation? Nineteenth century man lacked experience in coping with urban problems. What is our excuse?

In other words, the problems that an industrialized society posed to the nineteenth century are similarly posed to us of the twentieth century.

India, China, and Japan
in the Nineteenth Century

# 20

# Western Impact

# and

# Asian Response

The nineteenth century was a period of transition from the old to the new for India, China, and Japan. In India the first half of the century was characterized by gradual British domination of the subcontinent. The second half of the century witnessed the establishment of a modern English colony that was governed by a handful of career British bureaucrats. In China, the corrupt and stagnant dynasty proved incapable of coping with domestic disorders and foreign encroachments. The last half of the century saw the Ch'ing retreat in the face of military defeats, humiliating unequal treaties, and the failure of the self-strengthening movement which looked to the past instead of the future. As a bewildered China stood on the threshold of the twentieth century she found her territories being carved into foreign spheres of influence and in 1912 a republican form of government replaced the traditional Confucian state and society. For Japan, too, the nineteenth century was a period of change. But unlike traditional India and China, which found themselves incapable of adapting to the rapidly changing realities of the world, Japan successfully made the transition from a traditional feudal state to a modern industrial nation.

## British India: The Era of Crown Rule

With the suppression of the Sepoy Mutiny in 1858 the Indian subcontinent once again came under foreign domination. For nearly a century the British ruled the subcontinent, and their impact on the peoples of the region can still be seen today. The first phase of British rule, from 1858 until 1919, saw the British government's assumption of the East India Company's holdings and the creation of an efficient colonial administration which brought even the most remote regions of the subcontinent under the influence of policymakers in far off London.

### India as a Crown Colony

The official transfer of the East India Company's holdings to the Crown was announced in a proclamation by Queen Victoria in 1858. The document confirmed direct British authority over sixty percent of the subcontinent and promised that the Crown would not annex territories that belonged to native princes and local rulers. This did not mean, however, that the British were willing to grant local autonomy to the nonannexed areas. On the contrary, the princely states were controlled more tightly than ever before through a number of unofficial understandings, which included British control of foreign relations and interstate relations within the subcontinent. Moreover, the Crown representatives kept a watchful eye on marriages and succession arrangements among the native princes. And in such cases they were not reluctant to exert strong pressures to depose those who were anti-British.

**Administrative Structure.** The Parliament in London exercised direct control over its Indian Empire after 1858 through a cabinet-rank secretary of state for India. Directly under the secretary of state was the viceroy (formerly the governor general) who actually resided in India. The viceroy was assisted in turn by two subordinate bodies, the Legislative Council and the Crown-appointed Executive Council. The Crown commitment to the growth of empire was reinforced when Queen Victoria added "Empress of India" to her title in 1876. After 1862 a few Indians were allowed to participate in both bodies, but ultimate power remained in the hands of the viceroy who possessed the right to veto all measures passed or recommended by the two advisory bodies.

**Civil Service.** The actual day-to-day administration of the subcontinent was performed by the Indian Civil Service. The members of this bureaucracy became an elite group because of their dedication and efficiency. Although the Civil Service was opened to Indians after 1868, the competitive entrance examinations were extremely difficult for those who did not have an English education. A majority of the bureaucrats came from England, and as they brought wives and children, and established residences in India, we see the growth of large overseas populations of Britains who had a vested interest in the continuation of their homeland's control over the native peoples and resources of the region.

**Examples of British Influence.** British influence in the subcontinent was felt in many areas outside the appointments of bureaucrats. A famine control system was begun by Viceroy Edward Lytton who governed India from 1876 to 1880. By anticipating food shortages and stockpiling surplus supplies in potential problem areas his system succeeded in eliminating large-scale famine problems until the disruption of World War II. Public health was improved through the construction of hospitals and dispensaries, and the introduction of innoculation and vaccination programs. In order to maintain close contacts with officials throughout the subcontinent, the British also built railroads, roads, and telegraph lines.

Improved transportation and communication also enabled the British Army to move quickly into areas threatened by riots or rebellion. India became a special chapter in the history of the British armed forces, for the Royal Navy could demand budgets to protect the sea-lanes "East of Suez," and the army would send its best junior officers to gain experience in battling the savage mountain peoples who harassed the northern passes of the subcontinent. The regimental colors of the British Army are laden with streamers that recall those battles, and the literature of late nineteenth-century England drew much of its most popular themes from the British in India (Kipling, for example).

**Education and the Stirrings of Nationalism.** British-style education was also introduced to India, and universities were established in Bombay, Calcutta, and Madras. Higher education was also available in England for those who could afford it, and many young Indians who later emerged as political leaders went overseas to study. As these students read about concepts such as democracy, individual freedom, and equality in their textbooks, they could not overlook the fact that these ideals were not being practiced in the land of their birth. Thus many of them such as Gandhi, Nehru, and Jinnah later became leaders of political movements against the British colonial presence in the subcontinent.

The majority of the young students who had opportunities to succeed within the colonial system were conscious of the barriers between themselves and the British. Signs reading "For Europeans Only" were posted in public places, and Indians were barred from entering the tightly restricted society that was reserved for the white population. In a land that had developed its own sharp distinctions between classes, the upper-class Indians found themselves treated as inferiors. But they were not alone in their frustrations, for in the process of educating and employing Indians from all social backgrounds in the civil service, the British colonial administration had created a sizable middle class among the Indian population. Literate, articulate, and sensitive to their thwarted aspirations for upward social mobility, the white-collar workers formed the backbone of nationalistic groups who demanded more status and real power in the government. No longer were they willing to serve as puppets of the colonial administration. Increasingly they issued demands for self-government and independence.

### The Nationalist Movement

The intellectual origins of nationalistic fervor during this period can be traced to the social and religious reform ideas of Ram Mohan Roy (1772–1833). Roy, who has often been referred to as the "father of Indian nationalism," argued that the Western concept of progress could coexist with traditional Hindu values. The Muslim counterpart of Ram Mohan Roy was Syed Ahmad Khan (1817–1898).

**National Congress.** Indian nationalism progressed from the realm of ideas to an organized phase when the Indian National Congress was formed in 1885. Its support came from the new professionals and bureaucrats who formed the growing middle class, and by 1900 two divergent elements had emerged. The Moderate element was led by Gopal Krishna Gokhale (1886–1915) and sought gradual reforms and eventual full partnership for India within the Commonwealth. The other group, who became known as the Extremists, looked to Gal Gangadhar Tilak (1856–

1920) and rejected moderation. While Gokhale and the Moderates requested changes, Tilak demanded them. Neither element could hope to succeed, however, for Indian nationalism was still a movement without sufficient strength to openly challenge the government. Its numbers were largely restricted to the Westernized middle class, without mass support. But in 1905 the British provided the catalyst that stirred the masses to back the middle class.

**Partition of Bengal.** In that year Lord George Curzon (viceroy from 1899 to 1905) made a decision that linked the masses to the middle-class nationalists and also created a problem that has only recently been resolved (formation of the new nation called Bangladesh). This was the partition of Bengal into two parts: East Bengal and Assam. East Bengal had a population of thirty-one million people and a capital at Dacca; but more importantly, it was mainly Muslim, while west Bengal was predominantly Hindu. The rumor quickly spread through the politically active Bengali middle class that Curzon and the British were trying to punish and eliminate the Bengalis by making them into a small minority in west Bengal while creating a new, Muslim dominated province in East Bengal. This argument appealed to the masses of Bengalis and they joined a protest movement led by Surendranath Bannerjea. When the movement boycotted British goods and burned Lancashire cotton, Tilak and the Extremists in the Congress—and even Gokhale and the Moderates—joined in supporting the Bengalis. For the first time, the middle classes had been joined by the masses in a common cause, and as the movement spread beyond Bengal, Indian nationalism moved from a mere movement to a potential nationwide force that had to be reckoned with.

The British and European population had cause for anxiety, for the spreading emotional appeal of the movement gave rise to terrorist groups who praised assassination in the name of the Goddess Kali. Curzon left India, and in 1906 the Liberals formed a new government in Britain. London's new appointments as secretary of state (John Morley) and viceroy (Gilbert John Minto) were not sympathetic to the growing sense of nationalism in India, but they were at least realistic in their recognition that concessions had to be made. This led to the Indian Councils Act of 1909, better known as the Morley-Minto Reforms.

**Morely-Minto Reforms.** While the Morely-Minto Reforms were made reluctantly, they contained certain features that moved the subcontinent toward eventual self-government through an increased participation of Indians in representative assemblies at all levels. The reforms recognized the principle of elections, although suffrage was still restricted to the upper classes. The reforms also paved the way for the appointment of Indians to the provincial executive councils (some were already serving in the viceroy's Executive Council). In response to the concern of the Muslim League (formed in 1906 with British approval) for protection of the Muslim minority, six separate Muslim constituencies were created— a move that foreshadowed the later difficulties between Muslims and Hindus when the subcontinent was divided into India and Pakistan in 1947.

Two years after the Morley-Minto Reforms were introduced, a sympathetic new viceroy, Lord Hardinge, reversed the partition of Bengal and moved the capital from Calcutta to Delhi. The transfer of the capital angered the large European community in Calcutta, but it was well-received by the non-Bengali Indian population because of the capital's location in the heartland rather than on the coastline.

**World War I and its Impact on India.**   The outbreak of war in Europe profoundly affected both the nationalist movement in India as well as British Crown rule. England's involvement in the war shattered her aura of invincibility as she fought for survival. The myth of British and Western superiority was a casualty of the war. Nationalists were further encouraged by the Russian Revolution of 1917 and the fall of the despotic czarist regime and by Woodrow Wilson's Fourteen Points which proposed the impartial adjustment of colonial claims. Lured by the prospect of concessions, the Indian National Congress supported the British. Others expressed their loyalty by fighting under the British—to the ultimate cost of 26,000 Indians killed and 70,000 wounded. The Indians believed—or were led to believe—that their sacrifice would result in expanded privileges.

**Tilak and the Congress.**   The movement also felt the effect of Gokhale's death in 1915. From 1915 to 1919 the movement and the Congress leadership belonged to Tilak. In 1916, Tilak and later Annie Besant, a British theosophist, began Home Rule Leagues which agitated for self-government after the war. Under Tilak's guidance the Congress and the Muslim League concluded the Lucknow Pact in December 1916. In exchange for the Congress's recognition of separate Muslim electorates, the Muslims agreed to support the Congress's demand for self-rule.

**Montagu-Chelmsford Reforms.**   In an attempt to appease the nationalists, the Montagu-Chelmsford Reforms were passed by Parliament in 1919. Briefly, the reforms included the appointment of three Indians on the viceroy's eight-member Executive Council; the Legislative Council became bicameral; and the franchise was extended. On the provincial level, a dyarchy or dual system of government was introduced which gave Indian ministers responsibility for such areas as public works, education, agriculture, and public health. The British, however, retained control of the departments that dealt with taxation, law, and order. And the viceroy still retained his veto powers.

While the details of the Montagu-Chelmsford Reforms were being finalized, the British enacted legislation that deprived the Indians of certain basic civil rights. The rationale was the need to protect lives and property in the face of mounting terrorism. Leading the protestors was a forty-nine-year-old lawyer, Mohandas Karamchand Gandhi (1869–1948).

**Amritsar Affair.**    On April 13, 1919, the Amritsar affair rocked India. Amritsar, which is located in the Punjab, was one of the many areas hit hard by the demands of the war. A British general broke up an illegal gathering of ten to twenty thousand unarmed Indians by firing on them. Over 1200 were wounded and 379 were killed. The significance of the Amritsar affair cannot be overemphasized for it marks a turning point in Indian history. Nationalism and the demand for self-rule had been supported by a small, Westernized middle-class minority. It now found a broad base of appeal. The massacre signaled the emergence of a new group of leaders such as Gandhi and Jwarlarlal Nehru (1889–1964) and the Muslim leader Muhammad Ali Jinnah (1876–1948). The next phase of the movement for independence, which culminated in 1947, would be dominated by Gandhi's nonviolent, noncooperation campaigns.

### Nineteenth-Century China: Foreign Incursions and Imperial Decline

The defeat of the Ch'ing (Manchu) Dynasty in the first Anglo-Chinese War, more commonly referred to as the Opium War, marked a turning point in China's relations with the outside world. After 1842, China was forced to retreat inward from her imperial borders to the heartland. Efforts at retrenchment followed retreat, but time was not on the side of the traditional Chinese state. Foreign pressures continued, and by the latter half of the nineteenth century the European powers were joined by the Japanese and Americans in demanding territorial, political, and economic concessions. Manchu leaders and traditional institutions proved incapable of meeting these challenges, and the series of external crises was compounded by the outbreaks of large-scale domestic disorders and natural calamities. By 1900, the Ch'ing government was a thin facade of traditional conservatism, and when revolution swept the land in 1911, the last dynasty slipped quietly into history.

#### The First Anglo-Chinese War (1839–1842) and Unequal Treaties

**Introduction of Opium.**    From the official Chinese point of view, opium was the chief factor in their final rejection of negotiations in favor of open confrontation with the British. The debilitating narcotic had been introduced into China by European sailors in the seventeenth century, and the habit had spread quickly among all the sectors of Chinese society. In 1729 and again in 1799 the government banned its importation, but the demand was so great that both Chinese and foreigners either bribed officials or resorted to smuggling to garner their share of profits. By 1833 the traffic in smuggled opium alone amounted to fifteen million dollars. The cost to China's population was even more staggering, for the Ch'ing government estimated that by that time more than ten million Chinese were opium addicts.

**Opium Trade.** The British, in the form of the East India Company and individual traders, cared little about the human suffering. As shrewd businessmen they were interested in statistics relating to profits and favorable trade balances. And opium provided the British with one commodity that the Chinese would purchase. Prior to their discovery of opium, the British had been forced to pay for Chinese goods with gold and silver because the West had little to offer to the Chinese. But now the trade balance shifted sharply to favor the British, with the Chinese economy increasingly threatened by a drain of silver to pay for opium.

Finally, in 1839 the Ch'ing government decided to take firm action. A hard-nosed official named Lin Tse-hsu was given specific orders to halt the trade. Lin moved decisively when he arrived in Canton. In addition to confiscating all existing opium in the harbor and extracting written promises (bonds) from foreign ship captains to stop the traffic, he surprised the foreigners by actually destroying over six million dollars worth of opium. Lin then announced that all trade in Canton would cease until he received bonds from all foreign merchants.

**"Opium War."** The British held out, and when Lin refused to exempt them from his ultimatum many English merchants had to send their goods into Canton aboard American and other non-British vessels. At this point, a minor incident served as a catalyst for the hostilities that followed. A group of British seamen had been punished by English law for having killed a Chinese during a scuffle. But Commissioner Lin demanded that they be turned over to the Chinese courts. Captain Elliot, the British superintendent of trade in Canton, refused and Lin in turn cut off water and food supplies to the British in Hong Kong and Macao. The situation became tense, and after weeks of deadlocked negotiations, fighting broke out between Chinese and British warships on November 3, 1839.

The British offered to halt hostilities if the Chinese would pay for the destroyed opium, acknowledge the principle of extraterritoriality, and cede them an island off the Chinese coast for a trading base. When the

Chinese rejected these terms, the fighting escalated with a British naval blockade and bombardment of Canton. In order to save the city from destruction, the Canton officials paid six million dollars as ransom to the British. But the British expanded the conflict by moving north and bombarding Nanking. When the Chinese government recognized the inferiority of their troops against the relatively small British forces involved they sued for peace. The Treaty of Nanking (1842) became the first of many "unequal treaties."

**Treaty of Nanking.** The British exacted such a harsh price from the Chinese in the Treaty of Nanking that other Western nations were envious. Among the Chinese concessions were the following: The opening of five ports to outside trade (Shanghai, Ningpo, Foochow, Amoy, and Canton); the establishment of British consular offices and merchant trading ports and residences in all of the treaty ports; abolition of the Co-hong system and direct contacts between British and Chinese merchants; Hong Kong ceded permanently to the British; Chinese acceptance of an *ad valorem* tariff with no provision for unilateral changes or abrogation; diplomatic contacts between Chinese and British to be conducted under British concepts of protocol and equality (to eliminate the *k'ou t'ou*); and a Chinese indemnity payment which eventually totalled over thirty million dollars. Two additional clauses added in 1843 (Treaty of the Bogue) granted the British a "most-favored-nation" position and extraterritoriality in criminal cases.

**Most-Favored-Nation Clause and Unequal Treaties.** While the Ch'ing government was still reeling from its disastrous encounters—both in battle and in the peace negotiations—with the British, the other nations with interests in China pressed for their own treaties. The United States was eager for trade, and Caleb Cushing was dispatched to secure the American position. On July 3, 1844, Cushing signed the Treaty of Wanghsia which included the basic provisions of the British treaties but superceded them by extending extraterritoriality to cover civil as well as criminal law. The French also signed a treaty with the Chinese in 1844 which was similar to the British and American treaties except for its focus on religious tolerance.

While the specific provisions of all the treaties gave the West a pivotal foothold in China, the most-favored-nation clause encouraged them to continue their pressure on the Chinese. A concession to one, after all, meant the extension of privileges to others as well. The extraterritoriality clause was also significant, for implicity in it was the assumption that Western concepts of justice were superior to those of China. Westerners would reinforce their belief that Western civilization was inherently more humane and "civilized" than that of the East. The implications of these assumptions concerning the relative merits of different societal values continue to plague us today.

### Internal Chaos: The Taiping Rebellion and the Extension of Unequal Treaties

Shortly after their series of humiliating bouts with foreign soldiers and diplomats, the Ch'ing were faced with an internal conflict which flared into perhaps the most destructive rebellion in history. The origins of the Taiping Rebellion (1850–1865) are shrouded in history, but we know that as the rebellion spread it contained several widely divergent goals and sources of support. The rebel forces included peasants seeking agrarian reforms, nationalists opposed to the Manchu dynasty because of its foreign origins, religious fanatics proclaiming a weird distortion of Christianity, and some who were simply bandits and pirates out for booty.

**Hung Hsiu-Ch'uan and the Taiping Rebellion.**  The figure who emerged as the leader of these disparate forces was himself an enigma.

**Figure 20-1.**  Taiping Rebellion. Rebellion of the Angle of North Fort immediately after its capture.

Hung Hsiu-ch'uan was a former school teacher who dreamed of rising from his position in a tiny village and entering the civil service. When he failed the examinations he turned to reading Protestant pamphlets. Shortly afterward he became ill, and in a serious of mysterious "visions" he announced that he was the younger brother of Jesus Christ. Moreover, Christ had allegedly sent him to save mankind. Hung plunged into a program of proselytizing with the aid of an American Baptist missionary named Issachar Roberts.

When the officials of Kwangsi province banned his activities in 1851, Hung began an open rebellion against the Ch'ing government. Infused with a fanaticism that swept the Manchu armies before them, the Taiping (from *T'ai-p'ing t'ien-kuo*, meaning "Heavenly Kingdom of Great Peace") rebels pushed north to the Yangtze and then sailed down the river to Nanking where they annihilated a Manchu army of 20,000 men and proclaimed the city as their capital. In Nanking, Hung delegated civil and military duties to his subordinates while he turned to further defining his religion and his plans to remake Chinese society. In essence, the religion that Hung devised was rooted in Protestant Christianity with elements of Confucian, Taoist, and Buddhist ceremonies. Hung himself was allegedly ordained by the God Jehovah to rule not only China but the entire world as well. The Taiping state was to be semicommunistic, with all wealth and property redistributed equally among all men. Herein we see goals that must have had great appeal to the discontented peasantry. And this explains the zealousness with which his followers fought.

Unfortunately for Hung, the armies that he dispatched to the north were defeated before they reached Peking by Mongols who had been called up by the Ch'ing. Hung's distortions of Christianity alienated other religious groups. His rejection of religious images led to their systematic destruction in both Buddhist temples and Catholic churches. Between 1853 and 1856 Hung's preoccupation with his religious studies led to a loss of coordination between the diverse ranks of the rebels. Nonetheless, by June 1856 the Taiping armies had cleared the Nanking area of Manchu forces and were on the verge of destroying the last reserves of the dynasty. At that moment Hung suddenly had many of his ablest commanders assassinated, and the Manchu forces launched a major offensive. The imperial forces were diverted, however, by the *Arrow* War which once again forced the Ch'ing to focus on foreign incursions. While Manchu armies turned to face the foreign threat, the Taiping were able to regroup and prepare for a return bout in 1860.

**Further Chinese Concessions to Foreigners.**   The unequal treaties had failed to ease friction between the Chinese and the Western powers. On the contrary, the conditions under which they had been negotiated resulted in a large number of violations on both sides. The opium traffic continued because of the continuing demand from Chinese addicts and the high profits to be made by both Chinese and Westerners; with the demand for cheap labor overseas, in America for example (railroads), a widespread traffic in illegal coolie labor developed within the foreign settlements; foreign flags were used also by pirates and smugglers to protect themselves from official Chinese harassment. It was such a situation that touched off the second war between China and the foreigners.

**Arrow War.**   In 1856, the Chinese High Commissioner in Canton sent a boarding party to the Chinese vessel *Lorcha Arrow* in search of a suspected pirate. The vessel flew the British flag, and when the Chinese refused to free the crew—who were all Chinese—and ignored British demands for an official apology for violating a vessel flying the British flag, British naval forces captured the Canton forts and bombarded the city. When the British withdrew to give the Chinese an opportunity to apologize, Commissioner Yeh reported to Peking that he had repulsed the invaders.

The situation was quiet until December 1857 because the British were preoccupied by the Sepoy Mutiny in India. When action was resumed the Chinese were quickly routed by combined Anglo-French forces who captured Canton and then moved north to Tientsin, the port city of Peking. After the easy capture of the Taku forts at Tientsin the Chinese sued for peace. During the negotiations, which culminated in the Tientsin Treaties of 1858, nonbelligerent nations such as Russia and the United States also sent representatives. The major new concessions made by the Chinese included the opening of additional coastal ports to foreigners as well as permission to trade and travel on the Yangtze River and inland areas, legalization of the opium trade, extensions of extraterritoriality, and toleration of Christianity.

Soon after the signing of the treaties the Chinese reconstructed the Taku forts and delayed their own ratification of the Tientsin Treaties. The Anglo-French forces organized an expeditionary force under Lord Elgin and moved toward Peking. During an armistice called by the Chinese a British diplomat named Harry Parkes was captured and eighteen of his staff were brutally tortured and killed. The Anglo-French force then marched into Peking, burned the emperor's summer palace and forced the flight of the emperor himself.

**Peking Conventions.**   In 1860, Prince Kung, the emperor's brother, was forced to sign the Peking Conventions which added the following conditions to the 1858 Tientsin Treaties: the right of foreign ambassadors to reside at Peking; legalization of the coolie trade; the opening of Tientsin as a treaty port; the addition of Kowloon to the British controlled port of

Hong Kong. In return for acting as mediator of the Peking negotiations the Chinese gave Russia northern Manchuria (including the port of Vladivostok) and wide-ranging commercial privileges.

**The End of the Taiping Rebellion.**    The Treaties of Tientsin (1858–1860) which permitted Westerners to travel and trade in the interior regions of China served as a stimulus for helping the Ch'ing suppress the Taiping rebellion. Regular units of the British and French armies joined with Manchu banner units in ejecting the Taiping from coastal areas, and in 1860 they were joined by a large force of Filipinos, Americans, and European mercenaries who were led by an American named Frederic Ward and later, Major Charles Gordon of the British Army (known as "Chinese" Gordon). Under pressure from these unlikely allies, the Taiping forces were steadily pushed back. The Taiping capital at Nanking fell in 1864 following the suicide of Hung Hsiu-ch'uan and the last Taiping forces were defeated in May 1865.

During the fifteen years of rebellion, the death toll surpassed twenty million. The Ch'ing dynasty was on the verge of bankruptcy because of the dual burden of suppressing the internal disorders while confronting the foreign incursions, and nine provinces lay completely devastated. Moreover, Hung's identification with Christianity, albeit distorted, created strong resentment among many Chinese toward Christians—a sentiment that appeared frequently later in the century.

**Hostility Toward Christians.**    Due to the various provisions of the unequal treaties, Christians claimed that they had the right to build churches and proselytize anywhere in China. Furthermore, they often insisted that extraterritoriality applied to their Chinese converts. Unhappy with this state of affairs but powerless to stop the missionaries, the Confucian-oriented bureaucrats encouraged the masses to drive the missionaries out of China. The average Chinese saw reasons to distrust and even hate the missionaries. Confucian ancestor worship had been attacked. And a variety of sordid rumors, such as the charge that orphans were eaten by nuns, resulted in direct attacks upon the missionaries and their churches. The most spectacular of these was the Tientsin Massacre of 1870. The Tientsin rumors persisted that the French Catholic orphanage bought children in order to tear out their eyes and hearts. Encouraged by local officials a mob invaded the church grounds and destroyed the furnishings. During the melee fifty people were killed. Western forces were mobilized but the Chinese government averted a full-scale confrontation by issuing an apology and agreeing to pay reparations and an indemnity. Nonetheless, the affair left a bitter aftertaste which precluded any possibility of close friendship between the European powers and the Ch'ing.

### Attempts at Reform: Self-Strengthening

The Ch'ing response to the increased Western presence took several forms after the signing of the unequal treaties and conclusion of the Taiping Rebellion. In order to meet the Western challenge, leaders such as Prince Kung, Tseng Kuo-fan, Feng Kuei-fen, and Li Hung-chang proposed to strengthen China along Western lines. In foreign relations the tribute system was discarded and a foreign office (Tsungli Yamen or "Office for General Management") was created to handle foreign relations at Peking. The Chinese Imperial Customs Service which was staffed primarily by the British was expanded to serve in all treaty ports. Headed by Sir Robert Hart, who served as inspector general from 1863 to 1908, the Customs Service provided the Chinese with an efficient, honest, and reliable source of revenue.

Other attempts were made to modernize China. In 1862 a language school for interpreters was established. Shipyards, arsenals, technical schools, railroads, and a telegraph system were constructed, but efforts to modernize and industrialize on a large scale were severely handicapped by opposition from the Confucian-oriented officialdom.

The problem was compounded by the need for massive reconstruction after the destruction caused by the Taipings. But rather than expand production and secure new sources of revenue, the Manchu government looked to a reallocation of the tax burden to solve the financial crises. The examination system was also resumed after being interrupted by domestic chaos. Unfortunately, all of these programs created an elite who had a stake in the old system rather than a commitment to modernization. Those who wielded power were ultraconservatives such as the Empress Dowager Tz'u Hsi (1835–1908). Others who played key roles in industrialization projects such as the scholar-bureaucrat Li Hung-chang did so to advance their own private ends.

### Foreign Relations After 1870: New Powers, More Demands

The Russian thrust in Central Asia during the 1870s was for the most part successfully parried by the Chinese. After Muslim and Turkish rebels were defeated by Chinese troops armed with Western weapons, the Russians were forced to withdraw from part of Chinese Turkestan. In 1884 the area became Sinkiang Province.

The Ch'ing were not as successful with the French, for by 1885 the area we now call Vietnam had been relinquished to become part of French Indochina. The Chinese were also unsuccessful in their relationships with Britain and the United States.

China lost parts of her empire to a sister Asian nation, Japan. In 1874 Japan invaded Taiwan to punish aborigines who had killed fifty-four shipwrecked Ryukyuans. Both the Ryukyu Islands and Taiwan were Chinese tributary states, but Peking paid an indemnity to the Japanese to compensate them for the murders and the cost of the expedition. By their action the Ch'ing recognized Japanese sovereignty over the Ryukyu Isdands.

**War with Japan.** It was over Korea that China and Japan clashed in 1894. When China sent troops into the peninsula at the request of the Korean king, Japan also ordered units into the area. Both sides refused to leave unless the other did so first and fighting erupted when the Korean court was forced to declare war on China. The Japanese victory was a surprise to a world that expected China to win.

The Treaty of Shimonoseki (1895) ceded Formosa, the Pescadores, and the Liaotung Peninsula to Japan. The Japanese also received a large indemnity and a commercial treaty which gave her all the rights other nations had in China. Korea was recognized as an independent state. Before the treaty was ratified, however, Japan was forced to return Port Arthur and the Liaotung Peninsula to China because of the intervention of Russia, France, and Germany (the Triple Intervention). In exchange Japan received an additional indemnity.

China's defeat signaled the beginning of the race for foreign spheres of influence carved from Chinese soil. For example, to the annoyance of Japan the Russians moved into Manchuria after the Triple Intervention. The Germans settled in Shantung and the British and French expanded their influence in southern China. Fearful of being excluded, the United States proclaimed the Open Door Policy in 1899.

On the domestic front, the defeat meant the end of the long period of self-strengthening against foreign encroachment. Reforms would now be attempted but they would be too few and too late.

### Imperial China: Reform, Rebellion and Collapse

**"Hundred Days Reforms."** The disastrous outcome of the first Sino-Japanese War compelled many scholar-bureaucrats to petition their government for basic reforms rather than "self-strengthening" programs. Led by K'ang Yu-wei (1858–1927), the reformers sought changes that would have resulted in the creation of a constitutional monarchy. Between June 11 and September 21, 1898, the emperor acted on K'ang Yu-wei's advice and issued a series of edicts known as the "Hundred Days of Reforms." They ranged from the formation of Western-style industries and schools to military reform and the abolition of sinecures.

Opposition was swift, as conservatives, especially the Empress Dowager Tz'u-hsi, feared the loss of their positions and vested interests. Tz'u-hsi who had retired in 1889 now returned to power and remained the most powerful person in China until her death in 1908. K'ang was forced to flee to Japan and the emperor went into seclusion.

**Figure 20-2.** The last Chinese Empress Tz'u-hsi.

**Boxer Rebellion.** The failure of the reformers precipitated another attempt to solve the problem of the foreign menace. Initially the Boxers (*I Ho-Tuan* or "Righteous Harmony Fists") were not only antiforeign, they were anti-Ch'ing as well. By 1899, however, they were joined by antiforeign Manchu officials and concentrated their fury on the foreigners in China. The Empress Dowager gave the Boxers tacit support; later her backing was more overt. When the Ch'ing refused to make a real effort to suppress Boxer attacks on foreigners in north China, the Western powers in Peking felt compelled to increase their legation guards. Soon

**Figure 20-3.**    Boxer Rebellion.

afterwards the Boxers destroyed the major railroad connecting Peking with Tientsin and by June 20, 1900, the foreign compounds in Peking were besieged. An international expeditionary force lifeted the siege on August 14. Humiliated, the Chinese government was required by the Boxer Protocol of 1901 to pay an indemnity of $333,000,000, apologize and punish those responsible for the outbreaks, destroy a number of forts, and revise commercial treaties and custom duties.

**Ch'ing Reforms.** The Empress Dowager, who had been driven from Peking, now returned and lent her support to reforms that she had previously opposed. Intermarriage between Chinese and Manchus was permitted. Other reforms sought to bring the military, judiciary, and civil administration up to Western standards. The Confucian civil service examinations were abolished and students were sent abroad to study. A ministry of education was established along with a Western style school system beginning with kindergarten. The Ch'ing were persuaded to accept a constitutional monarchy based on the Japanese model which in turn had been constructed with the Prussian system in mind.

The Nine Year Plan of 1908 laid plans for a national parliament and constitution. Despite Tz'u-hsi's death in the same year, provincial assemblies and a national assembly were convened by 1910. On the other hand, the proposed changes were no longer satisfactory to a growing number of revolutionaries.

**Sun Yat-sen.** The leader of the revolutionaries was Dr. Sun Yat-sen (1866–1925) who had been educated in Hawaii and was forced to flee from China in 1895 after an abortive uprising aimed at toppling the Ch'ing. While overseas (primarily in Tokyo) where he was encouraged by the Japanese to overthrow the Ch'ing, Sun produced his *San Min Chu-I* ("Three Principles of the People") which included "nationalism," which was anti-Manchu and anti-imperialist; "democracy," which included a constitution; and "socialism," which meant "equalization of land rights" rather than redistribution of land. In 1905 Sun founded the *T'ung Meng Hui* ("Three League of Common Alliance") which played a key role in the revolution of 1911. Sun proposed to create a republican China in three phases: a period of military rule while the Manchus were being suppressed, a period of tutelage to educate the people, and finally constitutional government.

**Revolution.** The revolution broke out in October 1911. Imperial troops mutinied when their secret anti-Manchu society was discovered. By December all of southern and central China declared its independence. Sun Yat-sen who was then in the United States returned to China via Europe where he sought European sympathy for his cause. On January 1, 1912, he was inaugurated as Provisional President of the Chinese Republic at Nanking. At the same time he offered to relinquish his post to Yuan Shih-k'ai who had been called in by the Manchus to suppress the rebellion. It was an important step, for Yuan was China's hope of avoiding a long civil war which would probably have resulted in foreign intervention. Thus in 1912 the Manchu emperor abdicated, Sun Yat-sen resigned, and Yuan Shih-k'ai, the northern Chinese strongman with the best army, became President of the Republic of China.

## The   Meiji Era: Japan Responds to the Western Impact

The collapse of the Tokugawa feudal system and the restoration of the emperor to the throne in 1868 was one outcome of Matthew Perry's opening of Japan in 1853. The Tokugawa shogunate, weakened by over two hundred years of peace and isolation, disintegrated in the face of crises produced by the appearance of Western gunboats. Unlike China, however, Japan's attempts to meet the threat of foreign encroachment would result in the creation of a modern industrial and military nation state that the West would have to reckon with.

### Bakumatsu: The Collapse of the Tokugawa Shokunate

**Opening of Japan.**   As early as the period 1780 to 1800 Japan rejected first American and then Russian and British attempts to establish commercial relations. Several more rebuffs in the early nineteenth century prompted the United States to dispatch Commodore Matthew Perry and a squadron of four ships to force Japan to open her doors. The dilemma posed by Perry's arrival in 1853 forced the Tokugawa shogun to take an unprecedented step: He consulted the imperial court and the *daimyo* to obtain a consensus on government policy vis-à-vis the foreigners. Although most were antiforeign and expressed a desire for resistance, the Tokugawa felt compelled to sign the Treaty of Kanagawa in 1854 especially when Perry returned with eight warships, including three propelled by steam. The treaty provided for an exchange of consular representatives, the opening of two ports, the most-favored-nation treatment, and humane treatment of shipwrecked American sailors. Other nations such as Great Britain, Russia, and Holland negotiated similar treaties. Once more the shogun conferred with the emperor and secured his approval of the treaties. It was clear that the Tokugawa were no longer absolute masters of Japan.

**Sonno-Joi.**   In 1858, Townsend Harris, the first American consul to Japan, concluded a commercial treaty. The Harris Treaty, the first of many unequal treaties Japan was to sign, included extraterritorial rights for Americans, the opening of additional trading ports, and permission for Americans to live not only in the treaty ports but also in Osaka and Edo. The shogun's approval of this treaty resulted in the polarization of the *daimyo*. There were those who supported the Tokugawa position. Men such as Ii Naosuke, the Tokugawa equivalent of a prime minister, signed the commercial treaties and worked for the resurrection of shogunal leadership. He was assassinated in 1860 by the Mito branch of the Tokugawa family. On the other hand, there were others from the anti-Tokugawa *tozama han* of Choshu and Satsuma who rallied around the emperor with the slogan *sonno-joi* or "revere the emperor and expel the barbarians." These loyalists did not hesitate to attack Europeans in Japan. For example, in 1862 Satsuma samurai murdered an Englishman named Richardson. After the shogun admitted that he could not punish the guilty persons, the British decided to exact retribution and bombarded Kagoshima, the Satsuma capital. Satsuma not only surrendered, but became admirers of the British and began to purchase British warships for its own navy. After 1868 most of the officers of the Japanese navy came from Satsuma. Choshu, which also fired on foreign ships in 1863, was in turn bombarded by a joint British, American, Dutch, and French fleet. Like Satsuma, Choshu was impressed by Western military might and purchased Western arms. Choshu samurai became the backbone of the Japanese army after 1868.

In 1866 Choshu and Satsuma entered into a secret coalition against the Tokugawa. The next year a new emperor was selected, and in January 1868, Choshu, Satsuma, and their allies proclaimed an "imperial restoration." After a very brief period of resistance, over two hundred years of peace and isolation under Tokugawa rule came to an end.

### Meiji Japan: The Building of a Modern Nation State

**Charter Oath.**  In 1868 the teenage Emperor Mutsuhito (1852–1912), better known by his posthumous name Meiji ("Enlightened Rule"), promulgated the Charter Oath which stated the goals of the new government. Clearly an effort to rally support around the emperor, the Charter Oath promised "deliberative assemblies" which would allow for greater popular participation in government, the end of feudal restrictions, and an official commitment to modernization. The Meiji leaders' basic goals were embodied in the phrase *fukoku kyohei* ("rich country, strong military").

**Administrative Structure.**  During the first years of the Meiji era, the capital city was moved from Kyoto to Edo, which had its name changed to Tokyo ("Eastern Capital"). In 1871, a Council of State and six ministries were created which governed Japan until 1885, when Ito Hirobumi (1841–1909) introduced the cabinet system. The real power during this period (1868–1912) rested in the hands of men from Satsuma and Choshu such as Ito and Yamagata Aritomo (1832–1922). After 1900 they continued to exercise authority as *genro* or "elder statesmen." As in the past, the emperor served as the symbol of power and left the decision making to his advisers.

**From Samurai to Soldier.**  In order to establish a strong centralized state, the new leaders had to deal with the feudal fiefs, the *han*. Thus the *daimyo* of Satsuma, Choshu, Hizen, and Tosa returned their *han* to the emperor in 1869 and set an example for other lords to follow. In 1871, an imperial rescript abolished the *han* and divided the country into prefectures. The *daimyo* received generous compensation for their losses and many were appointed governors of their respective territories. The samurai, on the other hand, did not fare as well for the new stipends they received were less than their pre-1871 income. The plight of the samurai worsened in 1876 when the government was forced to commute the stipends into bonds because of financial difficulties. Insult was added to injury when in the same year the samurai were forbidden to wear swords.

Samurai discontent began to mount. Not only were they facing poverty and the loss of their feudal status symbols, they did not have the skills or capital to invest in business. Several proposals for overseas military expeditions were suggested as a means of solving the unrest and low morale. An expedition to Korea was vetoed; and the punitive Formosan expedition of 1874 (which forced China to relinquish the Ryukyu Islands) was a fiasco. The frustrations of the samurai class were reflected in their support of the 1877 Satsuma rebellion. The crushing defeat of the samurai rebels was significant, for the government forces were comprised of conscripts from the common classes and trained to fight with Western-style arms and modern tactics. Opponents of the new government now turned to other means to express their discontent.

**Movement for Representative Government.** The decade of the 1870s also witnessed an early movement for representative government led by men such as Itagaki Taisuke (1837–1919) of Tosa. Itagaki resigned his government post in 1873 over the issue of the Korean expedition. He and others formed political clubs which pressured the government for a popular assembly. This movement for people's rights was supported by unhappy samurai, tax-paying landholders, and Westernized intellectuals. The government tried to suppress the movement through legislation such as the Press Law of 1875 (which gave it the right to censor newspapers and periodicals).

It should be noted that the leaders of the new government were not opposed to a representative government. In 1879 members of prefectural assemblies were elected by restricted franchise. Gradually other local bodies were also elected. The basic question which divided the Meiji political leaders was whether the new government was to follow the British or Prussian model. The debate was resolved as a result of the Crisis of 1881.

In 1881, Councilor Okuma Shigenobu (1838–1922) of Hizen submitted a memorial that asked for elections in 1882, a parliament in 1883, and a British-style cabinet. Okuma was dismissed, but not before the emperor was forced to issue an imperial rescript which promised a national assembly by 1890. The outcome was actually a victory for Ito Hirobumi who proceeded to draft a constitution on the Prussian model without Okuma's interference. Okuma's departure also meant that the reins of the government rested in the hands of men from Choshu and Satsuma *han.*

Okuma and Itagaki now turned to political parties as a means of influencing government policy. In 1881, Itagaki formed the Liberal Party

(Jiyuto) and, in 1882, Okuma established the Constitutional Progressive Party (Rikken Kaishinto). Hampered by factional disputes and strong government action against them, the parties began to disintegrate by the middle of the decade. The party movement was also hampered when Okuma was enticed back in 1888 to serve the government as foreign minister.

When Ito returned from Europe in 1883, he called for basic changes that would lay the groundwork for the Constitution: in 1884, a new peerage system was created to provide the membership for a House of Peers; in 1885, a cabinet system began to operate along the Prussian model, with the prime minister directly responsible to the emperor; in 1887, a civil service examination system was established; in 1888, the Privy Council was appointed to advise the emperor.

**Constitution of 1889.** The constitution was promulgated in 1889. The emperor was the supreme head of state who could veto or initiate legislation. A Diet or national assembly was established with an upper house, the House of Peers, whose members were appointed; and a House of Representatives which was elected. The Diet's power of the purse was restricted by the constitutional provision which provided that the previous year's budget would go into effect if the government's new budget proposal should be refused.

Ito and his cohorts were anxious to see their efforts at constitutional government succeed. Failure would mean loss of face in the eyes of the West and the continuation of the humiliating extraterritoriality clause. The Choshu-Satsuma clique relinquished its control of the cabinet in 1898 to a coalition party (the Kenseito or Constitutional Party) formed by Itagaki and Okuma who occupied the posts of foreign minister and prime minister respectively. Unprepared for the enormous task and without the support of the Choshu-Satsuma clique, the Itagaki-Okuma coalition collapsed after five months. General Yamagata Aritomo then assumed the post of prime minister for the second time. Much of his efforts were spent on measures that would make the military independent of the Diet and the bureaucracy. In 1900 Yamagata pushed through a law that stated that the positions of army and navy ministers could be filled only by generals or admirals on the active lists of the armed services.

In 1900, Ito finally organized a government party, the Rikken Seiyukai (Constitutional Government Party). A few months later Yamagata resigned and Ito became prime minister. Although the Seiyukai had a majority in the lower house, Ito was not without problems. Frustrated by the lack of unity among the *genro*, a stubborn upper house that did not support his measures, and internal party disputes, Ito resigned in 1901.

From 1901 to 1912, the Meiji government was characterized by the end of the *genro* monopoly of high positions such as prime minister. The earlier period had see the post of prime minister alternate between men from Choshu (Ito and Yamagata) and Satsuma (Kuroda and Matsukata) clans. Now it would alternate between the young proteges of Ito and Yamagata—Prince Saionji and General Katsura. Saionji and Katsura were able to cooperate from 1901 to 1912, but in 1912 the Saionji cabinet fell when the army minister resigned. This had serious implications for the future of constitutional government in Japan for it was the first in a series of events that led to military domination of the government by the decade of the thirties.

### Transformation of the Economy and Society

In order to realize the goal of *fukoku kyohei,* the Meiji leaders assigned a high priority to the development of industry and a modern economy. The decimal system was adopted and the yen became the standard coin in 1871. The government pioneered in the development of railroads, strategic industries such as shipyards and steel mills, and consumer goods such as textiles. At the same time, private entrepreneurs from the merchant, samurai, and peasant classes also played an important role. These entrepreneurs, who were motivated by patriotism as well as profit, received help from the government in the form of subsidies, credit, and technical aid.

**Birth of the Zaibatsu.** The cost of industrialization, development of the northern home island of Hokkaido in the face of expanding Russian interests, as well as earlier mentioned payments to the samurai and expenses incurred by military expeditions led to a major financial crisis in 1880. The land tax, which accounted for eighty percent of the overall revenue, could not be increased without severe repercussions from the peasants. The government was reluctant to borrow from abroad and it was decided that the government should sell its industrial enterprises with the exception of public utilities, communications, and military industries. From the group of daring investors who purchased many of the government industries would emerge the industrial combines known as *zaibatsu.* By the death of Emperor Meiji in 1912 Japan had a diversified and highly productive industrial base to support her overseas ventures.

**Educational Reforms.** The Meiji leaders realized that modernization along Western lines had to be accompanied by reforms in education. In order to acquire skills and knowledge as soon as possible, the government brought foreign advisers to Japan and sent students overseas. Initially, the highly centralized French educational system had the greatest influence over the Ministry of Education which was established in 1871. After the arrival of David Murray in 1873, however, liberal American ideas began to prevail. The decade of the 1880s saw a dramatic shift in Japan's educational system. No longer was the emphasis on individual development. Instead loyalty to the throne and the welfare of the nation were placed above all virtues. The "morals" courses which were introduced in the elementary schools during this decade and the Imperial Rescript on Education of 1890 reflected this change. Education was becoming a means of state indoctrination through a Ministry of Education which controlled textbooks and course content.

As Japan entered the twentieth century her children were entitled to six years of compulsory schooling. Thereafter, the males who managed to work their way up through middle and higher schools could attend the prestigious imperial universities or private institutions such as Waseda and Keio if they passed the entrance examinations. Girls who wished to continue their education attended separate girls' schools and colleges. Through a centralized educational system, Meiji Japan produced a literate, disciplined and skilled population while individual freedom was subordinate to the needs of the state.

**Westernization.** Many Japanese realized that they had to adopt Western customs as well as technology if they wished to be accepted as equals by foreigners. Above all, they did not wish to be objects of ridicule. The Meiji leaders introduced the Gregorian calendar. Postal service and electricity were made available. With government encouragement the Japanese began to brush their teeth, eat beef, and wear Western hairdos and clothes. The craze for things Western hit its peak in the 1880s. After this, many superficial aspects of Western living such as ballroom dancing fell into disfavor as the Japanese began to emphasize their own cultural traditions.

### Learning From the West: Sino-Japanese War and the Beginning of Modern Japanese Imperialism

The Meiji era was also characterized by Japanese expansion overseas in the direction of China and her tributary states. Some of Japan's early successes included international recognition of her rights to the Ryukyu Islands (1874) and the use of gunboat diplomacy to open Korea to foreign intercourse (1876). It was the Sino-Japanese War of 1894–1895, however, that clearly demonstrated the imperialistic objectives of Japanese foreign policy in Asia.

**Sino-Japanese War.** The conflict broke out in Korea where both the Chinese and Japanese were deeply involved in political intrigues. The better equipped and trained Japanese army and navy were constantly on the offensive. By November 1894 Ch'ing forces had lost Korea and in the spring of the next year the Japanese were in Manchuria and the Liaotung Peninsula. The peace treaty of Shimonoseki (1895) brought the war to a close.

**Russia and Great Britain.** The Triple Intervention had been instigated by Russia and it introduced a period of intense Russo-Japanese rivalry in Manchuria and Korea after 1895. In addition to its underdeveloped natural resources, Manchuria was of special interest to the Russians who saw it as the terminus of their Trans-Siberian Railway as well as the answer to their long-sought-after warm water port. In 1896, China gave Russia permission to build the eastern portion of their Trans-Siberian Railway across Manchuria, and in 1898, Russia secured her warm water port when she leased the Liaotung Peninsula. Japanese and British anxiety mounted when Russia used the Boxer rebellion to occupy Manchuria. The result was the Anglo-Japanese Alliance of 1902 which acknowledged Japan's preeminence in Korea and Britain's dominant role in central China. The pact stated that in the event that either party became involved in a conflict, the other would remain neutral. The target of the agreement was obviously Russia, but in the eyes of the Japanese people the mere fact that Great Britain had signed the bilateral pact was a symbol of Japan's rise to world power status.

In the meantime Japan was also disturbed by increasing Russian influence over the Korean court. Japanese leaders had long viewed Korea as a potential dagger aimed at Japan. Therefore Japanese influence and control of the peninsula was essential for the security of the nation. When the Japanese attempted to reform the Korean government and legal system after the Sino-Japanese War, the Korean queen protested. She was killed and her husband was seized but he managed to escape to the Russian legation. After this incident Russian influence rose while Japan's position deteriorated. Russian businessmen secured timber and mining concessions; Russian advisers served the Korean army and administration. Tensions were eased when Russia recognized Japan's economic interest in Korea in 1898, but Russian occupation of Manchuria after the Boxer rebellion rekindled Japanese fears of Russian encroachment on Korea.

**Russo-Japanese War.**   Four months after the signing of the Anglo-Japanese Alliance in 1902 Russia agreed to withdraw her troops from Manchuria. When the second phase of withdrawal did not occur in 1903 as promised, the Japanese proposed to solve their differences with Russia by offering to recognize Russia's influence over Manchuria's railroads in exchange for Russian recognition of Japanese rights in Korea. While the negotiations continued, Russia sent troops into Manchuria. Suspicious, the Japanese broke off the talks in 1904 and executed a successful surprise attack on the Russian fleet in Port Arthur.

Russian forces were no match for the modern Japanese army and navy. Through President Theodore Roosevelt's efforts the Russo-Japanese War came to an end in 1905 after the defeat of the Russian Baltic fleet in the Tsushima Straits. The Treaty of Portsmouth gave Japan half of Sakhalin Island, the Russian leasehold of Liaotung and railroad concessions, and recognized Japan's sphere of interest in Korea.

The Japanese victory in the Russo-Japanese War had significant implications for the future. It offered encouragement to Asian nationalists who were seeking to overthrow the yoke of Western colonialism. It marked the beginning of Japan's overseas empire. Korea was annexed in 1910 and Japanese interests in Manchuria grew in the twentieth century. It also signaled the beginning of anti-American sentiment in Japan, for the Japanese blamed the United States for their failure to receive more concessions from Russia. On the other hand, American perceptions of Japan began to shift from admiration for the underdog to distrust and fear of a potential threat to American interests.

By 1912 Japan had been transformed from a feudal regime to a modern Westernized nation-state. The Meiji leaders had succeeded in their original goal: *fukoku kyohei.*

## Summary

The end of the nineteenth century saw the once great traditional civilizations of Asia either overwhelmed or on the verge of disintegration. Indeed, by 1900 almost all of Asia had been carved up and incorporated into the imperial schemes of the European powers, the United States, and a Japan that had adopted Western imperialism. The British had reduced the entire Indian subcontinent, Burma, and the Malay peninsula to the status of colonies within their vast worldwide empire. Southeast Asia was largely under French domination, with the exception of American control of the Philippines and the Dutch in the East Indies. Germany, a latecomer to the race for Asian empires, held a number of Pacific islands. Japan had annexed Formosa, and both Russians and Japanese coveted Korea and Manchuria. And with few exceptions all of the imperial powers had spheres of influence in China.

By the eve of World War I, little more than a decade into the twentieth century, the old order was dead in India and China. But there were signs that the pendulum had begun to swing slowly back toward a balance between East and West. In India a growing sense of nationalism had already led to organized demands for independence. China had recently experienced a great revolution in which the accumulated corruptions and flaws of the Confucian system had been swept away. Japan had emerged as a force on the international scene with her defeat of Russia, and the fact that Asians had defeated Europeans served as an impetus for nationalist movements throughout Asia. Moreover, the awesome and ruthless destruction of property and lives during the Great War raised doubts about the alleged superiority of Western civilization.

The West, because of its technological superiority, had overtaken and overwhelmed the traditional societies of Asia, but World War I revealed the inability of Western man to control the use of science and technology for human progress. The moral decadence and hypocrisy of

**Asia and the Pacific, 1910**

- British territory
- British protected states
- Dutch territory
- French territory
- German territory
- Japan and Japanese territories
- United States and possessions

**Figure 20-4.**

Western ideals were again demonstrated clearly at Versailles when the Japanese request for a racial equality clause was denied. When the bankrupt imperial nations turned their attentions back to their colonies they discovered that their authority was increasingly challenged. And within a half century the pendulum would continue to swing toward Asia with growing momentum.

# Reform,

# Nationalism,

# and

# War

Great Britain
  Victorian Compromise
  House of Lords
  Irish Question
France
  The Second Empire and Napoleon III
  The Third Republic
  Constitution of 1875
  Age of Scandal
Italy
  Victor Emmanuel
  War of 1859
  Garibaldi
  Unification
Germany
  William I
  Bismarck
  War of 1864
  1866: Preparations
  Seven Weeks' War
  North German Confederation
  Franco-Prussian War
  Unification Completed
  The New Empire

European international conflict, which had been mimimized by the Congress system in the early decades of the post-Napoleonic period, began to intensify again during the last half of the nineteenth century. Although some significant political, social, and economic reforms were instituted in Britain, France, and other countries, the *dominant* theme in Europe after 1850 was nationalism and nationalistic rivalry. Established nation-states competed aggressively with one another for territory and power, while scores of nationalist and ethnic groups struggled to achieve unification of nationalist and ethnic groups struggled to achieve unification and to gain their independence from these established states. The connected forces of blind nationalism, imperialism, and militarism resulted in a series of preliminary crises and clashes around the turn of the century, and ultimately led to a full-scale global conflict more destructive than any previous war in man's history.

## Great Britain

### Victorian Compromise
In Britain the three decades following the reforms of the 1830s are known as the period of the Victorian Compromise. The wealthy middle class joined with the old aristocracy to form a new power structure, one that kept the lower classes "in their place." In the latter half of the 1800s, two men dominated English politics: Benjamin Disraeli (1804–1881) and William Gladstone (1809–1898).

**Disraeli's Reforms.** Disraeli, leader of the Conservatives, was the converted son of an Italian Jew. He was a noted Victorian novelist, whose mode of dress and speech were called "dandy" in his day—the counterpart of our "mod." Included in Disraeli's reforms were the Second Reform Bill (1867), which gave the vote to most city workers and redistricted Parliament; the Public Health Act (1874) improving sanitation conditions in the cities; the Dwelling Act (1876), which condemned unsafe buildings; and, the Factory and Workshop Act (1878) codifying existing labor laws.

**Gladstone's Reforms.** Gladstone, leader of the Liberals, was the son of a wealthy merchant and had been educated at Eton and Oxford. Gladstone's reforms included The Forster Education Act (1870) which created the first free elementary schools; the introduction of the Australian Ballot (1872) which made secret voting compulsory; and the Third Reform Bill (1884) giving the vote to agricultural workers.

### House of Lords
The extended franchise made it easier for reformers to gain election to the House of Commons, but the aristocratic House of Lords stood as a

barrier against reform legislation. In 1909, for instance, it delayed passage of a government budget bill. In 1910, the Lords tried to "amend to death" a Parliamentary reform bill and finally agreed to pass it only under the threat that the King would create 250 new peers if they continued to block it. This bill virtually eliminated the final veto power of the Lords. From this time forward if a measure passed the Commons on three successive sessions, it would become law without approval of the Lords. The bill transformed Parliament into a virtually unicameral body and cleared the way for its consideration of one of England's most vexing problems—the Irish question.

### Irish Question

The Irish question, which had plagued the English since the time of Henry II, had become politically critical for her by the nineteenth century. After 1800 the growing population of Ireland forced the redivision of tenant farms into smaller parcels; absentee landlords raised rents as they reduced land size. To add to these economic difficulties, the potato crop failed in 1840, leading to famine and a mass migration, mostly to the United States. Under the leadership of men such as Charles Parnell, the Irish party in Parliament worked for Home Rule. Gladstone, recognizing the issue, strove to improve conditions in Ireland, but his bills for Home Rule failed to pass in Parliament in both 1886 (Commons) and 1893 (Lords) and Irish national discontent continued to mount as the clouds of war began to gather over Europe.

### France

#### The Second Empire and Napoleon III

Generally when the actions of a contemporary leader defy evaluation, time eventually brings into focus the results of his actions. However, it has been over one hundred years since Napoleon III was deposed, yet he still eludes conclusive evaluation.

His liberal economic policies stimulated all aspects of the French economy: heavy industry, agriculture, transportation, and internal improvements. The French railroad system was outstanding, and industrial output in coal and iron was second only to Great Britain's. Napoleon was dedicated to the modernization of French cities, climaxed by the beautification of Paris. His economic policies extended to French planning and financing for the building of the Suez Canal.

**Imperial Diplomacy.**    It is in foreign relations that the extremes of Napoleon are demonstrated. He was a nationalist in the broadest sense; that is, he favored the nationalistic aspirations of Germans, Italians, Poles, and others. Yet in the end he lost the friendship of Italy and fought a war with Germany. He desired a balance of power in European politics, aiming his early wars toward restricting the power of Russia (1854–1856) and Austria (1859). He also wanted to extend French territorial holdings, but he only acquired Nice and Savoy, and the instigation of the tragic Maximilian Affair in Mexico almost caused a war with the United States and a loss of prestige from which he never really recovered. His last involvement in foreign affairs, the Franco-Prussian War, cost him more than prestige: he lost his imperial throne.

### The Third Republic
Unlike the First and Second Republics which were born in revolution, the Third happened by accident. The assembly that was elected following the overthrow of Napoleon III was dominated by monarchists. The Commune of Paris reacted by seceding from the remainder of France (March 1871). A second siege of Paris (April-May) was worse than the first: public buildings were burned; the Archbishop of Paris was assassinated; and few prisoners were taken. The actions of the Commune of Paris discredited radical groups (communists and anarchists) and greatly reduced their numbers. The reconvening assembly was for restoration, but which king: the Count of Chambord (Bourbon) or the Count of Paris (Orleanist)? It was finally agreed that the Count of Chambord would become Henry V, when he announced that he would be an absolute ruler and abolish the tricolors. The moderate and liberal monarchists then agreed to a temporary republic until Henry died.

### Constitution of 1875
The assembly elected Marshall MacMahon president (November 1873), and then prepared a constitution. Inasmuch as it was to be a temporary document, it was simple. Surprisingly, the Third Republic lasted until 1940.

### Age of Scandal
The remainder of the nineteenth century was a struggle between monarchists, clerics, and the military on one side, and republicans on the other. Each was determined to discredit the other, yet tended to discredit themselves through some sort of scandal: MacMahon, a royalist, eventually resigned because he was unable to hand the government to the Orleanists (1879); François Grevy, the next president and a republican, resigned because his son-in-law was selling Legion of Honor Medals (1887); Georges Boulanger, a monarchist disguised as a republican, attempted to overthrow the government with the help of army leaders (1889); and, the Panama Canal Scandal demonstrated corruption in the government at high levels (1894). Yet these scandals and others that

plagued the Third Republic during its first two decades appear insignificant compared to the Dreyfus Case.

**Dreyfus Case.**   The case contained elements of monarchist-military-cleric versus republican-Socialist, with an added ingredient: anti-Semitism. Captain Alfred Dreyfus, a republican, a Jew, and a member of the general staff, was convicted of spying and sentenced to life imprisonment on Devil's Island (1894). Dreyfus's conviction was based on military secrets supposedly in his handwriting that had been meant for the Germans. In 1896 the new head of army intelligence, Colonel Picquart, discovered more documents in the same handwriting. His investigation showed that it was the handwriting of a Major Esterhazy (a monarchist). Esterhazy was tried, found innocent, and Picquart was sent to North Africa (1898). Evidence against Dreyfus presented at Esterhazy's trial were forgeries by a Major Henry. He confessed, was arrested, committed suicide, and Esterhazy fled from France.

Support was growing for Dreyfus, including the radicals, such as Georges Clemenceau, and the noted author Emile Zola. Zola was eventually tried and found guilty of libel because of his attacks. In 1899, the French Supreme Court ordered a new trial for Dreyfus. At the retrial the army, in spite of all contradictory evidence, still found Dreyfus guilty, but with a recommendation for clemency. Dreyfus was pardoned by President Loubet (1899) and in 1906 the Supreme Court reversed the decision. After twelve years Dreyfus was cleared.

**Results of the Case.**   The consequences of the Dreyfus case are interesting: Dreyfus was promoted and given the Legion of Honor; Zola, who had died in 1902, was given a state burial; Picquart became Minister of War in 1908; Clemenceau became Prime Minister in 1907; and Esterhazy died in exile. There were other significant consequences of the case. The monarchist movement was completely discredited. Almost all anti-republican military leaders were purged from the army. The Church, which endorsed the army throughout the entire affair, found itself now persecuted by the anticleric forces of the Republic. A law in 1901 closed thousands of church schools and replaced them with public ones; in 1905 the Concordat of 1801 was ended; and another law made it illegal to teach Church doctrine in the schools. Thus the Republic survived, but it was so politically fragmented that every ministry was a coalition and none lasted longer than three years.

### Italy

Italy apparently emerged from the revolutions of 1848 and 1849 little changed. Every revolt and anti-Austrian movement was crushed, and the only liberal ruler (Charles Albert) was forced to abdicate. The only visible gain was that Victor Emmanuel II, Charles Albert's son, retained Piedmont's liberal constitution.

### Victor Emanuel

Victor Emmanuel II was a pleasure-seeking playboy (nicknamed the "cavalier king") determined to be king of a united Italy, dedicated to constitutional government, and able to select outstanding men to serve him. The most outstanding was Cavour.

**Cavour.** Count Camillo Benso di Cavour (1810–1861) was a man of many talents: a graduate of a military academy, engineer, agriculturalist, economist, journalist, and political scientist. Among his accomplishments before becoming Prime Minister of Piedmont-Sardinia were his plans for a railroad system for Italy; and an experimental farm that became a model in Italy. He was a recognized expert on the British parliamentary system; founder of the newspaper *Il Risorgimento,* which was the voice for Italian unification; and Minister of Finance and Agriculture for Piedmont.

Cavour realized the necessity of foreign help against Austria. His first move was to join with Great Britain and France against Russia in the Crimean War. Cavour was a representative at the Treaty of Paris (1856), where he was able to expound Italian nationalism and also make contact with Napoleon Ill.

**Cavour and Napoleon.** Cavour perceived Napoleon as a potential ally for Italian unification. At Plombières in 1858 a secret agreement was made between Napoleon and Cavour. The provisions called for the creation of a four-state Italian confederation under the presidency of the Pope. The four states were to be (1) Naples (unchanged); (2) Papal state (cut down to Rome and its immediate area); (3) Kingdom of Central Italy (from the territory removed from the Papal State, plus Lucca and Tuscany, with Napoleon III's cousin Victor Napoleon as king); and (4) the Kingdom of Northern Italy under Victor Emmanuel to include Piedmont-Sardinia, Lombardy, Venetia, Parma, and Modena. France was to receive Savoy and Nice from Piedmont, which would make France's southern border the Alps. A marriage alliance was included under which Napoleon's cousin married Victor Emmanuel's daughter. The key part of the agreement was the military provision. War with Austria was necessary to create the Italian Confederation, but Napoleon insisted that for purposes of public opinion Austria had to appear as the aggressor.

### War of 1859

Cavour easily duped Austria into declaring war. He openly made Piedmont a refuge for deserters from the Austrian army, and he secretly helped revolutionary groups in Lombardy and Venetia. When his "secret" aid was discovered by Austrian agents, Austria handed Piedmont-Sardinia an ultimatum which was rejected. On April 27, 1859, Austria declared war and Napoleon personally led the French army against Austrian "aggression."

Although the battles at Magenta and Solferino were not decisive, they gained most of Lombardy for the allies. Revolts in Tuscany, Parma, and Modena expelled the pro-Austrian rulers, and these states demanded to be part of a united Italy. Napoleon then backed out. Fearing that he had gone too far in creating a strong nation on France's boundary and also fearing possible loss of Catholic support because of danger to the Pope, Napoleon secretly met with Franz-Joseph and agreed on a peace treaty. Under the treaty, Sardinia retained Lombardy, Austria kept Venetia, and the other states were to be returned to their rulers. Victor Emmanuel, having lost his ally, agreed to the treaty at Zürich (November, 1859) and Cavour resigned in protest.

**Treaty of Turin.**   Circumstances changed defeat to victory. The populations of Parma, Modena, Romagna, Lucca, and Tuscany refused to accept the return of their previous rulers. Instead they held plebiscites where almost unanimously the people voted to join Sardinia. Cavour, who had returned to office, convinced Napoleon to recognize the annexations by giving him Nice and Savoy. Most of northern Italy was not unified and plans were in motion for expansion.

### Garibaldi

There is great disagreement among historians on the events that followed. Garibaldi and one thousand red-shirted volunteers did sail from the island of Sardinia to Sicily. But what was Cavour's role? As a head of state, Cavour was responsible for stopping any aggressive act originating on Sardinian territory against another sovereign nation, yet he claimed he knew nothing of Garibaldi's preparations. Garibaldi landed on the island of Sicily and by the time he reached the mainland his original 1000 men had grown to 60,000. He marched on Naples and captured it with a force of 100,000. Meanwhile, Cavour convinced Napoleon that he had to stop Garibaldi by driving through the Papal state to Naples. Garibaldi could have been king of Naples-Sicily, but following a meeting with Cavour, he endorsed the plebiscite that joined the northern and southern parts of Italy.

### Unification

The eastern two-thirds of the Papal state was retained, which united all of Italy, except for Venetia and the area surrounding Rome. At the Parliament of Turin in March, 1861, Victor Emmanuel was proclaimed king of Italy. Unification was not yet complete, and Cavour would not live to see it. Three months after the Parliament of Turin, Cavour died.

Italy found a new ally in Prussia and in the War of 1866 received Venetia for her part in the war. Rome was important as a symbol of nationalism, but so long as French troops were protecting the Papal state, little could be done. During the Franco-Prussian War, French troops were withdrawn, and the Papal state was occupied, except for Vatican City, where Pius IX proclaimed himself a "Papal Prisoner" and refused to recognize the Italian Kingdom. Italy's success and Cavour's diplomacy meanwhile had become a model for Germany.

## Germany

The German and Italian situations following the revolutions of 1848 were similar: Austria was the enemy of unification, Napoleon was a potential ally, and there was a change of rulers in the leading state before anything was accomplished.

Leadership had been a problem in Prussia since Frederick the Great: Frederick William II (1786–1797) was defeated by the French; Frederick William III (1797-1840) was defeated by Napoleon I and dominated by both Metternich and Alexander I; and Frederick William IV (1840-1861) was frustrated by the Humiliation of Olmütz, so frustrated that he went insane.

### William I

Frederick William IV's brother was first regent, then king. William I, like his predecessors was neither an outstanding administrator nor leader, but unlike them, he had been trained in the military, and recognized his own limitations. As a military leader, dedicated to unifying Germany under Prussia, he was determined to build up the army for the eventual conflict with Austria. But to expand and modernize meant money, and the liberals in the Prussian Parliament refused to vote it. On the advice of his friends, William appointed Otto Edward Leopold von Bismarck as Chancellor.

### Bismarck

Otto von Bismarck's preparation for leadership (1815–1898) differed extensively from his Italian counterpart. A member of the Junker class of East Prussia, he gained more of a reputation for drinking beer than studying at the University of Berlin. Entering the Prussian civil service he was dismissed for "breach of discipline." Marriage at the age of thirty-two changed him completely. He entered the Prussian Diet (1847-ff); served as Prussian ambassador to the German Diet (1851–1858), then, to Russia (1859–1861), then to France (1862), and was foreign minister

(1862). His policies as chancellor were called "blood and iron" from a speech to the Prussian Diet.

Upon becoming chancellor in September, 1862, he worked on the legislature to raise the money for military reform, but neither bribes, threats, nor tricks could acquire enough votes for the funds. He then ran Prussia in 1863 without a budget—laid and collected taxes anyway. The diet's reaction? Although they condemned him in 1863 for destroying parliamentary government in Prussia, in 1867 they voted for the 1863 budget *ex post facto*.

### War of 1864

The army was soon put to use. The King of Denmark was also the Duke of Schleswig-Holstein. The duchies were German and part of the Confederation. Although Danes had promised in 1852 not to make the duchies part of Denmark, in 1863 King Christian IX of Denmark issued a liberal constitution that incorporated them. The duchies protested, other German states protested, and Prussia and Austria did more than protest. Bismarck convinced Austria to join Prussia in a war defending the German duchies. The combined Austro-Prussian armies easily defeated the Danes and annexed the duchies. Under the Convention of Gastein, Prussia received Schleswig and Austria acquired Holstein.

The anexation of Schleswig was a small step toward unification, the next step was much larger.

### 1866: Preparations

Bismarck knew that in order to eliminate Austria from Germany, the other powers had to be neutralized. Great Britain favored a united Germany because it weakened both France's and Austria's position. Inasmuch as Bismarck had developed a closeness with Alexander I when he had been ambassador to Russia, which he had reinforced by offering troops to Russia during a Polish uprising in 1863, Russia was not a problem. Bismarck had also gained insight into Napoleon's character when he was in France. Knowing Napoleon was interested in territorial gain, he agreed "verbally" at Biarritz (October, 1865) to endorse French acquisition of Luxembourg and Belgium in exchange for neutrality in case there was an Austro-Prussian War. Italy desired Venetia to complete its unification and agreed to a defensive alliance with Prussia against Austria. Next, Bismarck had to provoke Austria.

### Seven Weeks' War

Bismarck used Holstein to goad Austria. Austria endorsed Frederick of Augustenburg as ruler of the Duchies, and when Prussia protested, Austria presented its case to the German diet. Bismarck claimed this broke the agreement of Gastein and sent troops into Holstein for protection. Austria was provoked, and probably knew what Bismarck was doing, but believed its larger army would be victorious.

The Seven Weeks' War in reality was a one-battle war: the Battle of Sadowa. After two preliminary engagements removed Austria's allies (for example, Hanover), the Austrians and Prussians met at Sadowa (near Prague). Although outnumbered, superior Prussian planning (General von Moltke), technology (use of telegraph and railroads), arms (breach versus muzzle loaders), and training gave Prussia a decisive victory of 9,000 Prussian casualties to 40,000 Austrians. With its armies defeated and its government on the verge of bankruptcy, Austria sued for peace.

### North German Confederation
The terms of the Treaty of Prague were lenient, considering the circumstances: Austria ceded Venetia to Italy and Holstein to Prussia, paid a small indemnity, and agreed to the dissolving of the German Confederation and its replacement by the North German Confederation.

The new Confederation consisted of the northern two-thirds of Germany (excluding Bavaria, Baden, and Württemberg). The constitution created a federal system with the king of Prussia as hereditary president; a lower house (*Reichstag*) represented according to population and elected by universal manhood suffrage; and an upper house (*Bundesrat*) representing the twenty-two member states. Foreign affairs and the armed forces were under the federation, but internal affairs were under the individual states. Prussia controlled the federation by having seventeen out of forty-three members in the *Bundesrat,* and only fourteen votes were needed to defeat legislation.

**1870: Preparations.** But unification was still not complete. Between 1867 and 1870 Bismarck cultivated Bavaria, Baden, and Württemberg. He invited them to remain in the Zollverein, which meant close economic ties. Defensive alliances were made between the confederation and the other German states.

Meanwhile Napoleon discovered Bismarck was "ignorant" of his promises from Biarritz. A war followed, but who was to blame? Napoleon who still believed in his destiny or Bismarck who desired further unification? Both were, they wanted the war and so did the nationalists in both countries.

The other powers stayed out of it for various reasons: Great Britain because Bismarck had delivered to them a memorandum Napoleon had written showing his desire to annex Belgium; Russia because Napoleon had aided the Polish revolt of 1863; Italy because Bismarck had been truer in his agreements than Napoleon; and Austria perhaps because of possible danger from Russian attack. All that was needed was an incident.

**Ems Telegram.**  Events in Spain supplied the incident both sides needed. In 1868, Isabella II had been overthrown and abdicated in 1870 in favor of her son. The revolutionists instead offered the crown to Prince Leopold, a Hollenzollern and relative of William II of Germany. Leopold turned down the offer the first time, and was reconsidering a second invitation when Napoleon intervened. Since Napoleon did not relish France between two Hollenzollerns, he instructed the French ambassador to Germany to approach William to intercede with Leopold. Ambassador Benedetti went to the Ems Spa where William was vacationing and presented Napoleon's request (July 12, 1870). William sent a telegram to Bismarck informing him of the meeting. Bismarck, with the aid of General von Moltke, changed the wording of the telegram to make it appear that Benedetti and William had been rude to each other. He also held the doctored Ems Telegram until July 14 so that it reached Paris at the height of Bastille Day. With nationalism at a high pitch the French National Assembly declared war on the North German Confederation (July 19, 1870).

### Franco-Prussian War

Napoleon's first surprise of the war was the entrance of Bavaria, Baden, and Württemberg into the war. His second was the superiority of the German forces over the French. Although the French army was larger and had been modernized its leadership was questionable and failed to improve its muzzle-loading artillery, and the German army's breach loading rifled artillery made the difference.

It was the superiority of the German artillery that defeated Marshall MacMahon at Wörth, who fell back to regroup. At this point, leadership broke down. Napoleon decided retreat would look bad and ordered MacMahon to advance. The opponents met at Sedan where both MacMahon and Napoleon were captured and an army of 82,000 surrendered (September 1 and 2).

The French Assembly made two decisions: first, to end the Second Empire; second, to endorse the continuation of the war. Although MacMahon's army had been captured, there was a 173,000-man army under Marshall Bazaine at Metz, and armies were forming in the provinces. Then Bazaine surrendered his entire army for no apparent reason (he was court-martialed following the war). The assembly was still determined to carry on the war, but with no organized French armies left the German army laid siege to Paris. After four and a half months, its population starving, Paris surrendered on January 28, 1871.

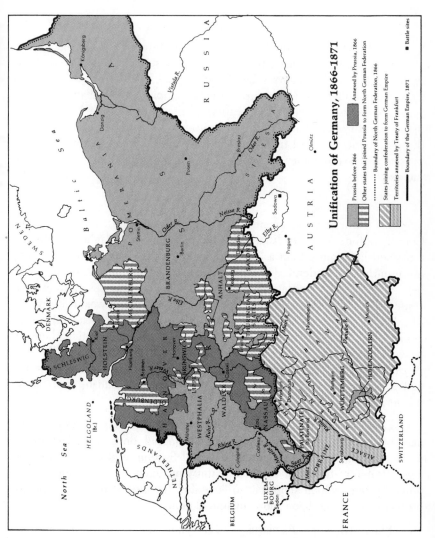

Unification of Germany, 1866-1871

| | |
|---|---|
| (shaded) | Prussia before 1866 |
| (dark) | Annexed by Prussia, 1866 |
| (light) | Other states that joined Prussia to form North German Federation |
| ····· | Boundary of North German Federation, 1866 |
| (hatched) | States joining confederation to form German Empire |
| (vertical lines) | Territories annexed by Treaty of Frankfurt |
| —— | Boundary of the German Empire, 1871 |
| ■ | Battle sites |

**Figure 21-1.**

**Treaty of Frankfurt.**   The treaty with France was harsher than Denmark's and Austria's. France ceded Alsace and most of Lorraine, paid Germany an indemnity of five billion gold Francs (one billion dollars), and accepted a German army of occupation until the indemnity was paid. Germany was victorious and France would neither forget nor forgive.

### Unification Completed

As the wave of national pride swept southern Germany, each state joined the confederation until every German state, except Austria, was unified. The day Paris surrendered, January 28, 1871, the North German Confederation legislature declared itself an empire and William, emperor. Thus 909 years following the creation of the Holy Roman Empire, Bismarck had through "blood and iron" initiated a second *reich*. Nationalism through unification had triumphed in Italy and Germany; however those people who were under the control of other nationalities enjoyed less success.

### The New Empire

The form of government of the Empire was almost identical to the Confederation: The *Reichstag,* elected by universal manhood suffrage, remained little more than a 397-member debating society; the *Budesrat,* representing the federated states, still contained enough Prussian members to block any legislation; and the Chancellor was selected by and responsible to the Emperor. The most significant change was in Bismarck. The "blood and iron" leader now became the man of peace. He had gained his objectives through war and now he sought to retain them by peace. Also, where his energies for almost ten years (1862–1871) emphasized foreign affairs, his next twenty years were devoted to internal matters. Bismarck saw three problems to overcome; localism, the "black" danger, and the "red" danger.

**Localism.**   The loyalties to local areas were easily overcome. Bismarck introduced unifying changes: an Imperial Bank and currency; a unified railroad system; an Imperial Postal System; and a single code of laws. Probably the most significant unifying agency was a free educational system, which emphasized love for the fatherland. The second problem may have been more imagined than real.

**Black Danger.**   Bismarck, a Protestant, believed Catholics were more loyal to the Church than to the state—therefore a danger. In order to end this "black" (Jesuit) danger, Bismarck had the legislature pass a series of anti-Catholic measures: no cleric criticism of the government was allowed; Jesuits were expelled; theology became a state university monopoly; and only civil marriages were legal. The Catholic membership forming the Center Party—ancestor to the present Christian Democratic Party—in the *Reichstag* continued to grow, and Bismarck, observing that repression did not work and desiring the Catholics as allies against another threat, began to repeal the repressive measures in 1878.

**Red Danger.** Bismarck attempted to suppress Socialism by two methods: coercion and kindness. The Socialists who had voted against and had not supported Bismarck's wars of unification formed the Social Democrat party in 1875. Appealing to the growing working classes, the Social Democrats increased their votes and membership in the *Reichstag*. Suspecting the Socialists' loyalty to the state, Bismarck attempted to pass repressive measures against them. Not until there were two attempts on William I's life, which Bismarck blamed on the Socialists, was he successful (1878). Although Socialist candidates were still allowed to run for office, no Socialist publications or public meetings were permitted, and the Social Democratic party was outlawed. Lasting from 1878 to 1890, these repressive measures appear to have aided rather than hindered the Socialists. The votes received by them went from 300,000 to 1,500,000, and they increased their membership in the *Reichstag* from twelve to thirty-five.

Bismarck, recognizing that oppression was not working, originated the concept of giving workers in small amounts what the Socialists promised, therefore lessening the appeal of the Socialists. Under Bismarck's leadership, Germany became the model for social legislation. Included in the enactments were sickness insurance (1883), accident insurance (1884), protection of woman and child labor (1887), and old-age benefits (1889). When Bismarck retired, the oppressive measures were repealed, and the Social Democratic party's growth was so extensive that by World War I it was the largest single political party in Germany.

### Frederick III

William I died in 1888, and the throne went to his son, Frederick III. A victim of throat cancer, Frederick died ninety-one days later. If he had lived, the history of the world would have changed drastically. Frederick was a liberal who advocated the English Parliamentary system, with the chancellor responsible to the legislature. Instead, Frederick's son, William, became emperor.

### William II

Born with a crippled arm, adoring his grandfather, rejecting his father, hating his maternal grandmother (Queen Victoria), resenting Bismarck, and looking upon himself as a reincarnation of Frederick the Great, William was destined to be in the spotlight of Europe for thirty years. Determined as George III had been to be a real king, William first had to remove Bismarck. For two years the young king and elder states-man fenced for position, then using the question of renewing the anti-Socialist legislation, William demanded and received Bismarck's resigna-tion (1890).

William used front men as chancellors and whenever opinion built up against his policies, he removed the chancellor. Many of his policies were extensions of Bismarck's, others were his own. Economic growth continued, and by 1914 Germany was the number three industrial nation. Bismarck had little interest in colonial expansion, but under William, Germany acquired extensive holdings in both Africa and Oceania. William continued military preparation and defensive alliances, but his failure to carry out the isolation of France proved disastrous.

### Austria-Hungary

#### Austria after 1848

The Austrian Constitution of 1851 was an attempt to Germanize the heterogeneous empire: Hungary was made a province; German became the official language of Hungary; and government posts in Hungary were filled by Austrians. The lack of Hungarian support during the 1859 War motivated Franz Joseph to reinstate the Hungarian Parliament (1860). When the offer of a new constitution was refused in 1861, the matter was dropped but the disaster of 1866 brought it into focus again.

**Ferencz Deak.** During the 1850s Ferencz Deak replaced Kossuth as the leader of Hungarian nationalism. An intelligent and gifted orator, Deak took a more moderate stand than Kossuth. Inasmuch as he was for equality within the empire, not separation from it, he did not take part in the revolutions of 1848 to 1849. In 1861 it was Deak that Franz Joseph summoned to Vienna, and following 1866 it was his work that brought forth the new constitution.

**Ausgleich of 1867.** The *Ausgleich* (compromise) of 1867 trans-formed the Austrian Empire into the Dual Monarchy of Austria-Hungary. Hungary was a separate nation with the provision that the emperor of Austria was the king of Hungary. Each state had its own parliament and prime minister for internal affairs. A joint ministry handled external affairs, such as foreign relations and tariffs and, common problems, such as finances and the armed forces. A joint parliament, with sixty Austrians and sixty Hungarians, meeting alternate years in Vienna and Budapest, oversaw the ministry.

The Hungarians gained their nationalistic goals, but the Slavic groups within the empire were still a minority that failed to reach theirs.

Not only were the Slavs within the Dual Monarchy frustrated, their cousins' problems in the Balkans eventually proved to be disastrous to European peace and security.

## Russia

At mid-nineteenth century, Russia was one of the most underdeveloped European nations. If comparable to another world power, it would be the United States. Russia was developing its eastern frontier as the United States developed its western, both were building their transcontinental railroads, both were freeing their slaves (serfs), and both were searching for a national philosophy separate from Western Europe.

### Russian Intelligentsia

The two groups that dominated Russian thought were the Westernizers and the Slavophiles. The Westernizers looked toward Europe as the model for Russia, while the Slavophiles saw Slavic origins for the future. Both groups were nationalistic, for reform of the government, and emancipation of the serfs. Inasmuch as the Slavophiles were more moderate, there was a tendency for the Westernizers to be jailed or exiled. For example, Alexander Herzen (1812–1870) from his exile in London sent his newspaper the *Bell* to Russia where it was widely read, even by the czars. Other exiles gathered around him, even the Anarchist Bakunin.

### Alexander and Emancipation

Alexander II (1855–1881) succeeded Nicholas I as Czar during the Crimean War. Once the war was over, he set in motion his plan to emancipate the serfs. Although he was a conservative, he believed emancipation was good for Russia. Unlike the freeing of the slaves in the United States, the liberation of the serfs was carefully planned and carried out. The serfs were given the opportunity to acquire land through purchase (forty-nine-year loans by the government) or accept a smaller free section. The former masters of the serfs were compensated for their loss of labor and land. Another interesting parallel between the United States and Russia is that the serfs in Russia were freed in 1861, the same year that the Civil War over slavery began in the United States.

### Other Reforms

Alexander did not stop with emancipation. He introduced numerous reforms, including reorganizing the budget system; introducing the jury system; expanding education to everyone, including females; and starting representative government. The legislatures, called *zemstva*, designated local *zemstva* elected by the people, and a province *zemstva* elected by

438 Europe in the Victorian Age and the First World War

local vote. There was no provision for a national body. Although Alexander did more to improve conditions than his predecessors, there were groups who pushed for faster change.

### Nihilism

Ivan Turgenev in his book *Fathers and Sons* (1862) coined and defined the term nihilist. A nihilist was one who accepted nothing on faith, whether it be religious, social, or political. Adopting this as their creed, many young intellectuals calling themselves the *Narod* (the people) began preaching to the peasants not to support the government or church (that is, financially). The *Narod* failed because the peasants did not understand it, and the secret police could easily spot and arrest members.

By the late 1870s a new Nihilist group formed, called the *Narod Volya* (the people's will), who took the rejection concept a step further. Their philosophy of ending government was to assassinate those in authority. Believing in what they were doing, the members were willing to die for their cause. In 1878 and again in 1879 they killed the chiefs of the secret police and other officials, then they decided to assassinate Alexander II. Two attempts in 1879 and another in 1880 failed, then in March, 1881, just as Alexander had agreed to a constitution, he was killed by a bomb.

Before the death of Alexander, the *Narod Volya* had the sympathy of the people, because they rid Russia of oppressive individuals. But the death of the "Little Father" shocked the people and caused them to turn against the Nihilists who were executed, imprisoned, or exiled, and the remainder quieted down. The movement was over, but the anarchists adopted both their philosophy and tactics, and the word annihilate became part of our vocabulary.

**Reaction of Alexander III.** Inasmuch as Alexander III (1881–1894) blamed the death of his father on liberalism, he was dedicated to restore the policies of Nicholas I. He replaced Alexander II's advisers with more conservative ones, and the most conservative and influential was Alexander III's former tutor, Konstantin Pobedonostsev. As Procurator of the Holy Synod (governing body of the Russian Orthodox Church), Pobedonostsev dominated the Russian scene until 1905. Alexander's reign was one of Russification, with non-Russian minorities discriminated against, particularly the Jews. The persecution of the Jews led to the mass migrations of the 1880s and 1890s to the United States

**Indecision of Nicholas II.** Nicholas II (1894–1917) had the desire but not the ability, to continue the work of his father. Weak and indecisive, Nicholas was dominated by his advisers, friends, and wife. He ruled as Louis XVI had, and his fate was the same.

**Revolutionary Groups.** Industrialization followed the emancipation of the serfs (because of the resulting cheap labor supply). Although far from becoming a major industrial nation, there was a growing working class. Founded in 1883, the Marxist Social Democrats grew with the proletariat.

At a meeting in London in 1903 the more moderate wing of the party split with the radical wing over the editorship of the party's newspaper. Lenin's radical group, who won the vote, took the name Bolshevik (men of the majority), and the moderates under Cederbaum and Martov became known as the Menshevik (men of the minority).

### Revolution of 1905

Because of dissatisfaction by both the peasants and workers over conditions in Russia, Nicholas I was convinced a "small war" would unite the people, but just the opposite occurred. The Russo-Japanese War (1904–1905) was a David and Goliath affair, with little Japan defeating the Russians in every battle. Then, as everything was going wrong on the war front, a group of workers marching on the Czar's palace to present a petition were fired upon by cossacks (January, 1905). The slaughter of hundreds of peaceful demonstrators aroused the radicals, who demonstrated, called strikes, and assassinated officials. By June, mutinies had started in the navy, and in October the St. Petersburg Soviet (workers' council) called a general strike which, as it spread, paralyzed both industry and railroads.

**October Manifesto.** Nicholas, fearing a revolution that would overthrow his government, issued a proclamation agreeing to a constitution and a national legislature (Duma) to carry out reforms. The Bolsheviki wanted to continue the revolution, but the moderates were satisfied.

**Work of the Duma.** The first Duma elected by universal manhood suffrage (May, 1906) was dominated by the liberal Constitutional Democrats (Kadets). Although their demands were moderate by Western standards, Nicholas, who no longer feared revolution, dismissed the Duma because he considered it too radical. In 1907 a second Duma was elected and dissolved; again, it was too radical. In order to guarantee a workable Duma, before the third election was held, property and literacy qualifications restricted the suffrage of workers, peasants, and non-Russians.

Along with a properly conservative Duma, Peter Stolypin was made Prime Minister. Although a conservative and loyal to the Czar, Stolypin's outlook was similar to Alexander II's. Under his leadership the Duma created free and compulsory education; passed a homestead bill giving free land to peasants migrating to undeveloped areas; ended the 1862 emancipation tax; and, created agriculture banks to make funds available to peasants wishing to improve their lands.

Stolypin was assassinated in 1911 and the reforms stopped. Russia once more started to drift. Dissatisfaction began to grow among the workers and peasants, and Nicholas was again convinced in 1914 to become involved in a "small war."

## The Balkans: Powder Keg of Europe

### Panslavism

With origins in both Russian imperialistic designs on the Dardanelles and the South-Slavic peoples' desires for independence from the Ottomans and Austrians, the ethnocentric movement of Panslavism drew the other European powers into conflict from the time of the Crimean War to World War I.

### Crimean War

Looking for an excuse to invade Turkey for the purpose of acquiring the Dardanelles, Nicholas I invoked a Russo-Turkish treaty from 1774. The Treaty ostensibly gave Russia a protectorate over Christians in the Holy Land, and Orthodox and Catholic Pilgrims had clashed there during Easter week (1850). Russian forces invaded the Danubian Provinces (future Rumania) in September, 1853; two months later they destroyed the Turkish fleet. France, Great Britain, and Sardinia came to the defense of Turkey, each for their own reasons: Great Britain because she was determined to frustrate any Russian imperialistic designs; Sardinia to draw attention to Italian nationalism; and Napoleon III to demonstrate the greatness of the Second Empire.

The war was the first since the Napoleonic and was poorly fought on both sides; Florence Nightingale was the only individual to become famous; and a military blunder, the "Charge of the Light Brigade," is the only battle remembered. After two and a half years of fighting, mostly on the Crimean Peninsula (322 days to capture Sebastopol), Alexander II, the new Czar, threatened with invasion by Austria, asked for peace.

**Treaty of Paris.** Napoleon III convened the most impressive gathering of diplomats since the congress system. Although his ambitions for a revision of frontiers in Europe came to naught, there were both short and long-range accomplishments. The only exchange of territory was the Danubian Principalities and parts of Bessarabia which were placed under the control of the allies. Russia's losses went beyond territory: she gave up her protectorate of Christians in the Ottoman Empire and agreed to the neutralization of the Black Sea (no warships or forts). International agreements were made between those involved: the Danube River was internationalized; neutral rights were guaranteed, including "freedom of the seas"; and, privateers were abolished. The long-range agreements became the basis for much international law, the short-range ones lasted less than twenty years.

### Balkan Nationalism

The next two decades marked a growing dissatisfaction with Turkish rule in the Balkan states. Rumania, in 1862, received autonomous status, but along with Serbia (also autonomous), Bulgaria and Bosnia-Herzegovina desired complete independence. Taking advantage of unsettled conditions in Turkey (two *coups d' état* in a year), revolutions started in 1875. In 1876, Abdul Hamid II became sultan and began crushing the revolutions with extreme cruelty, so much so that the major European powers protested. When the Turks ignored the complaints, Russia decided to act.

### Russo-Turkish War

Russia in 1870 started rebuilding its fortifications in the Black Sea area (contrary to the treaty of Paris). Desiring both to weaken Turkey and to aid the Slavic peoples in the Balkans, Russia declared war on Turkey on April 24, 1877. Crossing the Danube (June) the Russians were held at Plevra by the Turks until December. The Russians, joined by Serbians, Rumanians, Montenegrins, and Bulgarians, captured Adrianople on January 16, 1878. With Constantinople threatened, and requests for aid rejected, Abdul Hamid asked for peace.

**Treaty of San Stefano.** The Treaty of San Stefano appeared to be the answer to Panslavism: Turkey recognized the independence of Serbia, Montenegro, and Rumania with enlarged territories; Bulgaria was created as an autonomous principality; the straits were internationalized; and Russia received part of Armenia, Dobruja, and an indemnity. Then other nationalistic aspirations, particularly British and Austrian, were exerted: Disraeli did not want Russia supreme in the area, and Franz Joseph desired expansion into the Balkans.

### Congress of Berlin

Disraeli and Franz Joseph argued that San Stefano was a revision of the Treaty of Paris, which could only be accomplished with the consent of the signatories of the Treaty of Paris: Great Britain, Germany, Austria-Hungary, France, Italy, Russia, and Turkey. Unable to face any combination of the major powers, Russia agreed to a meeting. The results of the Congress of Berlin (June 13–July 13, 1878) little resembled those of the Treaty of San Stefano: Russia was allowed to keep Armenia and was also given Bessarabia from Rumania; Rumania was compensated for the loss of Bessarabia by receiving Dobruja from Russia; Austria was authorized to occupy Bosnia-Herzegovina; Great Britain acquired Cyprus; Greece was granted Thessaly; and Bulgaria was divided into three parts. The northern section remained autonomous; the middle (Eastern Rumelia) semi-autonomous under Turkey; and the southern (Macedonia) returned to Turkey. None of the Balkan states was happy with decisions at Berlin.

**Revisions of Berlin.**    Bulgaria was one Balkan state that did something about the decisions. In 1885 she reannexed Eastern Rumelia, and in 1908 declared her independence. This was countered that same year when Austria annexed Bosnia-Herzegovina outright. The final revisions of the Congress of Berlin were accomplished in 1912–1914 and, as we shall see, supplied the last steps to World War I.

### Europe's Peaceful Century

The nineteenth century has been described as a century of "peace, progress, and prosperity," and in many ways it was. At the beginning of the century only Great Britain and France had any form of representative government, yet by 1914 every European nation, except Turkey, had some form of elected national legislature. The majority of states had universal manhood suffrage, and in some, even women's rights were being recognized.

### Small Nations

Because of limited space, it has not been possible to delve into the histories of the various states of Europe, but it was the little states that introduced many political reforms. Switzerland was the first to have universal manhood suffrage, and use the initiative and referendum. Finland, as an autonomous Russian Duchy, gave women the vote in 1906. Norway not only gave women the vote in 1907, but even allowed them to run for political office.

### Era of Peace

It has been stated repeatedly that the nineteenth century (1815–ff) was one free from war. Compared to every other century of man's history it was. The tally sheet is interesting:

1815–1853, no war
1853–1856, Crimean

1859,  Austro-Franco-Italian
1864,  Prusso-Austro-Danish
1866,  Seven Week
1870–1871,  Franco-Prussian
1877–1878,  Russo-Turkish
1878–ff,  no war.

There were six wars, five lasted less than a year, and in none of them were all major powers involved; they were short, and they were localized.

Man was also organized for peace. Alfred Nobel, who made his money from manufacturing explosives, left his fortune for the creation of the International Peace Prizes. Individuals such as Tolstoi, Zola, Kipling, and organizations such as the Institute of International Law, the International Peace Bureau, and most socialist organizations preached peace. Two meetings were held by organized governments at The Hague (Netherlands) in 1899 and 1907, where the present International Court of Justice was founded and agreements were made attempting to provide a legal alternative to the horrors of war.

Writers exalted peace and attacked the stupidity and wastefulness of conflict. Norman Angell, in his book, *The Great Illusion* declared that it was an illusion to believe that even a "victorious" nation could profit from any future war. And the British statesman, Lord Haldane, declared "There is far greater prospect of peace than ever there was before. No one wants war."

## Causes of World War I

### Introduction

Tragically, however, by 1900, these hopeful signs of increasing unity and enlightenment were already being overshadowed by other historically more familiar, but less hopeful portents, such as increasing nationalism, militarism, and imperialism. Within less than a score of years into the new century these latter forces would smother the hopes of the peace lovers and produce a global conflict more sweeping and consequential than any the world had yet seen. In Europe this conflict is sometimes called The Great War. Since the Second World War it has more frequently been termed World War I.

### Nationalism

The causes of World War I, like the causes for most broad historical events, were rooted deep in the past but they began to become more clearly defined and more virulent from the 1870s onward. Perhaps the central cause of the war was narrow nationalism—the belief that one's own nation is superior to all others and that its interests, right or wrong, must be placed before all others. During the last quarter of the 1800s nation-state rivalries became particularly intense and dangerous because of the appearance on the world stage of several newly unified national powers—Germany and Italy in Europe, Japan in Asia, and the United States in the Americas. Each was determined to win its "place in the sun" beside the established nations.

### Ethnocentrism

Closely related to nationalism as a cause of the war was ethnocentrism—the belief that all people of a particular race or ethnic stock should be unified. Since ethnocentrism is usually a separatist concept, implying racial superiority, it tended, like narrow nationalism, to generate hatreds and tensions wherever its influence was felt.

### Press Jingoism

Another cause of the war, emanating from nationalism, was the work of the so-called jingoist or nationalist press. In the years prior to 1914 the newspapers of many countries launched frequently inaccurate, chauvinistic propaganda attacks on one another, continually inflaming public opinion and creating an atmosphere uncongenial to reason, negotiation, or compromise.

### Militarism

Militarism was another product of nationalism and another cause of the war. Motivated both by dreams of national glory and by fears for national security, most European countries during the late 1800s began to arm themselves to the limit and to threaten one another with this armed force. "Sabre rattling" unfortunately became an increasingly popular and dangerous practice in the years preceding the war.

### The Alliance System

Probably the final catalyst among the causative factors leading to a full-scale world was was the European Alliance System. This system has been described in earlier chapters, and we will not go into all of its intricacies again here. It must, however, be remembered that after the Franco-Prussian War (1870–1871) Europe moved into an especially complicated period of diplomatic maneuvering and intrigue. This diplomacy primarily revolved around the efforts of France and Germany to protect themselves against one another by forming mutual aid agreements with other countries. To simplify a very complex story—by 1914 most of Europe and some other parts of the world were divided into two heavily armed alliance systems. At the center of one alliance web were the so-called Triple Entente nations—France, Britain, and Russia, with their vast imperial holdings. Ultimately they would be joined by Japan, Italy, Belgium, Portugal, Greece, Rumania, Serbia, Albania, and Montenegro. At the center of the other web were the Central Powers—the German and Austro-Hungarian Empires. Italy was formally linked to them in a Triple Alliance until 1915 when she shifted allegiance to the Entente. Other German allies were Turkey and Bulgaria. The very existence of these two great armed camps in Europe sharpened war fears and created the harrowing possibility that any small war between two nations might result in the final involvement of all those nations' allies in a cataclysmic world war.

### Preliminary Crises

Prior to 1914 there were, in fact, several preliminary crises, near-wars, or small wars which did not expand or escalate but did heighten international tension. Some examples of these nationalist, imperialist encounters were the Anglo-German rivalry in East Africa (1890); the Sino-Japanese War (1895); the Anglo-French clash in the Sudan (1898); the destructive, but localized, Russo-Japanese War (1905); the two Moroccan Crises of 1906 and 1911 which twice brought France and Germany perilously close to war. So many threatening nationalist clashes occurred in the Balkan area around the turn of the century that it came to be called "the powder keg of Europe." The large nations viewed these constantly bickering, comic-opera states as relatively unimportant pawns in their game of power and sought to draw them into their orbit either by treaties of alliance or by force. In 1908, the Austrian annexation of Bosnia and Herzegovina embittered Russia and exacerbated Austro-Russian relations. The two so-called Balkan Wars of 1912 and 1913 found the Balkan states at first battling Turkey and then one another—Bulgaria against Rumania, Serbia against Albania, and so on. Only diplomatic intercession by Britain and Germany helped head off another Austrian-Russian crisis.

### Sarajevo

Once again, war itself had been contained within the Balkan frontiers, but avaricious, paranoic nationalism and the spirit of war remained at least as intense as before. Serbian nationalists hungered for more territory, feared the intentions of Austria (yet baited her), and looked to Slavic, big-brother Russia for support. Austria, although she feared the reaction of Russia and the other powers, yearned to annex Serbia and to check Serbian nationalist agitation before it would infect the many minority groups within her shaky, polyglot empire. In the summer of 1914 the heir to the Austrian throne, the Archduke Franz Ferdinand, began a "good will tour" through the southern provinces to counter separatist sentiment and encourage loyalty to imperial Austria. On June 28, as his entourage was crossing a bridge in the little town of Sarajevo in Bosnia he was shot and killed by a Serbian-inspired student nationalist. Few suspected then that this tragic incident was the spark that would finally detonate "the powder keg of Europe" and set off a series of events that would ultimately engulf a large part of the world in the flames of war.

### The Final Crisis

Once again British and German diplomats, in particular, sought desperately to prevent the explosion but apparently the forces of reason, patience, and compromise had spent themselves and the forces of blind reaction, fear, and destructiveness had replaced them. Austria declared war on Serbia on July 28, and two days later Russia began to mobilize. Germany, viewing the Russian mobilization as too great a threat to her security, joined her Austrian ally and declared war against Russia on August 1. On August 3, to avoid an almost certain "surprise" attack from the rear, Germany also declared war against her arch-antagonist and Russia's ally—France.

Within a few months all the other nations that had been previously tied to one another in defensive alliances were drawn, one by one, into the vortex. A local conflict had become a world conflict. The Great War had begun.

## World War I

### Introduction

The conflict lasted more than four years and before it had run its bitter course it involved most areas of the globe—the Middle East, the Far East, Africa, America, and the seas surrounding them. But the focal point of the war was Europe, and more specifically, central Europe. The three major "fronts," or fighting lines, practically circumscribed the boundaries of central Europe. The "Western Front" ran roughly from the North Sea southward through Belgium, France, and western Germany to Switzerland. The "Eastern Front" ran southward from the Baltic Sea through Russia, eastern Germany and Austria, and into the Balkans. The southern, or "Italian Front," ran through the Italian and Austrian Alps.

### The Western Front

Although Germany was no more responsible for the outbreak of World War I than any of the other powers she was much better prepared for it materially and strategically. The training, equipment, and

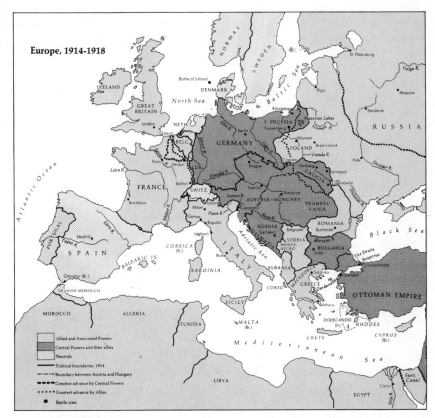

**Figure 21-2.**

logistical support given to her armed forces was superb and as early as
1905 she had developed a master strategy, called the von Schlieffen Plan,
designed to meet the likely eventuality of a two-front war against both
France and Russia. Immediately upon the outbreak of war it was planned
to wheel the weight of the German armies through neutral Belgium and
northern France to Paris, take this vital city and knock France out of the
war within a few weeks, just as Prussia had done in 1870. The idea was
to eliminate France quickly, thus ending the period of a two-front war
and enabling Germany to concentrate most of her forces on Russia before that nation could mobilize her ponderous might.

At first the plan operated with Germanic precision. Richard Harding Davis, an American newspaperman, reported "The German army
moved into (Brussels) as smoothly and as compactly as an Empire State
Express. There were no halts, no open places, no stragglers. . . ." The
German Chief-of-Staff, General von Moltke declared, "In six weeks it
will be over." Several things occurred, however, which drastically al-

tered the von Moltke timetable. On August 4, Britain entered the war, spurred by Germany's cynical violation of Belgian neutrality, and immediately sent a British expeditionary force across the Channel to help toughen Belgian and French resistance and to slow the German military machine. The juggernaut was indeed slowed down, and von Moltke himself slowed it further when he transferred several army corps to the Eastern Front to face a feared Russian invasion of Prussia. It was finally stopped altogether at the First Battle of the Marne River, only 30 miles from Paris, in one of the most heroic and crucial actions of the war. Paris (and probably France) was saved; the Germans were forced to drop back, abandoning the von Schlieffen Plan; and the war on the Western Front settled into a grim, strategic stalemate.

### Trench War

During four long years the two armies faced one another, dug into parallel lines of muddy, rat- and lice-infested trenches, stretching 500 miles from Belgium to Switzerland. It was the worst kind of war, marked by interminable periods of debilitating trench-dwelling, punctuated by intermittent and destructive efforts to cross a few hundred yards of shell-pocked morass (called "no-man's-land"), and to "break through" the enemy's lines. Until 1918, however, the balance of power remained so even that neither side was able to win this costly game of "breakthrough" despite constant and ingenious effort. The British enlarged and modernized their fleet and merchant marine; the Germans countered with their own modern fleet and the lethal submarine, or U-boat. Germany experimented with poison gas; the Allies developed the gas mask. Britain produced the tank; Germany soon countered with her own tank force. In the course of four years both sides made similar revolutionary advances in heavier-than-air-craft. In 1914 the airplane was little more than a motorized box-kite used for observation. By 1918 it had become a compact, maneuverable, and powerful military instrument (with tremendous commercial potential), able to carry bombs and machine guns syncronized to fire through the propeller arc. Both sides also kept pace in "improving" the destructive capability of small arms, grenades, machine guns, and artillery pieces.

Many felt that the balance of power might be tipped when Italy switched allegiance to the Allies in 1915, but the Italian effort along the southern front never became a determining factor in the war. In 1916 the Germans launched a great offensive designed to break through the center of the Allied lines, but they were finally hurled back by the incredible French resistance at Verdun. To ease the pressure on Verdun the British launched a counter-offensive along the Somme which also failed, after several months of costly fighting. Hundreds of thousands

**Figure 21-3.** British soldiers were victims of a German gas attack in April, 1918.

died in major campaigns such as these (70,000 at Verdun alone) and other hundreds of thousands died in minor skirmishes or in the trenches, victims of "war-connected" causes such as gangrene, tuberculosis, pneumonia, rat bites, mental breakdown, or exhaustion. Yet the deadly stalemate continued and was not broken until 1918 when America's aid finally tipped the balance of power in favor of the Allies.

### The Eastern Front

Meanwhile events of great importance were taking place on the Eastern Front and in Russia. The outbreak of war had unified the Russian people as they had not been unified since the Napoleonic Wars. They immediately began a two-pronged offensive into the Austrian province of Galicia in the south and into the German province of Prussia in the north. The Galician campaign went well and there were initial successes in Prussia, but with von Moltke's transfer of six German army corps to the Eastern Front in September of 1914 the tide quickly turned, and the Russian Armies were decimated by the German Generals von Hindenburg and Ludendorff in the campaigns at Tannenberg and the Masurian Lakes. Between 1914 and 1917 Russia, valiant but misguided, undertook at least one campaign per year against her Germanic foe and they all followed approximately the same pattern—initial heroics and successes, quick exhaustion of supplies, a battering German counter-offensive, terrible losses, and, inevitable retreat. The pattern is easily explained. Even though the Russian army was the largest in Europe and the Russian soldier notably hardy and courageous, the autocratic government of Russia under Nicholas II was corrupt and weak and could not give adequate support to Russian armies in the field. This continuing political failure, with its resultant military catastrophes and huge loss of life and land, began to convert the early patriotic fervor into a dark mood of disillusionment and resentment.

The resentment turned to anger during the unsuccessful offensive of 1916 when Nicholas personally (and disastrously) took over military command at the front leaving the government in the hands of his unstable wife, Alexandra, and their wildly eccentric and profligate "religious adviser" Rasputin. In February (or March) of 1917 the anger became rebellion and in a spontaneous, almost bloodless, rising the people deposed the autocratic Nicholas (ending 300 years of Romanov rule) and set up a liberal, Provisional Government. Unfortunately, this government was neither truly representative of the people nor responsive to their rising clamor for peace. Under great pressure from the Allies it doggedly continued the fight against Germany even after the failure of its so-called Brusilov (or Kerensky) offensive in the summer of 1917. Popular fury mounted again and this time there was a strong leader on hand to channel it. He was the brilliant Russian Communist, Vladimir Lenin.

Probably no man has had more impact on twentieth-century Russia and the world than Lenin. He was a combination of the man of thought and the man of action. He took the socialist philosophy of Marx, modified it to fit Russia's needs, added some of the revolutionary techniques of the Russian radical groups, as well as his own notions concerning the "dictatorship of the proletariat," and forged them all into a strikingly successful revolutionary instrument. He and his Bolshevik party had opposed the war from its inception and now he saw his opportunity to end it and seize power. In October (or November) he launched Russia's second revolution of 1917—the Bolshevik Revolution—and in four weeks, with a force of no more than 300,000 men, he had overthrown the Provisional Government and declared a "victory for socialism" in Russia. He immediately withdrew Russia from the war and in March, 1918 signed with Germany the harsh Treaty of Brest-Litovsk which lost Russia most of her western provinces and the Caucasus, one quarter of her population, three quarters of her arable land, and one half of her industry. Germany, Austria, and Bulgaria stood triumphant on the Eastern Front.

**Figure 21-4.**   Lenin in Red Square, Moscow, 1920.

### The Middle East

In the Middle Eastern theatre, however, Germany's other ally, Turkey, found herself in a generally uncomfortable position from the beginning to the end of the war. Like Russia, Turkey's military forces were potentially strong but her autocratic, imperial government was incredibly decadent and corrupt. It simply could not adequately cope with the problems of a disintegrating empire under the stresses of war. It constantly feared a major Russian drive against its shaky northeastern provinces. It feared another unified Balkan attack upon its small remaining European territory, and The Straits. Although this Balkan attack never materialized, the British did try, unsuccessfully, to take The Straits, in their ill-fated Gallipoli (or Dardanelles) campaign of 1915 to 1916. In the long run, however, Turkey's crucial problem, and the ultimate focus of the Middle Eastern conflict, was the emergence of Arab nationalism within the Empire. British agents, like the famous Colonel T. E. Lawrence

(Lawrence of Arabia), encouraged this nationalist sentiment and stirred revolt among the Arab tribes. By 1918, Arab and British forces had occupied most key centers in the Arabic portions of the Empire, and Turkey was compelled to sign an armistice with the Allies.

### The War at Sea

Naval events between 1914 and 1918 had a tremendous impact upon the course of the war and its outcome. When the conflict broke out Britain was still clearly "mistress of the seas" and her powerful fleets were assigned the same task they had been called upon to perform against the Napoleonic Empire. They were asked to establish a naval blockade that might ultimately "starve out" the Central Powers. It functioned throughout the war but was apparently not decisively effective. One of the reasons for its only moderate success was German naval power. Prior to 1914 the Germans had built a surface fleet which many felt could challenge British supremacy and the British blockade. For reasons that historians are still debating, the core of this surface fleet ventured only once (in 1916) out of the Baltic to confront the British. After a dramatic but indecisive engagement off Jutland in the North Sea they retired once again to their Baltic haven leaving the future challenge of the blockade to their "under-the-sea-boats," or U-boats. These lethal marauders of the deep not only weakened the British blockade but created a devastating blockade of their own by sinking more than 5 million tons of Allied shipping to the end of 1917. At one point in 1917 the British had only a six-week supply of food left to them.

### United States Entry

Happily for the Allied cause, this U-boat activity, along with other factors, began to turn public opinion in the "neutral" United States increasingly toward the Allies and against Germany. As early as 1915 the torpedoing of the British vessel, the *Lusitania,* with the loss of more than 100 American lives, brought the United States and Germany close to war. Again in 1916, the sinking of the British *Sussex* with American passengers aboard created another crisis which dissolved only after the German pledge to President Wilson to cease "unrestricted" submarine warfare. Wilson was reelected president in 1916 with the slogan "He kept us out of war." However, by 1917 Germany had become so convinced of the unrivaled effectiveness of U-boat activity that she determined to recommence all-out submarine war, and between January and April, eight American vessels were sent to the bottom. Most Americans enthusiastically backed their government in April of 1917 when it declared the existence of a war "to make the world safe for democracy."

### End of the War

Germany had recognized the probability of the United States entry into the war after her violation of the Sussex pledge but she gambled that she could defeat Britain and France before the tremendous material resources and manpower of the United States could become effective. She was able to transfer large forces from the Eastern Front after Russia's withdrawal from the war in October, 1917, and to pull some units away from the Italian Front after Italy's defeat at Caporetto, also in October. And in March of 1918 the German High Command ordered its greatest offensive of the war which almost succeeded in breaking the Allied line—but not quite. . . . Thanks to the heroic last-ditch resistance of the British and French, bolstered by the crucial and timely support of the United States, the German drive was stopped. Then, spearheaded by General Pershing's fresh American Expeditionary Force, the Allied armies under the command of French Field Marshal Foch launched their own massive counter-offensive in July, 1918. They gradually hammered back stubborn German resistance in the bloody encounters at Chateau-Thierry, Belleau Wood, St. Mihiel, and the Meuse-Argonne. By October the Germans were broken and in full retreat out of France, the Kaiser abdicated, and a provisional government sued for peace.

On November 11, 1918, an armistice was signed, finally terminating the terrible conflict four years and four months after the "Sarajevo incident." It has been estimated that this war cost in monetary terms—350 billion dollars; in more important, human terms—20 million dead, 20 million wounded, 5 million displaced.

## The Peace

### The Fourteen Points

Germany and her partners had accepted peace on the basis of Wilson's Fourteen Points, enunciated in January, 1918, in an effort to win world opinion for the Allies by the promise of a postwar peace settlement with justice for all people and vengeance against none. In general, it pledged open treaties, freedom of the seas, trade equality, arms reduction, equitable ethnic and territorial adjustments, and the establishment of a "league of nations" to preserve international peace and justice. In January, 1919, representatives from 27 nations met in Paris and after six months of hard, often bitter, negotiation they produced the controversial Paris Peace System. The defeated nations were not invited to attend any sessions except the final signing ceremony.

### The Big Four

The so-called Big Four powers dominated the proceedings. Woodrow Wilson was, of course, president and representative of the

United States. He was a very religious and idealistic man, almost messianic at times, but genuinely dedicated to the concepts of a just and lasting peace. Some of his words spoken at the beginning of the conference will illustrate this idealism: "The cause being just and holy, the settlement must be of like quality. A supreme moment of history has come. The eyes of the people have been opened and they see. The hand of God is upon the nations." Georges Clemenceau was premier and representative of France. He was an emotional, loquacious lawyer and politician; a fiery, militant nationalist with a deep devotion to anything Gallic and a vengeful bitterness toward Germany. He respected Lloyd George but could not accept the Puritanical self-righteousness of Wilson: "Wilson has Fourteen (Points); the Good Lord himself had only ten!" David Lloyd George was prime minister and representative of Britain. He was an honest, practical, hard-headed statesman, dedicated to winning Britain's fair share at the peace table but congenial to compromise and reason. He generally liked Wilson but not some of his "holier-than-thou" attitudes. He enjoyed Clemenceau but not his pomposity and emotional displays of chauvinism. He is reported to have said one day after a particularly exasperating session with his fellow delegates: "What am I to do between one man who thinks he is Jesus Christ and another who thinks he is Napoleon?" Vittorio Orlando was premier and representative of Italy, but both he and his country tended to be viewed as rather unimportant, "honorary" members of the Big Powers club, and had small influence at the sessions.

### The League of Nations

Wilson had very little experience with the nasty in-fighting of national politics. He had no experience with international bargaining and maneuvering. It is a small wonder, then, that the Paris Treaties were much more the product of the vengeful, cynical power-politicians of the Old World, like Clemenceau, than they were of idealistic visionaries like Woodrow Wilson. Wilson and the idealists achieved only one major victory at Paris, but, it was an important one. They insisted on including, as an integral part of the treaty, a provision for Wilson's cherished League of Nations. If a nation signed the treaty it automatically accepted The League. Its founders hoped that as a world forum it would help to remedy inequities in the peace settlement, check international aggression, and promote world peace and understanding. It was made up of a small executive Council, dominated by the great powers; a large Assembly, representative of all member nations; an administrative Secretariat; a Permanent Court of International Justice; and a variety of other organizations designed to carry out humanitarian social and economic services around the globe.

## The Paris Peace System

There were five Paris peace treaties, one for each of the five defeated nations, and each one named after the particular suburb or quarter in which it was signed. The most important one was the Versailles Treaty with Germany. It was signed on June 28, 1919—intentionally or unintentionally—five years exactly from the date of the assassination of the Archduke Franz Ferdinand. It was certainly not the kind of treaty that the Germans had expected on the basis of the Fourteen Points. It contained a clause placing prime responsibility for the war on Germany. It required huge war reparation payments—between 30 and 50 billion dollars. It ordered almost complete demilitarization of Germany. It stripped her of large areas of her European empire and of all her colonial possessions. It forbid any future union (Anschluss) with Austria.

By the Treaty of St. Germain, 1919, Austria lost Hungary and all her Balkan holdings, leaving her a small, postage-stamp state centered on Vienna. The Treaty of Trianon, signed with Hungary in 1920, made her an independent country about the same size as Austria. The Treaty of Neuilly, signed with Bulgaria also in 1920, took away her access to the Aegean, and cut back her territories to the benefit of Rumania, Greece, and other Balkan Allies of the Entente. And the Treaty of Sèvres, signed with Turkey in 1920, left her with little more than Constantinople in Europe; and only Asia Minor, out of her once vast holdings in the Middle East. It also lost her The Straits, but she recovered these in 1923.

## Summary

World War I, and the peace settlement that followed, undoubtedly did more to aggravate or create world problems than to solve them. The nineteenth-century forces of blind, militant nationalism and imperialism which had been prime causes for the war, were not diminished but rather intensified in the postwar period. Bitterness, cynicism, and disillusion over the war and the peace were rampant everywhere. The defeated nations, of course, were bitter but so, too, were many of the so-called "victorious" or "beneficiary" nations who had either been hurt by the war or disappointed by the peace. Many of the colonial peoples of Africa and Asia, encouraged either by vague European wartime pledges or by the seeming European postwar weakness, began to form incipient, nationalist independence movements. The "harvest time" of colonial nationalism did not come till after the Second World War but the period between the wars was the crucial "seed-time" of colonial independence—and the "autumn" of European imperialism.

# Africa,

# Asia,

# and

# America

The non-European world between the wars was in a state of ferment. World War I had encouraged nationalist independence movements everywhere because it both seriously weakened the European imperial powers and sharply stimulated the nationalist aspirations and expectations of the colonial peoples. Only a few countries, such as Egypt and Turkey, actually achieved independence in the interwar period, but nationalist sentiment was growing and anti-colonial pressures increasing throughout Africa and Asia.

The only two major nations that had emerged from the war stronger than they were before it were Japan and the United States. By the 1920s the balance of economic power was shifting toward them and away from Europe. They began to become dominant political forces in the East and the West respectively, despite their refusal to take on the real responsibilities of world leadership. The crash of 1929, however, precipitated a tragic depression in both countries and across the globe. Japan reacted to this crisis with a surge of militarism and aggression, while the United States retired deeper into its isolationism. Colonial tensions and economic depression, as well as the negative responses of Japan and the United States, helped to create conditions which led inevitably to another disastrous world conflict.

## Africa

### Continued Colonialism

The war, and the peace treaties that followed, had relatively little immediate effect on the peoples of Africa. Contingents of European-trained African troops served the Allies on several fronts during the conflict but no major military action ever took place in Africa itself. By the Treaty of Versailles, Germany's African colonies were taken from her, but were simply mandated to the allied powers—Britain, France, and Belgium. When the treaties were signed in 1919, Ethiopia and Liberia were the only independent nations on the entire continent. With the exception of these two countries and Egypt, which gained a kind of semi-independence in 1922, Africa remained completely colonized through the whole span of the interwar years.

### Incipient Nationalism

Ironically, however, this very process of colonization led to a concomitant process of Europeanization, especially among the upper classes of African society. Many Africans received a European education, learned European languages, and adopted European customs, institutions, and ideas. Perhaps most significantly they took European notions concerning liberty, equality, national sovereignty, and enterprise and began to translate them into incipient African nationalism. Some nationalist independence movements were organized in both sub-Saharan Africa and North Africa during the twenties and thirties but, with the exception of the great Rif rising of Abd-el-Krim in Morocco (1919–1926), they were amateurish in conception and generally easily controlled by the colonial authorities. The full force of the anti-imperialist storm would not break until after the Second World War.

## The Middle East

### Turkey

No people in the world was more deeply, completely, or durably affected by the war than the Turks. In 1914 the decaying Turkish Sultanate in Constantinople still reigned over a very backward but very large empire stretching southeast from the Black Sea and the Mediterranean across Asia Minor and the Arabic Middle East to the Red Sea, Persia, and the Persian Gulf. After Turkey's defeat, however, the victorious Allies by the Treaty of Sèvres (1920) stripped away all of her Arabic Middle Eastern holdings and her unilateral control over the crucial Straits area. They manipulated the "Sultan's government," occupied Constantinople, policed the Straits, and did nothing to discourage a Greek invasion of Turkish Asia Minor itself.

**Kemal Ataturk.**   For decades prior to the war, resentment and frustration had been building in the Turkish people against the corruptness of the Sultanate and its weakness in the face of foreign pressures. The terrible events of the war and the added humiliations of the peace finally brought this popular discontent to the boiling point and, in 1919, there began one of the most strikingly successful nationalist revolutions in modern history. The prime architect of this constructive revolution was also one of the most admirable leaders in modern history. His name was Mustafa Kemal—later called Ataturk (Foremost Turk). He was an army officer who had first gained fame for his successful defense of the Dardanelles against the British in 1915. After the war he became the charismatic rallying point and the organizing force of a rising nationalist reform movement called the "Young Turks." Between 1919 and 1923 he miraculously transformed the plucky but thoroughly beaten and disorganized "imperial" Turks into the inspired and unified citizenry of a more compact and homogeneous "New Turkey."

**Foreign Affairs.**   Kemal's inspirational leadership, plus the resilient courage of the Turkish people, had brought about the defeat and eviction of the hated Greek invaders by the end of 1922. His ability and moderation won him not only respect but important treaty concessions from the

Allied powers. The unpopular Treaty of Sèvres was renegotiated, and in 1923 the new Treaty of Lausanne cancelled Turkish reparations payments, made certain territorial and population adjustments favorable to Turkey, and once again restored to her important control of the Straits area. Kemal did not request, nor did the Allies ever consider, a return of any of the Arabic territories to Turkish control—this wise leader placed national unity and homogeneity before territorial aggrandizement. Also by 1923 Kemal had, with minimal bloodshed, completely disposed of the remains of the long-lived but unlamented Ottoman Sultanate (or Caliphate) and in October of that year he formally proclaimed the establishment of the new Turkish Republic and became its first President.

**Domestic Reforms.** But his revolutionary zeal did not stop short with his final acquisition of power, as is the case with so many military "strongmen." Ataturk now proceeded to the work that marks his true greatness—an incisive, sweeping reform of Turkey's outmoded institutions. The antique political and religious machinery of the Caliphate was abolished and the minions of the Ottoman dynasty banished. A new, representative parliamentary system and western-style legal institutions were established. Arabic script was replaced by the Latin alphabet. Place names were changed and the capital was moved from Constantinople (Istanbul) to Angora (Ankara) in the center of Turkey. Women were liberated and enfranchised; and many social remnants of the Moslem past, such as the veil and pantaloons and the fez, were abandoned. By the time of Ataturk's death in 1938 Turkey had been transformed from a decrepit, backward, medieval despotism into the strongest and most progressive modern nation in the Middle East.

### The Arabic Middle East

During the war the Allies had woven a very tangled web of secret treaties concerning the disposition of the Ottoman Empire. There were actually three distinct sets of agreements, each conflicting with the others and each marked by certain internal contradictions as well. One set consisted of agreements of the Allied powers to divide up among themselves all of the Turkish Empire. A second set of internally conflicting commitments were made between the British government and two different Arab nationalist leaders. In return for his pledge of assistance against the Turks, the eminent Emir Hussein was promised independence and sovereignty for all Arab peoples of the Middle East. At the same time a rival leader, Ibn-Saud, was promised separate sovereignty over a large and undefined area of Arabia. These pledges conflicted with one another and also with the plans of the powers. The third set of understandings developed out of talks, beginning in 1914, between the Allied powers and the leaders of the World Zionist Organization and concerned the creation of a Jewish homeland in the Palestine region of the Middle East. In November, 1917, Lord Balfour of Britain wrote to the Zionist leader, Lord Rothschild, that his government would approve the establishment in Palestine of a "national home for the Jews . . . it being clearly understood that nothing shall be done which may prejudice the . . . rights of existing non-Jewish communities in Palestine." This Balfour Declaration was clearly in conflict with both the imperialist ambitions of the powers and the pledges made to Hussein. It carried within it (as we now know) the greatest potential threat to the future peace of the Middle East.

**Uneasy Colonialism.** After the war, the pledges made to both Arabs and Jews were generally ignored and most of the Arabic Middle East and North Africa was dominated by the two great European powers —Britain and France. France continued to control French Morocco and Tunisia in the Maghreb and was additionally mandated, by the League of Nations, the former Turkish territories of Syria and Lebanon. Britain continued to dominate "independent" Egypt and the "independent," oil-rich sheikdoms of Arabia and received League mandates over the former Turkish territories of Iraq (Mesopotamia) and Palestine.

Naturally, the Arab peoples in these areas were bitterly disappointed with the broken promises and the new colonial arrangements of the powers, and, in the early postwar years, they rose frequently in protest and open revolt. The results were invariably the same—Britain and France would respond with superior organization and fire-power, crush the revolt, gradually restore order and authority, then grudgingly grant some extension of autonomy to appease nationalist sentiment. In Palestine, the nationalist-imperialist problem was seriously compounded by the Arab-Jewish problem. The postwar British governments tried valiantly to solve the dilemma that the wartime British governments had created. They did open Palestine to the Jews. But they cut out of Palestine a separate and independent state east of the Jordan River called Trans-jordan which was closed to Zionist settlement; and they tried to restrict Jewish immigration to Palestine itself, after witnessing the unexpected influx caused by Hitler's rise to power in the thirties.

This combination of force and diplomatic concession pleased neither Jew nor Arab but enabled the British and the French to hold the rising tide of nationalism in check and maintain a tense, uneasy "peace" in the Middle East in the decades between 1919 and 1939.

### Persia (Iran)

The only other nations in the Middle East to gain genuine independence between the wars were Persia and Afghanistan. In the years prior to 1914, Persian history had been most inglorious. Like Turkey, she was weighted down with an anachronistic, despotic government and an antiquated social and economic system. Her destinies were largely controlled by Britain, France, and Russia—all of whom were interested primarily in her oil resources. While the powers were deeply involved in the war and its aftermath a military strongman emerged in Persia to lead a nationalist reform movement against the old order. Colonel Reza Pahlevi admired Kemal, and his career consciously paralleled that of the brilliant Turkish leader. In 1921 he led a successful *coup d'état* against the corrupt regime of the old ruler, or Shah. He made himself Shah, set up a new Pahlevy dynasty and launched a thoroughgoing reform program which within a few years had begun to convert medieval Persia into a more modern and progressive "Iran." He abdicated in 1941 leaving the throne to his son, Mohammed Reza Pahlevi, who is the present ruler of Iran.

### Afghanistan

The postwar history of Afghanistan was similar in many ways to that of Turkey and Iran. A strong man, Amanullah Shah, succeeded to power in 1919 and in that same year obtained British recognition of Afghanistan's independence. He (and his successors) maintained this independence during the interwar years by playing off Britain against Russia and by forming alliances with Turkey, Iran, and Iraq to resist pressure from the European powers and India. He also launched a series of domestic reforms to modernize his country—but here the historical similarity ends. Amanullah was no Ataturk or Pahlevi. His reform program failed and he was forced to abdicate in 1928 leaving the way open for a long period of civil strife, power struggle, political assassination, and frustrated reform.

## Asia

### India

At the turn of the century the huge, populous subcontinent of India seemed to be one of the brightest and most securely fixed jewels in the British crown of Empire. Britain had established in India during the latter half of the 1800s probably the most enlightened and progressive colonial system in the Afro-Asian world. It boasted at least token Indian autonomy in local government. It sponsored substantial economic and social reform programs in such areas as public health, agriculture, and land usage, water control, and transportation and communications. It attacked certain outmoded or barbaric practices such as infanticide, *purdah* (seclusion of women), *suttee* (burning of the widow on her husband's funeral pyre), and *thuggee* (professional assassination). Very importantly, it encouraged India's upper and middle classes to obtain a British education and to be trained to participate in the administration of British India.

**British India.**    The mass of the Indian people seemed reasonably content under this stable and benevolent imperial system and, in 1912, they enthusiastically rejoiced at the coronation of George V as King of England and Emperor of India. There did exist an Indian nationalist movement which had been formally organized in 1885 as the National Congress Party of India. But its leaders were largely moderate, middle-class British-trained lawyers and ex-bureaucrats who talked in terms of gradual, orderly emancipation. During the war, inspired by British promises of ultimate autonomy, most of these leaders and the Indian people contributed generously in money, materials, and manpower (over one million men) to the Allied cause.

**Postwar Problems.**    This hopeful and cooperative relationship began to deteriorate rapidly in the immediate postwar years. Initiating the tragic deterioration was a series of terrible natural catastrophes—drought, famine, influenza, and plague—which destroyed more than 20 million lives and engendered a desperate mood in India. The impact of the war itself made matters worse. Thousands of men who had never left their villages before 1914 returned from their wartime travels with new ideas and expectations, recalling imagined British wartime pledges of a new, more prosperous and autonomous India and finding instead fear, disease, hunger, and unemployment. The Indian people naturally, and irrationally, blamed the ruling British government for all their misery and joined in nationalist protest riots across the country. The British government unfortunately also reacted naturally and irrationally. In March, 1919, it issued the repressive Rowlatt Acts which allowed the suspension in India of the rights of assembly, habeas corpus, and trial by jury. Further riots led to stronger British police action, climaxed by the bloody Amritsar Massacre of April, 1919, in which 379 unarmed political protestors were shot to death.

**Mahatma Gandhi.**    It was in this grim period that the Indian nationalist movement and the Congress Party truly came to life. They were, of course, reinvigorated by the tragic events of the time but also by the emergence of a new, inspirational leader—Mohandas K. Gandhi—who took the city-bred intellectual nationalism of the Congress Party and converted it into a simple, practical yet spiritual program to move the hearts of the religious, peasant masses of rural India. This frail, ascetic lawyer-guru, building upon the Hindu principle of pacifistic reverence for life, and playing off India's numbers against Britain's technology, developed the uniquely effective revolutionary technique of "passive resistance" or "non-violent civil disobedience." He and his dedicated followers taught the peasant workers that they could win home-rule and ultimate independence not by fighting the better equipped British but by refusing to work for them (*hartal*) and refusing to buy their goods (boycott), thus threatening the sensitive British economy and at the same time stimulating Indian village industry.

**Passive Resistance.** When the British hopefully put forward the first Government of India Act in 1919, allowing some extension of self-government in the provinces, but none at the national level, Gandhi's nationalists rejected it as inadequate. Massive protest strikes and boycotts were carried out as Gandhi had instructed, but many of them, to his horror, ended in violence and bloodshed. The Mahatma or "Holy One" was jailed several times during the twenties and thirties and he frequently responded by fasting for long periods of time to dramatize British callousness and the cause of Indian independence. The news media made him an international celebrity and hero. The British who knew how to handle force did not know how to handle the strange, "unfair" tactics of this gentle, saintly man. He and his passive resistance embarrassed and confounded them. They made some concessions but they were usually too little and too late.

Finally in 1931 they invited Gandhi and other Indian nationalist leaders to a series of Round Table Conferences in London to discuss the whole span of India's problems. The end result of these conferences was the second Government of India Act issued in 1935. It provided for a federal system, with a national government broadly representative of all India and autonomous in national, domestic affairs. It also set up eleven representative, provincial governments with complete autonomy in provincial affairs.

**The India Act.** This Act was envisioned by enlightened British leaders as a penultimate step on the road to total unification and complete independence of all India. Gandhi and his now moderate wing of the All-Union Congress Party approved the Act and went to work within the new system to achieve its final goals. Unfortunately they were confronted with several formidable barriers. First was the opposition of the radical wing of the Congress Party led by Pandit Jawaharlal Nehru who wanted immediate independence and the establishment of a socialist system for India. Nehru began to emerge in the last half of the twenties as heir-apparent to Gandhi within the Congress Party. He revered Gandhi as a man and as the foremost contributor to the success of the Indian nationalist movement, but he was very different from his leader in most

Figure 22-1.   Gandhi.

ways. He was a handsome, wealthy, aristocratic intellectual, educated in the law at Cambridge and almost more European than Indian. He believed that the world would be changed through reason, science, and religion, and he was impatient with the traditionalism and gradualism of Gandhi and the British government.

Another barrier in the way of Indian unity was the absolute opposition of some fifty Indian princes, or *rajahs,* who had been allowed by the British to remain outside of British India and retain special feudal privileges and perquisites. Now they refused to join the new union because it would mean relinquishing this special power and wealth.

**Religious Problems.** By far the most serious and explosive threat to a unified, independent India, however, was the religious problem between Hindus and Moslems. Approximately three quarters of India's population was of the Hindu faith and the dominant Congress Party was essentially Hindu. Most of the other quarter of the population was Moslem and its rights had been well protected since the British takeover of India in the 1700s. An All-India Moslem League had been formed in 1919 as a counterpoise to the predominantly Hindu Congress Party but until 1935 it had little purpose and a small following. With the establishment of a federal union and increasingly serious talk of independence from Britain the Indian Moslem began to consider fearfully what his lot might be in a unified India without Britain, and dominated by the huge Hindu majority. Membership in the Moslem League increased and its leadership was taken over by the very able Mohammed Ali Jinnah who began immediately to infuriate Hindu nationalists by demanding that, if the Indian subcontinent were to become independent, it should be divided into two separate states, one Hindu and the other Moslem.

All controversy over independence became temporarily academic in 1939 when Britain entered World War II. The British government unceremoniously declared India in the war, ordered a moratorium on nationalist reform activity, and governed India by decree till 1945.

### Southeast Asia

Although during the interwar years the histories of the various colonial peoples of Southeast Asia differed greatly in detail they were similar in broad outline. Throughout the whole period the imperial powers retained control over their respective holdings despite the growth of nationalist, independence movements in each of them. As in Africa, India, and the Middle East, the grip of imperialism in Southeast Asia was weakened by World War I but not finally broken until World War II.

**Philippines.** Almost from the time the United States wrested the Philippines from Spain in 1898 it had, guilt-ridden, begun the process of preparing the islands for independence. There was nationalist resistance at first but it gradually disappeared in the face of the sincere and effective American effort to bring economic prosperity and political reform to the Philippines. A flourishing agriculture and trade developed. Filipinos were educated in self-government and given representative institutions and political responsibility. Autonomy was extended, step by step, and in 1935 the United States government promised complete independence within ten years. The outbreak of war and the ensuing Japanese occupation delayed, until 1947, the fulfillment of Philippine nationalism and the consummation of a uniquely enlightened imperial experiment.

**East Indies.**    Nationalism in the Dutch-controlled East Indies did not meet with the same kind of imperial sympathy and support as it had in the Philippines. Indonesian nationalism between the wars survived, not because of the Dutch colonial attitude, but in spite of it. Across the 3000 miles of her island domain Holland had constructed a very efficient and prosperous colonial system which brought tremendous benefits to her and to a few favored Indonesians, if not to the large mass of the Indonesian people. She looked upon nationalism as a potentially serious threat to this rich empire and stamped out its manifestations whenever they appeared, whether Moslem, Chinese, or Marxist inspired. By the late thirties thousands of alleged nationalists had been killed or arrested in suppressive police actions and the Indonesian independence movement seemed to be mortally wounded, if not dead.

**Indochina.**    The French imperial system in Indochina was perhaps the least enlightened in Southeast Asia. French rule was marked by tight political suppression, relentless economic exploitation, and a smothering cultural arrogance. Nationalist parties were outlawed and nationalist aspirations had no outlet except through sporadic outbursts of violence and terrorism. In this environment it was natural that the revolutionary concepts of Marx took root and began to grow. One of the chief exponents of this Marxian philosophy was a Vietnamese who had been trained in China and the Soviet Union. His name was Ho Chi Minh, and during the thirties he built a Communist organization which was to become the chief inspiration and vehicle for Indochinese nationalism through World War II and into the postwar period. But prior to 1940 there was little question that France was the imperial master in Indochina.

**Malaya and Burma.**    Britain managed to maintain control of her two Southeast Asian provinces, Malaya and Burma, through the interwar period, using much more enlightened and flexible policies than those employed by France and Holland. Partly because of these policies and partly because of many diverting ethnic rivalries, nationalism never became a serious problem in Malaya. But Burmese nationalism was as intense as Indian nationalism and was partially a consequence of it. The Burmese were as eager to be free of age-old Indian dominance as they were to be independent of British controls. After years of gradual reform, Britain, in 1937, responded more fully to Burma's Buddhist-oriented nationalist demands by splitting her off from India and giving her a responsible parliamentary government, largely autonomous in domestic affairs. Britain still ruled, but Burma had a start on the road to independence.

**Siam.** Siam was the only Southeast Asian nation that was never colonized by the imperial powers. It was left as a buffer state between French Indochina and British Burma and Malaya. Between the wars it remained independent and, building on the solid foundation left by its capable nineteenth-century kings, it became one of the most modern, prosperous, and progressive states in Asia. In the 1930s however, political power passed into the hands of an aristocratic-military junta which became increasingly anti-western and pro-Japanese as the decade progressed.

**China.** In 1900, China was the doddering, helpless giant of Asia, wasted by the cancer of antiquated tradition and pride, and plagued by the depredations of younger, more dynamic industrialized societies. All that was left of the once-great Manchu dynasty was the child-Emperor, Henry Pu Yi, who was manipulated by his effete courtiers and by the decaying dowager Empress, Tz'u-hsi, dubbed "Old Buddha." The Chinese peasant masses, like the village-peasants in most of the Afro-Asian world, were politically detached from their ineffectual government but were callously exploited by it, and, by almost everyone else—rapacious provincial "warlords," landlords, intellectual Mandarin aristocrats, and the so-called "foreign devils." Even into the twentieth century the life of the peasant was typified by constant labor and impoverishment, frequent hunger and sickness—and early death. These conditions engendered growing popular resentment.

*The Revolution of 1911.* Unfortunately, even by the early 1900s, neither the work of nationalist leaders like Dr. Sun Yat-sen. nor the mounting pressures of popular discontent had succeeded in weakening foreign influence or prompting meaningful Manchu reforms. The fabled patience of the Chinese people was wearing thin—and in 1911 it snapped. A minor incident involving use of foreign capital set off a series of risings which within a few weeks had become the first great Nationalist Chinese Revolution. The Manchus were forced to abdicate and a republican government was established with a Parliament controlled by Dr. Sun's Kuomintang Party. For the sake of national unity Dr. Sun Yat-sen stepped

aside and permitted a former Manchu general, Yuan Shih-kai to become
the first president of the Republic of China. Although Yuan died in
1916, his tyrannical efforts to create a new imperial dynasty caused more
revolutionary turbulence in China and led to another decade of civil
war, anarchy, and "warlordism." The torn young republic entered World
War I, in 1917, largely to secure the support of the western Allies, Britain,
France, and the United States, against the demands and depredations of
her eastern "ally," Japan. But not only did the Western powers fail to
support her against Japan, they continued their own imperialist activities
in China into the postwar period and turned aside all Chinese pleas for
economic assistance.

*The Republic of Sun Yat-sen.*   Finally, in 1921, Sun Yat-sen was
elected president of the Republic by the southern Cantonese government,
and, within the next few years he was able to restore relative peace to
China and to begin the first program of real unification and reconstruction since the 1600s. Disillusioned with the western European states, he
turned for desperately needed help to anti-imperialist, socialist Russia.
He received little material aid but much sympathy and advice from
Moscow. A group of Soviet advisers led by the very able Michael Borodin
played a major role in creating the first nationalist Chinese army and in
remodeling the Kuomintang party structure. The Russians also influenced
his formulation of the famous three goals, or Three Principles of the
Chinese People: (1) The Principle of Nationalism—to establish a unified
nation-state free of foreign domination; (2) The Principle of Democracy
—to achieve ultimately, through popular education, a true government
"of the people, by the people and for the people"; (3) The Principle of
Livelihood—to assure economic security for all, through industrialization
and equitable land distribution.

Dr. Sun died prematurely in 1925 before he could begin imple-
mentation of these Principles, and there ensued another long period of
civil strife which again destroyed any real hope for Chinese unity,
democracy, or security. This time the power struggle grew out of an
ideological split which had been evident within the Kuomintang Party
itself. In 1924, Dr. Sun had invited all Chinese Communists to join the
Kuomintang. Many had done so but they naturally began to advocate
more radical approaches to unification and socioeconomic reform than
the Kuomintang moderates could accept. When Sun's moderating influence was gone, this split became an open break and the moderate, so-
called Nationalist wing came under the leadership of the rising young
military commander, Chiang Kai-shek.

*Chiang and Mao.*   Chiang, was the son of a petty landlord raised
in the conservative Confucian tradition (though later Christianized),
trained to military stiffness and arrogance, and forever detached from

the Chinese masses by background, success, and marriage—to the west-ernized daughter of a wealthy Shanghai merchant. His governing drive was the unification of China and he perceived only two serious barriers to this unification—warlords and Communists. Military power, he felt, would eliminate them both. In 1926, he swung his armies north from Canton and carried out a successful campaign against the warlords, crushing most of them or forcing them to terms. In 1927, he discarded Dr. Sun's pact with the Communists and launched a savage attack against the major Red enclaves in the cities. In 1928, he took the northern center of Peking and set up his capital at Nanking. By 1930, he had driven several million Communists into a huge "pocket" in southern China, centered on Kiangsi province. Here a brilliant peasant leader by the name of Mao Tse-tung was effectively drawing the peasants (contrary to orthodox Marxist theory) into his rural Communist organizations by confiscating properties of the large landlords and redistributing the land among the poor. In five campaigns during four years, Chiang's armies mercilessly hounded the Red contingents until, by 1934, most of them had been slaughtered or entrapped. Only 90,000 escaped and began what has been called "The Long March" toward the inaccessible north-west mountains of China. A year later, 7000 survivors who had endured the incredible hardships of the 6000-mile march arrived at Yenan in northern Shensi province. Here, once again, Mao's concern for land re-form and the problems of the poor began attracting peasant support to him. He trained revolutionary cadres to fight guerilla war and waited —gathering strength for a time when Chiang would not be so strong.

*War with Japan.* Chiang had not yet secured China internally from the warlords and Communists when the external menace of Japan began to loom. In 1931, the Japanese attacked and seized the Chinese province of Manchuria. China was not strong enough to act unilaterally and all of her pleas to the League and the Western powers for action against this aggression brought only a diplomatic reprimand for Japan. The Western response was the same when Japan launched her conquest of China proper in 1937. This time Chiang fought the Japanese and so did Mao's Communist forces, in a half-hearted wartime alliance. But neither force fought full-out, seemingly holding themselves in reserve for one another. By 1939, the much superior Japanese armies had thrust the Chinese back into the northern and western mountains, taking most of the key cities and major rail and river links in eastern China—but this is a story for the next chapter.

Chiang brought some reforms to China during the thirties—some building and industrialization; some tariff and currency reform and some concessions from Western nations; and he did reunify China for a short while, by military force. But he did not bring real national unity nor did

**Figure 22-2.**   Mao Tse Tung (left) and Chou En-lai (right), *c.* 1930s.

he make more than a gesture in the crucial areas of land reform and political reform. China, between the wars was not only the victim of internal strife and Japanese aggression, she was also the victim of indifference, lack of understanding, and antiquated thinking in her leadership.

**Japan.** Among the peoples of Africa and Asia, the Japanese had been by far the most successful in modernizing their institutions and defending themselves against Western dominance.

*World War I.* Japanese confidence and strength continued to increase during the World War I period. Her favorable position as an Entente ally, and the preoccupation of all the Western powers in the conflict, enabled her to secure most of the Asian holdings of Germany and to bring great pressure to bear on coveted, weak China. In 1915, she issued the remarkable Twenty-One Demands against China which revealed clearly the growth of Japanese imperial ambitions and which would have made China a virtual satellite of Japan except for the diplomatic intervention of the United States and the end of the war. Although she was not satisfied with her share of the Paris Peace Settlement, she managed, despite the treaties, to maintain postwar control over most of those areas she had seized during the war—the German islands, Shantung, Manchuria, and southern Mongolia. Her territorial, trade, and investment interests in China and other regions mounted so rapidly that Britain, Russia, and the United States, in particular, began to feel that their preserves in Asia were being threatened.

*The Liberal 1920s.* During the 1920s, however, Japanese aggressiveness remained under control and was primarily economic rather than military. This period has been called Japan's "liberal decade." The older, aristocratic, traditionalist leadership, which had ruled the country since the 1880s, had died off by the end of the war and a younger, generally more liberal leadership began to replace it in both the political and economic spheres. The first commoner ever to hold the position of prime minister, Hara Takashi, was appointed to that office in 1918. He and many others like him believed that the future greatness of Japan lay in the continuation of enlightened reform and legitimate business expansion, instead of in imperialist adventuring. They attacked Japanese intervention in Siberia (1918) during the Russian Civil War. They worked for Japan's entry into the League (1919) as a step toward guaranteeing world peace. They urged the signing of the Washington (1921), Geneva (1927), and London (1930) Naval Limitations Agreements, and of the Four Power (1921) and Nine-Power (1922) Pacts pledging Japan and the other major powers to respect one another's interests in the Pacific as well as the economic and territorial sovereignty of China.

At home, the liberals worked diligently to expand agricultural, and particularly industrial, production, shipbuilding, and export trade. Hundreds of new factories, machines, and ships were built and inexpensive goods, mass-produced by low-paid Japanese workers, began to flood the markets of the world. By the end of the decade Japan was the foremost exporter of matches, cotton, rayon and silk textiles, and raw silk. The reformers also tried to liberalize the law and democratize the government, and they did succeed in expanding the suffrage from 3 to 15 million, in 1925, by giving the vote to most males 25 years of age and older.

*Problems.*   Unhappily for world peace, a combination of domestic and foreign problems undermined and then destroyed the liberal movement in Japan. Her arable land area was too small to support a population which had grown from about 55 million in 1920 to almost 65 million in 1930. The average peasant land holding was less than 3 acres per family. Peasants, driven off the land, crammed into congested, high-cost, urban centers where jobs were limited and low paid. Land-hunger was omnipresent in Japan.

Japan's own very limited natural resources could neither support this population nor her industrial economy. She was largely dependent on foreign purchases of her ever-increasing volume of manufactured goods to provide credits to buy raw materials to meet the ever-increasing demands of her people and machines. Fear of economic dislocation was a constant specter in Japan. Helping to create this dependence on foreign markets was the shrinking purchasing power of the Japanese themselves, and this shrinkage was partially caused by the fact that more and more wealth was passing into the hands of a very few lords of industry and finance, called the zaibatsu, while less and less, proportionately, was reaching the mass of workers and peasants.

*Mounting Discontent.*   Many common people began to lose faith in their liberal, business-oriented leadership and turned to more "positive" leaders, steeped in the old militarist tradition of the Samurai. These traditionalists were still present in large numbers in Japan and had only been thrust into the background during much of the twenties. They believed that the real answer to their country's problems was not peaceful, evolutionary, economic growth but military conquest and imperial expansion. Most prominent among these military elitists was the Baron Tanaka who had allegedly proposed in 1927, while prime minister, a rather ambitious plan for Japanese imperial expansion. This so-called "Tanaka Memorial" though probably a fiction, represents fairly accurately what many Japanese imperialists had in mind—the conquest first of Manchuria and Mongolia, then of all China itself, and, with the aid of China's resources, the whole of Asia and perhaps Europe too.

*Economic Crisis.*   Until 1929, however, Japan's problems were not serious enough nor was the militarist faction strong enough to act openly to change liberal policies. But in that year came the Great Crash and an ensuing world-wide depression that hit the vulnerable Japanese economy with terrible force. Foreign markets dwindled, tariff barriers and boycotts replaced "open doors" and "free trade." Between 1929 and 1931, Japan's foreign trade was cut in half. Many of her people were unemployed, hungry, and afraid. Into this crisis moved the forces of violence and extremism, attacking the liberals for their alleged weakness in both domestic and foreign affairs, especially their dependence on foreign trade and markets instead of on foreign conquest and self-sufficiency.

**Manchuria.** In a sense, these extremists were ushering out the relatively peaceful, liberal twenties and setting the tone for the violent, tragic thirties. In the very first year of the decade, 1930, a nationalist fanatic assassinated the liberal prime minister, Hamaguchi, on the ground that he favored disarmament and conciliation with China. In the next year, 1931, a crucial event occurred which could be viewed as the first preliminary crisis on the road to World War II. A group of Japanese Army officers, acting without approval of their government, determined to create a "Manchurian Incident" which would serve as an excuse to invade and secure that rich province before China or the Soviet Union could do so. They planted a bomb on the tracks of the South Manchurian Railway (September, 1931) and when the bomb exploded, ordered their troops in to "protect" the line. By March of 1932 they had occupied the entire province, recreated it as the "independent" Empire of Manchukuo and placed on its throne as puppet Emperor, the last evicted ruler of Manchu China, Henry Pu Yi.

*Failure of the League.* As we have noted, Chiang was too weak to act against Japan himself and appealed to the League to restore Manchuria to China. The League met in emergency sessions, talked a great deal and ended by appointing an investigative committee (The Lytton Commission) to go to Manchuria. The Commission did not arrive till after Manchukuo had been set up and its report, issued in late 1932, simply reprimanded Japan for aggression, but did not order her out, and declared Manchuria an autonomous state under both Chinese sovereignty and Japanese control. In 1932, the United States issued its own meaningless statement called the Stimson Doctrine, pledging not to recognize any treaty violating Chinese independence or territorial integrity. The Japanese, of course, ignored both declarations just as they had ignored the League Charter and all guarantees and peace pledges signed in the twenties. They remained in Manchuria but, in 1933, they withdrew from the League, having cast much doubt on the League's efficacy as a peace-keeping body and having provided a magnificent example of successful aggression to other revisionist nations such as Italy and Germany.

*The Militant 1930s.*   In 1932, the last of the liberal, interwar prime ministers was assassinated and the last liberal government collapsed—partly out of fear. With the coming of the conservative Admiral Viscount Saito to office, responsible party government virtually ceased to exist in Japan and from 1932 until 1945 political power rested entirely in the hands of the military clique. Under its leadership Japan developed an intense nationalism. Her educational curriculum was narrowed and regimented, her press, radio and religion were closely censored and, after the National Mobilization Law of 1938, all civilian workers were organized and controlled like a military force. Considering the temper of the new expansionistic leadership, the memory of the easy conquest of Manchuria, and the pressing economic needs of the country it is small wonder that Japanese foreign policy through the middle and late thirties became continually more aggressive, following the course of "Kodo," or, "The Imperial Way."

Finally, in 1937, the Japanese militarists felt the time was right for the second major step in their plan to establish the New Order in Asia— the conquest of China—proper. Without a declaration of war they threw the full weight of their well-disciplined and equipped modern armies against the tattered legions of Chiang. Within a few weeks they had set up a tight naval blockade along the Chinese coast, had taken the city of Peking, and were threatening Chiang's capital at Nanking. He was forced to abandon it and set up his wartime capital at Chungking in the western mountains. By 1940, Japan controlled most of the eastern plains of China but was never able to take all of it or to dislodge Chiang or Mao from their mountain retreats. In 1940, Japan formed a triple military alliance with Germany and Italy and signed a neutrality pact with Russia. Also, in 1940, after the fall of France, she took over French Indo-China.

### The Americas

#### The United States

In 1900, the United States was still generally considered a "second-rate" power. Only two decades later, at the end of World War I, she was universally acclaimed as a world leader and recognized as the wealthiest and most powerful nation within the family of nations. The war, of course, was instrumental in hustling her to this sudden eminence since its demands had brought forth the flood of national energies and resources responsible both for her new affluence and for the final Allied victory. In a manner of speaking, the war speeded her passage as a nation from childhood to adolescence. During her postwar adolescence she began to realize and experience her developing powers but did not yet understand them or know how to use them. Still naive and inexperienced, she struggled desperately toward pseudo-sophistication and adulthood. The interwar period contains many illustrations of this awkward, immature use of wealth and power. For example, she failed to use the great bargaining power available to her at Paris, in 1919, to create a more equitable peace settlement. Then, when the peace settlement failed to please her, she turned her back on it and the "cynical" Old-World forces that had fashioned it and retired into a mood of self-indulgent, reactionary isolationism.

**Domestic Affairs in the 1920s.** Due to this reactionary immaturity the ensuing decade of the 1920s, although superficially prosperous, confident, and often boisterously gay, was actually a time of great torment and stress for the United States. Justifiable pride in national achievement sometimes turned into blind, chauvinistic nationalism; and this narrow nationalism, combined with bitterness against the Old World, produced an atmosphere strongly antipathetic to everything "foreign" or "different" or "un-American." During the twenties, for instance, the Congress passed its first laws sharply restricting European immigration. In the early twenties a panic fear of "alien" Communism swept the country resulting in a period of Red "witch hunts." Wartime Sedition Laws were used to arrest and detain, without benefit of habeas corpus, scores of person accused of advocating radical, foreign ideologies. Two aliens, Sacco and Vanzetti, were found guilty of murder, not so much on the basis of the flimsy evidence brought against them but primarily because of the fact that they were foreign anarchists. In the famous Scopes "Monkey Trial" of 1925 a high-school teacher was found guilty of teaching "anti-Christian," "un-American" Darwinian evolution in his classes. The Ku Klux Klan and other hate-groups also had a revival in the twenties. Beginning as primarily an anti-Black movement, the Klan ultimately opposed everyone who was not a white, Anglo-Saxon, Protestant American. The Klan claimed a peak membership of five million in 1925.

**Escapism.** Also due to reactionary immaturity, the twenties was a period of ideological retrenchment (or retreat) and escapism. Millions of Americans had been wearied by the demands of war and of Wilsonian progressivism, and they had been disillusioned by a peace that had failed "to make the world safe for democracy." They were "fed up" with idealism, visionary reform programs, and government planning. They decided to return ideologically to the "good old days" of nineteenth-century, *laissez-faire* materialism and isolationism. For many, this came to mean the escape from all socio-political responsibility (national and international) and a full-time dedication to "making money" and "having fun." The only two constitutional reforms in the whole postwar decade, therefore, came just at the end of the war, a residue of wartime idealism. One was the crucial Nineteenth Amendment which for the first time extended the vote to all women across the nation. The other was the Eighteenth, or Prohibition, Amendment which not only failed to check alcoholic consumption but actually increased it and led to bootlegging, widespread gangsterism, and a diminishing regard for the law and its custodians throughout the twenties.

**Harding.**    Another unfortunate condition of American life during the 1920s was the general lack of public interest in government and politics. This public indifference and disdain naturally resulted in consistently weak government and the election to office of many mediocre, or downright inferior politicians, not only on the local level but on the national level as well. Of the three Republican presidents elected in the twenties, the first was, by general agreement, inferior, and the second was mediocre at best. Warren Harding should never have become a president of the United States. He was essentially a small-town politician whose highest qualification for the job seemed to be that he "looked like a president." He was swept into office in 1920 on the popular theme of "a return to normalcy," which apparently meant a return to the traditional nineteenth-century principles of isolationism and *laissez-faire* materialism. The only notable domestic developments during his administration were the increasing dominance of business over government and a series of graft scandals which only superficially stirred the lethargic American people but deeply affected Harding himself, helping to undermine his health and to bring about his premature death in 1923.

**Coolidge.**    His vice-president, Calvin Coolidge, now stepped quietly into the presidency to fill out Harding's unexpired term. They called him "Silent Cal" and his character was very different from that of his inept but affable predecessor and very different also from the contemporary, collective character of the American public. He was a dour, stiff New Englander, long on morality and integrity, short on speech and personality. But apparently the electorate found his honesty, curtness, and colorlessness refreshing, and his almost-fanatical support for their cherished *laissez-faire* principles highly laudatory. He believed completely that "the business of the United States is business" and that "the best government is the least government." He believed that government should not "rock the boat" but should function primarily to "keep the peace" so that business could operate with optimum efficiency and profit. Naturally then, during his administration big business expanded dramatically and government did almost nothing. The people loved it. They elected him again in 1924 on his own merits and probably would have reelected him in 1928 had he desired to be a candidate. But when said unequivocally "I do not choose to run," the Republican party was forced to search for another representative.

**Hoover.** They found him in Herbert Hoover, called the "Great Engineer," a very successful millionaire-businessman who had organized humanitarian war-relief programs in Belgium and Russia, served as Food Administrator under Wilson, and as Secretary of Commerce under Harding. He appealed to many Democratic liberals as well as to Republican conservatives and was swept into office with the largest majority to that time in American electoral history. Having risen from humble-country-boy to millionaire-president by his own hard work and within the framework of the American free enterprise system, he believed as firmly in the principles of "rugged individualism" and *laissez-faire* as his precursors. He believed that these principles, supplemented by government subsidies, low taxes, and high protective tariffs, were largely responsible for the booming prosperity of the twenties. In his inaugural address on March 4, 1929, he said ". . . given a change to go forward with the policies of the last eight years we shall soon with the help of God be in sight of the day when poverty will be banished from this nation. . . . In no nation are the fruits of accomplishment more secure."

Hoover's optimism was supported by many experts and by many economic indicators such as continually rising industrial and farm production, increasing bank loans, and soaring stock market prices. Other signs, however, did not read so hopefully. One negative factor was the growth of economic nationalism, or the drive for economic self-sufficiency, during the twenties. Nations like the United States raised high tariff barriers to keep out foreign goods and this action led to tariff wars and a drastic decline in American and world trade. The inability of Germany to pay her reparations to the Allies and the consequent, alleged inability of the Allies to pay war debts to the United States resulted in the Dawes (1924) and Young (1930) and Lausanne (1932) Agreements, drastically reducing both reparation and debt payments, but causing new economic stresses and dislocations. Extreme concentrations of wealth, declining purchasing power, overproduction, over-extension of credit, and over-speculation were further indicators of approaching disaster for the American economy.

*The Great Crash and Depression.* Only eight months after President Hoover's euphoric inaugural, the disaster struck. In October, 1929, the worst stock market crash in the nation's history occurred. Paper fortunes were wiped out in a matter of hours. Businesses and banks closed down. Suicide rates shot up. Panic ran rampant. The shock waves of this "Great Crash" and of the ensuing "Great Depression" were felt in all parts of the world, particularly in the industrialized nations.

Its political, social, and economic effects in the United States were, of course, cataclysmic. The Hoover administration had been conditioned to expect and to deal with prosperity. It did not know how to handle wholesale poverty and depression. It responded with well-meaning, half-way measures and outworn shibboleths. Hoover declared that there was nothing basically wrong with the nation's economy, but that the depression was "psychological" and could be cured with the proper reapplication of the principles of free enterprise and rugged individualism. "Prosperity," he said, "is just around the corner." Three years later, even with the aid of business loans and public work projects, production and trade had declined by a third, thousands of banks and businesses were closed, and 15 million were unemployed.

**Roosevelt.**   In 1932, the American people were desperate and they turned in their desperation not to violent revolution or to "the man on horseback" but to the democratic political process. They gave the Democratic Party and its presidential candidate, Franklin D. Roosevelt, a resounding mandate to take positive action against the depression. The man in whom they had placed their trust was a New York patrician, educated at Groton and Harvard, former Assistant Secretary of the Navy, vice-presidential candidate, and, Governor of New York. He was one of the strongest, most controversial, most persuasive, and colorful presidents in American political history. This charming statesman and consummate politician was elected president four times by sweeping majorities and held office from 1933 to 1945. He brought no blueprint or set doctrine to the hard task of salvaging America but he felt that government had to play a major role in the reconstruction. He was a liberal pragmatist who worked by "trial and error" within the framework of American experience. In 1932, he said "The country needs and . . . demands bold, persistent experimentation. It is common sense to take a method and try it. If it fails, admit it frankly and try another. But above all, try something."

*The New Deal.*   A massive body of legislation, collectively called the New Deal program, was developed by the Administration and enacted into law by a vitalized, cooperative Congress within Roosevelt's first term—the core of it, within Roosevelt's first "hundred days" in office. Its avowed purpose was to bring "relief, recovery and reform" to all groups within American society. The unemployed, destitute, and homeless were given immediate relief in the form of food and lodging. Public

**Figure 22-3.** After the Crash. Photo by Dorothea Lange, Oakland Museum Collection.

works projects were developed to provide jobs for the jobless, to stimulate the economy, and to conserve or beautify the environment. Long-range programs of social security were provided for the aged, the sick, and the disabled. The long-suffering farmer was finally given aid through government subsidies, extension services, crop insurance, and land resettlement. The industrial laborer came into his own during the New Deal period, thanks to legislation in support of unions, collective bargaining, and fair labor standards. Business growth and cooperation were encouraged through codes of fair business practice, government "pump priming," subsidies and loans. Laws were passed regulating banks and stock exchanges to provide more adequate protection for depositors and investors.

The economic effects of these New Deal reforms are hard to judge. Real recovery began in the late 1930s, but how much of that recovery was due to prewar orders from Europe and how much was due to New Deal planning we can never be certain. Whatever its economic effects, the New Deal certainly had major psychological and intellectual effects on the American people. Through positive, vital action, it lifted Americans out of numbing despondence, fear, and hopelessness and gave them, perhaps, a more mature purpose and self-confidence than they had in the frenetic twenties. Also it influenced a movement away from the philosophy of pure *laissez-faire* materialism and toward an acceptance of more government planning and social reform.

**Foreign Affairs in the 1920s.**   As we have noted, the United States came out of World War I a major world power and potential world leader. But because of her disillusionment over the war and the punitive peace treaties, and her desire to avoid further foreign entanglements, she once again fell back into her traditional policy of isolationism, losing herself in fun, affluence, and "normalcy." By rejecting the responsibilities of world leadership, she foreordained the doom of collective security in the interwar years and therefore must bear a fair share of the blame for World War II.

The first clear and shattering evidence of her isolationist mood came with the Senate's refusal to approve the Peace Treaty and the League of Nations. They were voted down twice (1919 and 1920) despite Wilson's warning that collective security and the League might be the only guarantees of future world peace. He said, "If we do not join the League, I can predict with absolute certainty that within another generation there will be another world war." The United States sent "observers" to some League sessions and gave some indirect support but never officially joined the organization. The Senate also rejected membership in the World Court even though an outstanding American jurist, Elihu Root, had helped to create it.

Except for the ill-advised and ill-fated intervention in the Russian Civil War (1918–1922) American policies were genuinely pacifist as well as isolationist between the wars. Secretary of State Hughes initiated the first naval disarmament conference in Washington (1921) and the United States attended the other two in Geneva (1927) and London

(1930). American disarmament probably went further than that of any other Allied power. American governments signed and adhered to all of the treaties concerning Chinese rights in Asia and signed the Kellogg-Briand Pact outlawing war.

**Foreign Affairs in the 1930s.** President Roosevelt's natural inclination was toward internationalism rather than isolationism but during his first term, at least, foreign affairs were completely overshadowed by domestic concerns related to the depression. He did restore diplomatic relations with the Soviet Union in 1933, and in the mid-thirties began to try to improve relations with the Latin American countries through reciprocal trade programs and his so-called Good Neighbor Policy. In the latter thirties, as his domestic problems diminished, his foreign concerns increased with the mounting aggressions of Germany, Italy, and Japan. He favored "quarantining" these aggressor nations and stepping-up aid shipments to Western Europe and China, but he was blocked by the strong isolationist "no-aid" sentiment of a majority of the American people. When the war actually broke out in Europe in 1939, public opinion then swung over to support his policy of "all aid to the Allies short of war," and between 1939 and 1941 the United States became what Roosevelt called "the arsenal of Democracy."

## Latin America

Space will not permit an examination of each of the Latin American countries individually but fortunately, or unfortunately, there are amazing similarities among them in broad outline if not in detail. We will examine the broad similarities and leave the detail to larger texts.

Eight Latin American states officially entered World War I, all on the side of the Allies. Generally they made a formal declaration of war or simply broke off diplomatic relations with the Central Powers but did not actually send troops to the battle lines. So the war affected them relatively little. Their ideas and institutions remained pretty much as they had been in the nineteenth century.

**Political and Social Systems.** Their political systems remained absolutist and authoritarian, controlled by a "strong-man" dictator or a military junta. They often called themselves "republics" but nowhere, except in countries such as Mexico and Uruguay, was there any real democratic growth in the interwar years. If elections were held at all, they were usually rigged and the loser rarely accepted the decision. Latin America has traditionally had "government by revolution" or "government by coup." There were only two social classes: on top, a small group of extremely wealthy exploitive, land-holding aristocrats; and below, the large mass of abysmally poor and exploited peasants and laborers. The upper class jealously guaraded its privileges and luxury, refusing to share any of its wealth in the form of taxes.

**Economic Problems.**   Underlying this anachronistic, socio-political system was a very backward economic system. The Latin American coun-tries had almost no industry and were generally dependent on a one-crop agriculture (for example, coffee in Brazil; bananas in Honduras; sugar in Cuba). When the crop failed or trading markets disappeared the peasants were left destitute and starving. Almost invariably these countries suffered from unfavorable trade balances, importing more in value than they ex-ported, and having to pay off the balance in always scarce capital. Latin America was drastically affected by the depression of the thirties when foreign markets and capital dried up.

**Foreign Affairs.**   Economic dependency was also at the bottom of her endemic and eternal dilemma in foreign affairs. Latin American coun-tries have always had to look to foreign countries for trade, for loans, for investment dollars, for skilled and educated technicians and advisers. But when they have done so they have opened themselves to foreign exploitation and intervention. Through the nineteenth century the chief threat came from Europe. In the early twentieth century it came from the United States, where "dollar diplomacy" and "gunboat diplomacy" governed relations with Latin America for more than two decades. As we have seen, however, in the thirties President Roosevelt launched an ambitious program to convert the Latin image of the United States from the "Colossus of the North" to that of the "Good Neighbor." This good neighbor policy, plus the growing threat of Nazi aggression within the Latin countries, had in fact brought considerably improved relations be-tween North and South America by the eve of World War II.

### Summary

Since the age of exploration and discovery Europe had been un-intentionally exporting the seeds of nationalism. By the nineteenth cen-tury these seeds had produced at least two potentially powerful new nations—the United States and Japan. The catalyst of World War I not only thrust these two non-European states into the forefront of world affairs during the twenties and thirties, but also created conditions which encouraged nationalist resistance to European imperialism in Africa, Asia, and the Americas. Although the peoples of all continents were deeply affected by the war and by economic crises in these two tragic decades, however, the most traumatically affected were the peoples of Europe.

# Democracy,

# Dictatorship,

# and

# Disaster

In terms of future world history, perhaps the most significant result of World War I was its effect on the peoples of Europe. While the war finally involved more than 30 nations and all areas of the globe, the greatest part of the fighting and of the destruction occurred in Europe. This grim ordeal weakened Europe more fundamentally than was realized at the time and marked the beginning of the end of her long period of world dominance. As a result of the war, her manpower and material resources were wasted, her trade and foreign investments debilitated, and her finances exhausted. This economic deterioration led to increasing political weakness and instability, as illustrated by the frequency of political crises and the rise and fall of governments.

Before she could fully recover from the effects of the war, the great crash of 1929 occurred, once again shattering her economy. Some nations, such as Russia, Italy, and Germany, sought escape from their desperate problems in dictatorship and aggression. Others, like Britain and France, seeking to avoid conflict at all costs, tried to ignore or appease these aggressors. But appeasement only encouraged further aggression and led Europe and the world, step by step, down the road to a second World War even more terrible than the first.

## Great Britain

### Domestic Affairs

The Great War of 1914 to 1918 was a climactic event in British history. It marked the peak of her greatness and the beginning of her decline. In the same sense that the United States entered the war in childhood and came out in exuberant adolescence, Britain entered the war in the prime of manhood and emerged in "later middle age." The 1800s had been the century when she "put it all together": the final victory over Napoleon and the French at Waterloo; supremacy of the seas; industrial, commercial, and imperial supremacy; the quiet evolutionary triumph of parliamentary democracy; Benjamin Disraeli, William Gladstone, Queen Victoria; the century of the Pax Britannica when "the sun never set on the British Empire."

**Economic Problems.** Britain's sun began to set during World War I when too many of her strong young men died and she had to pour out her vast wealth on nonredeemable machines of death and destruction. In 1914 she was the banking and credit capital of the world. By 1918 she was deeply in debt to the United States and her financial supremacy had passed to New York. Merchant shipping and trade, which was her life's blood, had been disrupted and decimated by wartime diversions and German U-boats. While she was preoccupied with war, the United States and Japan cut seriously into her carrying-trade, her markets, and her investment centers. This deterioration of her finances and trade led to business failures, cutbacks, and massive unemployment. Labor unrest was continual. In 1926, a great General Strike threatened to bring the economy to a complete stop, but British moderation prevailed. The Great Depression made matters even worse. Unemployment rose to one quarter of the total work force in the early thirties. The government had to resort to the "dole," and bread lines and soup kitchens appeared, just as in the United States.

**Political Problems.**   Also, just as in the United States and other parts of the world, conditions seemed dangerously ripe for the widespread outbreak of violent extremism and even revolution. Why such outbreaks did not occur here, but did occur in other countries, we do not know for certain. Maybe conditions were unbearably worse elsewhere, or, perhaps the established traditions of moderation, good-natured give-and-take, compromise, and orderly democratic change had a decisive tempering influence. What did happen politically in Britain was distinctly not traditional. Her governments began to rise and fall with unusual frequency, as her people sought desperately for leaders who would give them answers to their trying problems. In 1918, manhood suffrage was extended to the industrial working class, and in the next general election of 1922 the Liberal, Lloyd George, and his wartime coalition were voted out of office. In fact, the middle-of-the-road Liberal Party almost disappeared in the interwar years and never again gained the power to elect a prime minister. British public opinion now polarized between the traditional Conservative Party, emphasizing protection and free enterprise and the new Labor Party, emphasizing socialization and planning.

The Conservatives, under the leadership of the ultracautious Stanley Baldwin, held power on three different occasions during the twenties but did absolutely nothing to improve conditions in England. Also during the twenties, the people turned twice to the Labor Party of Ramsay Mac-Donald, hoping that it might have a magic socialist solution to their proliferating economic problems. It did not. In fact, at the beginning of MacDonald's second term in office he ran head-on into the Great Depression, and foundered. Since partisan governments had proved ineffective, a series of Coalition cabinets were tried during the thirties, but they were equally unsuccessful in coping with the rising tide of difficulties besetting England. Perhaps no leadership could have solved such heavy problems, but certainly the inert and unimaginative interwar governments of Britain were incapable of it.

## Foreign Affairs

Between the wars, Britain seemed to have two dominant goals in the area of foreign affairs: (1) to stay clear of Continental entanglements, and (2) to hold the Empire together.

**The Irish Problem.** One part of the Empire which had given her trouble from the beginning was Ireland. The "Irish problem," as England called it, came from Catholic Ireland's efforts to leave the Empire, and England's efforts to keep her in. By 1914, the Irish seemed on the verge of a giant step toward independence. An Irish Home Rule Bill had been passed approving self-government and a separate Irish Parliament, but the act was never put into effect. World War I broke out and Britain demanded that the Act be held in abeyance till after the war. Also, the measure had aroused strong opposition from the six northern Protestant-Irish countries of Ulster which did not want to be governed by the Catholic-Irish majority and wanted to remain within the British realm.

The strong Irish activist movement, Sinn Fein, which had been relatively quiet in anticipation of Home Rule was infuriated by this British retraction and renewed its militant activities. Clashes occurred throughout Ireland and reached their bloody climax in the Easter Rebellion of 1916. The British finally subdued the rising but not before scores of people had been killed. The writers and intellectuals of the movement continued to write and speak for Irish independence and began to revive and emphasize everything Gaelic. Three very famous literary men were members of this Gaelic League: W. B. Yeats, J. M. Synge, and James Joyce. Finally in 1921, the British grudgingly cooperated in the creation of The Irish Free State which was a union of all Ireland, except Ulster, under an independent government and with dominion status in the British Empire. But this arrangement did not satisfy the more extreme nationalists who wanted an Ireland entirely detached from Britain. Under the leadership of Eamon de Valera they worked and fought through the thirties to accomplish this end, and in 1937 converted the Irish Free State into the completely independent Republic of Ireland, or, Eire.

**The Empire.** The rest of Britain's "European" dominions overseas—Canada, Australia, New Zealand, and South Africa—remained formally within the Empire but achieved virtual independence between the wars. In recognition of their great individual contributions to the Allied war effort, and of their final maturation as nation-states, they were declared, by the Statute of Westminster in 1931, to be autonomous states within the British Commonwealth of Nations, equal to one another and to Great Britain and held together only by common language, law, culture, mutual economic interests, and loyalty to the British crown. Their pattern of development between the wars was similar to that of the United States.

They enjoyed considerable prosperity in the twenties because of healthy world trade and demand for their special products, but when the depression came in the thirties they were affected by it too, though not so extremely as the highly industrialized United States and Britain.

We have already surveyed what was happening in Britain's "non-European" empire in Africa and Asia during the interwar years. By 1939 she was still in control of most of the imperial dependencies she had held in 1919, but it was no longer a comfortable control. The war and nationalist independence movements had weakened her imperial grip everywhere. "The white man's burden" was becoming unbearably heavy and less profitable to carry; and Britain was preparing herself, with considerable anxiety and regret, to put it down.

**Isolationism and Balance of Power.**   Considering her painful memories of the war, and the urgency of her own domestic and imperial problems, perhaps it is not surprising that Britain should have tried to isolate herself from European affairs during the postwar period. She gave lip-service to the principle of collective security and she did join the League of Nations and other international bodies, but was almost as wary as the United States of making any real commitments that might lead her into conflict again. She refused to form meaningful defensive alliances with Russia and France even after the German threat had become evident in the 1930s. Some have felt that she hoped Nazi Germany and Communist Russia might "kill one another off" if left to themselves. British isolationism, appeasement, and unenlightened national self-interest played a major role between the wars in destroying collective security, encouraging the rise of totalitarian aggression in Manchuria, Ethiopia, Austria, Czechoslovakia, and Poland, and ultimately in precipitating World War II. The detail of this tragic course of events we will examine later.

### France

#### Domestic Affairs

Of all the western European nations France suffered the greatest physical damage from World War I. She lost four million men, or one-tenth of a total population of 40 million. Her eastern border regions, where the heaviest part of the fighting had taken place, were almost completely devastated. Over a thousand towns had been leveled. Thousands of homes, factories, and bridges had been destroyed and thousands of acres of land laid waste. She immediately began an energetic program of reconstruction—but the costs were huge. She also began to build along her entire eastern frontier a defensive wall designed to safeguard her against any possible, future German threat. It was called the Maginot Line and was an incredible concrete network of gun emplacements and connecting underground railways. Unfortunately it created a false sense of security in the French and was tremendously expensive.

**Economic Problems.**   She had borrowed heavily from the United States and other countries during the war and was now forced to put herself deeper into debt to help pay for these ambitious postwar reconstruction and defense projects. As a result, she suffered almost continued financial crises between the wars, and was wracked with the problems of high taxation, very low living standards, inflation, unemployment, and constant popular unrest. The fairly even balance of agriculture and industry in France made her less dependent than Britain on foreign trade and helped make her recovery in the twenties more rapid than Britain's. During the last half of the twenties France, like many other nations, enjoyed her best interwar years. But also, like many other nations, she was hit hard by the Great Depression of the thirties and her economic, social, and political institutions were once again badly shaken, and the morale of her people undermined.

**Political Problems.**   Great political instability also plagued France. It was caused not only by the economic failures of the time but by factors rooted in the history and constitution of the Third French Republic. The Republic had been torn by factional squabbles ever since its inception in 1870. The war temporarily unified the country but the guns had barely cooled when factionalism reasserted itself. There were, of course, scores of republican party groups, but there were also many Frenchmen who still opposed democratic republicanism. On the right wing there were groups like the Bonapartists, Bourbonists, and Orleanists who still desired a restoration of the monarchy. On the left were innumerable groups like the Anarchists, Communists, or Socialists advocating various degrees of socioeconomic change.

This political multiplicity was reflected in the multiple or "splinter" party system of the Third Republic. No single party in the interwar decades was ever large enough to control a majority in the French parliamentary Assembly. Groups of parties came together in temporary alliances around certain issues so that a majority could be created and a government formed. The alliances seldom held together for long and when they broke up the government usually fell or was, at least, reshuffled. So, France was shakily governed between the wars by these unstable coalitions or blocs, each one roughly representing the then current mood of the nation.

**Interwar Governments.**   The Sacred Union of the fiery Georges Clemenceau had represented the French spirit of patriotic unity and devotion during the course of the war. In 1919 the Sacred Union collapsed and the National Bloc of forceful, Raymond Roincaré, came to power. It stood for the intense spirit of national pride that permeated the early twenties and it acted to make France strong and to keep Germany weak. It enforced demilitarization of the Rhineland and ordered French occupation of the rich industrial Ruhr valley of Germany. The mid-twenties saw the rise of Edward Herriot's Left Cartel which reflected a popular desire for economic liberalization and the easing of world tensions. Herriot failed in his minor socialist experimentation with the French economy but agreed to reductions in German war reparations through the Dawes Plan, withdrew French forces from the Ruhr, and signed the conciliatory Locarno Pacts with Germany in 1925. After the Crash of 1929, a series of inept French governments rose and fell with dismaying rapidity, none of them able to pull the nation out of its economic spin. Popular disaffection increased and finally in 1933 the ultraconservative, rightist National Union came to power determined to bring order, unity, and direction to France. Under Pierre Laval, however, it went too far in its virtual support of Italian Fascist aggression in Ethiopia and it was driven out of office in 1936. A center-leftist reaction resulted in the election of Leon Blum's Popular Front coalition which tried desperately to repair the French economy but found itself blocked by frequent labor strikes and growing extremism on both the left and the right. Communists urged the overthrow of the whole "rotten," bourgeois, capitalist system. Fascistic groups, like the Croix de Feu (Cross of Fire), urged the establishment of a stronger authoritarian government which could crush the "vicious" leftists and restore order. The totalitarian countries (particularly Germany) began sending in agents to encourage and organize these extremists into "fifth columns" which would spread confusion in France and soften up her citizenry. By the time the Center Coalition of Edouard Daladier took office in 1938 the French were, in fact, a frightened, bitter, uncertain, and thoroughly disunited people; not a small part of their fright, bitterness, and confusion came from the knowledge that while they were mired in inertia their arch-foe, Germany, had somehow managed to become once again a powerful, unified, and threatening state. The new premier had inherited an impossible situation.

### Foreign Affairs

The two major motivating forces in French foreign policy after the war were generally the same as they had been before the war: (1) to maintain the Empire, and (2) to contain Germany.

**The Empire.** As we have seen, her imperial situation between the wars was similar to that of the British. She, too, had expanded her holdings as a result of the new mandates in the Middle East and Africa, and she, too, managed to cling desperately to most of her colonies despite her own domestic weaknesses and the rising tide of nationalism.

France would have liked to do what Britain tried to do in relation to Europe. She would have liked, for awhile at least, to insulate herself from world affairs and concentrate on internal rebuilding and imperial affairs. But her geographical position on the Continent and her almost psychopathic fear of German revival and révanche would not permit her this luxury. So once again her major foreign affairs pursuit on the Continent came to be the containment of Germany.

**The German Psychosis.** Beginning with the Treaty of Versailles, she had done everything within her postwar capability to strengthen herself and to keep Germany weak and isolated. She penalized Germany with impossible reparations, disarmed her, demilitarized her western frontier, stripped away her colonies and occupied her richest industrial and coal regions. Then in the middle twenties France began a more conciliatory approach which seemed to be working, at least up to 1929. In the meanwhile she rebuilt herself, and constructed the mighty Maginot Line—the most impressive defensive fortification built to that time. She joined the League and all other international bodies for collective security. She signed all disarmament pacts and peace treaties, such as the Kellogg-Briand agreement to outlaw war. She worked assiduously to put together a new system of alliances that would encircle Germany, and managed to bring Belgium, Czechoslovakia, Poland, and finally Russia into the system.

She could do nothing, however, about the Great Depression, which debilitated her but ultimately had the effect of rehabilitating and revitalizing Germany. Nor could she convince the United States and Britain of the danger of Nazi Germany, and without their support her new "Entente" was as useless as the Maginot Line turned out to be. When Premier Daladier went to Munich in 1938 to "appease" Hitler, he went because there was little else he could do. His country had no vital power left, and it had no effective allies.

### The Smaller Countries of Europe

Almost all of the smaller countries of Europe had been touched by the war in one way or another and in the interwar decades most of them were affected by economic and political instability in much the same way as the larger powers.

#### Democracy

A few, like the wartime neutrals, Switzerland, Holland, Denmark, Norway, and Sweden, remained relatively peaceful and continued their evolutionary development of democratic institutions that had been in existence before the war. Switzerland was a federal republic. Holland and the Scandinavian countries were democratic, constitutional monarchies. The only new successful democracy created out of the Paris Treaties was Czechoslovakia. Under such capable leaders as Edouard Benes and Thomas Masaryk this little country, cut out of the Austro-Hungarian Empire, and containing a dozen different ethnic groups still managed to prosper and maintain its democratic institutions till 1938.

### Authoritarianism

All other lesser states failed to retain or develop democracy and had become either dictatorships or military monarchies by 1935. The effects of the Great Depression pulled many of them under during the thirties. The Baltic states were cut out of the Russian Empire and became dictatorships—Lithuania in 1923, Latvia and Esthonia in 1934. Poland, after a weak experiment with democratic reform and constant struggle with minority problems, became a military dictatorship under Marshall Pilsudski in 1926. Stricken, truncated little Austria lasted till 1933, then became a virtual dictatorship under Chancellor Dollfuss. Her former imperial partner, Hungary, now also a postage-stamp state, passed the same way under Julius Gombos in 1932. All of the Balkan states managed to hold together despite economic malaise and minority conflicts, but they all had become military monarchies by the mid-thirties: Albania (King Zog, 1925); Yugoslavia (Alexander I, 1929); Rumania (Carol II, 1930); Bulgaria (Boris III, 1935); and Greece (George II, 1935). Portugal was a frail and turbulent republic from 1910 to 1932 when it was converted to a still poverty ridden, but orderly, dictatorship, under the tutelage of a former professor of economics, Oliveira Salazar. He remained absolute dictator from 1932 to 1968, but effected few important social or economic reforms.

### Spain

Spain continued to be a pitifully weak and backward monarchy through 1931, under Alfonso XIII. During the war she wisely remained neutral and profited considerably by supplying both sides. After the war, conditions returned to grim normality. To save the monarchy, a right-wing leader, Miguel Primo de Rivera made himself dictator and ruled till popular discontent forced his resignation in 1930, and the King's abdication in 1931. To the surprise and delight of democrats, Spain reversed the European trend and set up a Republic. The conservative, liberal, and radical left factions, which had been in constant conflict during Rivera's rule, continued to divide and plague the country during the period of the Republic. The liberal republicans prevailed, however, and ran the government adequately till 1936. In that year a civil war was sparked by the Fascist right-wing groups under General Francisco Franco who claimed that they wanted to protect the country from a Communist takeover. The Spanish Civil War lasted through three long, destructive years. Franco received much material aid and personnel from his Fascist allies, Hitler and Mussolini, who looked upon the war not only as a chance to advance Fascism but as an opportunity to test new weapons, techniques, and tactics. Russia was the only nation that gave aid to the Republican Loyalists. The West remained aloof and detached as the Fascist forces defeated the Republicans in 1939. Collective security had failed again.

## Russia—The Soviet Union

No nation was more vitally affected by World War I and its consequences than Russia. She suffered 10 million in human losses, terrible devastation of land and property, economic collapse, and social disintegration. She experienced two war-precipitated, political revolutions which brought down her 300-year-old Czarist autocracy and launched her into the world's first perilous experiment in Communist government. She bought her way out of the war in 1918 at the treaty price of one-quarter of her European territories and population and three-quarters of her developed mineral resources. These wartime travails largely determined the course of Russian history for the next two decades, and beyond.

### Civil War

The ink had barely dried on the Treaty of Brest-Litovsk when civil war broke out. This was the Russian Civil War of 1918 to 1922, and before its end Russia had suffered further devastation and the loss of another 10 million people. It was caused by war-connected bitterness and frustration and by cumulative resentment against the new Communist regime. Czarist loyalists wanted a restoration of the old Czarist regime. Middle-class liberals feared the Bolshevik plans for communizing Russia and wanted the return of representative, parliamentary institutions. The non-Bolshevik, leftist majority resented the Bolshevik minority's arrogant seizure and arbitrary use of power. All resented the "sell-out" at Brest-Litovsk.

At first it seemed that this ill-assorted array of so-called "Whites," with the help of foreign intervention, might defeat the disorganized Communist "Red" forces. But, in late 1919, the tide began to turn, thanks to growing dissension among the Whites and the increased effectiveness of the Red Army and of Red propaganda, which convinced many Russians that they were fighting to drive out the foreigner and establish a "worker's paradise." By 1922, the White armies had been shattered, the small contingents of American, British, French, and Japanese forces driven out, and Lenin's Bolsheviks were left finally in complete command in Russia.

### Lenin's NEP

Lenin had won a ruined land. The people were desperate from pain, hunger, and sacrifice. Production and trade were almost at a standstill. His program to communize Russia (War Communism) had failed to stimulate the economy. He realized that the people needed new economic incentives and that a quick and drastic change in plan was necessary to prevent a complete breakdown. In 1921, against strong opposition from doctrinaire Marxists within his own party, he developed what came to be called his New Economic Policy (NEP), which permitted a large degree of private ownership and free enterprise within the socialist framework of national ownership and government control. To the amazement of many of his capitalist and socialist critics this hybrid, patchwork system, within three years, had restored some areas of production to the levels of 1913.

### Power Struggle

When Lenin died in January of 1924 he had managed to solve some of Russia's economic problems but had failed to provide an answer to her chief political problem—the question of who would succeed to power after his death. The two major competitors in the ensuing power-struggle were Leon Trotsky and Josef Stalin. Trotsky was an eloquent firebrand and a brilliant theorist who supported the theory of "world revolution"— the idea that the Communist revolution could, and should, be spread around the world at the same time it was being consolidated in Russia. To many he seemed to be Lenin's natural heir-apparent. On the other hand, Stalin was a stolid, shrewd organizer who advocated the opposing theory of "communism in one country," which maintained that the Party should concentrate on completing the revolution in Russia before it began to devote itself to world revolution.

Lenin had felt that Stalin was too personally ambitious. Stalin proved the point by using his position as First Secretary of the Party to begin organizing support for himself as Lenin's successor. Upon Lenin's death, Stalin launched a successful, all-out campaign to strengthen himself and discredit Trotsky. In a struggle that shook the Party and the state, Stalin finally managed to drive his adversary out of the Party in 1927 and out of the country in 1928. Between 1928 and 1931, and again, between 1935 and 1938, Stalin carried out two thoroughgoing purges that ended all effective opposition, and left him absolute dictator of Russia.

## Political System

The political system of Soviet Russia had pretty much crystallized by the thirties and was formally represented in the "Stalin Constitution" of 1936 which according to Stalin himself was a liberalization of the 1924 Lenin Constitution and "the most democratic constitution in the world." It is still in effect today. The Constitution provides for a federal union called the Union of Soviet Socialist Republics (USSR) made up of the several constituent Union Republics (15 in 1972). In this Union, property is either owned outright by the state or can be "reclaimed" by the state at any time. Actually the Soviet system today is transitional state-socialism, not communism; an extensive list of civil rights and civil obligations includes the right and the obligation to work, to receive an education, and to have leisure time. The trouble is that such rights as freedom of speech, assembly, and the press do not extend to criticizing the system. All citizens 18 years of age and older have the right to vote— and 95% of them do. But only one candidate is put forward for each office so there is no voting choice.

At the heart of the formal government structure is a system of Soviets, or legislatures, arranged in pyramidal form, with many local Soviets at the bottom, then the 15 Republic Soviets and finally, at the top, one national Supreme Soviet. Each of these Soviets elects executive officers, or Ministers (formerly called Commissars), and judges. There is no separation of powers here. Actual political leadership, however, does not lie in this formal Soviet framework at all. The real power in Russia resides in the Communist Party which is only mentioned briefly in the Constitution, but whose members control three quarters of all key positions in the Soviet Union. Its structure is pyramidal also, beginning at the lower levels with local party Committees, then up to the Republic Party Congresses, and at the apex, the All-Union Party Congress. This All-Union Congress is so large and meets so seldom that it delegates power to a Central Committee, which in turn is broken up into smaller administrative offices. It is in one of these smaller bureaus, the Politburo, where final power is to be found in the Soviet Union. Sometimes the Politburo members share power, sometimes one of them dominates the others, and then we have an absolutism like the Stalin dictatorship of the forties and fifties.

## Economic System

While Stalin was busy consolidating political powers he also had to attend to the urgent needs of the Soviet economy. Despite the fact that the NEP had been an important stimulus, Stalin felt uncomfortable with its free-enterprise elements, and in the late 1920s he began to completely "re-socialize" and rebuild the Russian economic structure with the aim in mind of ultimately overtaking the West. The amazing system he used to bring about his ambitious end was called the "Five Year Plan," and it is the most important Soviet contribution in the economic sphere. A nation, state planning board (Gosplan) in Moscow established stiff production goals in all areas, to be achieved within a certain time— usually five years. It controlled every sector of the economy and drove the Russian people, whether voluntary or "slave laborers," to the limit to accomplish its set goals. Incentives, propaganda, and punishments were used to goad the worker to an ever-faster pace.

The main focus of the Stalin Five Year Plans was on industrialization, and especially the production of heavy machinery and armaments rather than consumer goods. The secondary concern was to increase agricultural production through mechanization and the collectivization, or combining, of small farms into larger units. Here Stalin encountered fierce opposition from the more prosperous peasants (kulaks) who resented the merging of their holdings with the poorer peasant's lands. When they resisted, Stalin ordered the "liquidation of the kulaks." Hundreds of thousands were killed in this so-called "second Bolshevik revolution" and hundreds of thousands more died in a resultant famine. In 1932, Stalin was forced to call a temporary halt to the "horrors of collectivization."

The results of the first Five Year Plans (1928–1940) were mixed. Collectivization was largely completed by the time the war broke out in 1939 but it had not succeeded in significantly raising agricultural output. It had succeeded in wiping out the most productive peasant class— the kulaks. Industrialization, however, had been dramatically successful. Between 1928 and 1940 the Soviet Union had risen from fifth to second largest industrial producer in the world and its gross national product had grown faster than that of any other country. Russia should have been materially ready for World War II. Up to 1940 the Stalin dictatorship and the Five Year Plans were the filtered results in Russia of Marx's notions of the "withering away of the state" and the socialist "worker's paradise."

### Foreign Affairs

In the early 1920s, Russia was a weak but belligerent outcast nation. Most other nations shunned her, or feared her, because she threatened to spread world revolution through the agency of the Third Communist International, which had been formed in 1919. The Western powers also were bitter toward her because she refused to pay off her heavy war debt to them. Russian belligerence was a product of many factors: her new Communist, anticapitalist doctrine; her fear of capitalist encirclement; her bitterness over Western wartime exploitation and intervention in the Civil War. The only mutual assistance agreement that she signed during this early period was the Treaty of Rapallo (1922) with that other outcast nation, Germany.

After Stalin took power and began to emphasize Russian affairs rather than world revolution, the Soviet government gradually commenced to normalize relations with other countries. She needed the trade, capital, and technical assistance that the outside world could give her. She was recognized diplomatically by one nation after another and finally, in the early 1930s, by the last anti-Communist holdouts, Japan and the United States. Her mounting fear of Japanese militarism in the Far East and of Nazi Germany's intentions in the West, led her into the League of Nations in 1934 and made her the foremost advocate of collective security during the latter half of the thirties. She formed defensive alliances with Czechoslovakia and with France but was constantly frustrated by the indifference and isolationism of the United States and Britain. The British-French appeasement of Hitler at Munich, in 1938, finally convinced her that she could not count on the Western Powers to help her against Fascist aggression and drove her into a non-aggression pact with Hitler in 1939.

## Italy

### Postwar Condtion

Conditions in "victorious" post-war Italy were grim. She had been left almost bankrupt by the costs of the war. Her population, despite emigration and wartime losses, was too large to be supported by her inadequate agricultural production. She had little industry and almost no indigenous mineral resources to support the growth of industry. By switching to the Allied cause in 1915 she had hoped to obtain certain Austrian territories in the Balkans and some of Germany's overseas colonies, to give her more economic strength and more national prestige, but her weak monarchical government was able to obtain few of these desired benefits from the Paris peace settlement. Massive poverty, unemployment, and popular bitterness resulted in widespread riots and strikes and the growth of extremist political factions, like the Communist, who urged the revolutionary overthrow of the "decadent" capitalist government and business classes.

### The Rise of Mussolini

In the early 1920s a strutting jut-jawed blacksmith's son and former socialist newspaper editor by the name of Benito Mussolini began with considerable demogogic skill, to exploit this ferment and discontent.

Drawing from the ranks of the disparate jobless, frustrated war veterans, and bitter nationalists, and implicitly encouraged by the conservative, anti-Communist representatives of the status quo, Mussolini started to put together a new militant rightist organization called the Fascist Party. It was spearheaded by a group of bully-boys, called the Black Shirts, and its avowed purpose was to crush the alleged Communist threat and restore order to the state. In 1922, pressured by a threatened Fascist "march on Rome," King Victor Emmanuel III "requested" Mussolini to form a "temporary government" to bring order out of chaos. By 1924, the strong-arm fear tactics of the Black Shirts had made the Fascist Party the only party in Italy and its leader, Mussolini, the unchallenged dictator of the Italian government and state.

### The Theory of Fascism

The name of Mussolini's party, and its political philosophy, was taken from the Latin word "fasces," referring to an axe in a bundle of sticks, which was a symbol of authority in ancient Rome. Accordingly, the central tenet in this unsystematic, arbitrary Fascist philosophy was the glorification of authority as represented by "The State" and "The Leader"— a kind of super-nationalism. It did not promise, as did theoretical Communism, that the state would ultimately "wither away." To the contrary, it declared that the absolutist state is the crowning achievement of civilization. It also glorified force, militarism, war, and imperial expansion. It was essentially antirational, appealing to the emotions of the people through parades, pageantry, and impassioned oratory. It was proudly elitist and intensely antidemocratic, as illustrated in the following comment by Mussolini: facism, he said, "denies the right of numbers to govern by means of periodical consultations; it asserts the irremediable and fertile and beneficent inequality of men who cannot be levelled by any mechanical and intrinsic device as universal sufferage." It believed, in direct contrast to democratic theory, that the individual was created to serve the state and would serve it with perfect obedience, and without concern for freedom and equality, as long as the state maintained political order and economic security. To Italians in the 1920s Fascism offered an escape both from the fear of Communist revolution and from the responsibiilties and inefficiencies of democratic freedom. Millions readily accepted the offer.

### The Fascist State

The government that emerged from this Fascist philosophy was a highly centralized totalitarian dictatorship. Mussolini from his position as absolute leader (Il Duce) attempted to establish total control over every aspect of the lives of his people. He had ruthlessly crushed all significant political opposition by the mid-twenties and ruled through the one party left in Italy—his Fascist Party. He had a council of ministers called the Fascist Grand Council but he dominated it completely. Through the Lateran Accords of 1929, he settled long-standing differences between the Catholic church and the state by allowing the creation within Rome, of an independent papal state, called the Vatican. But Mussolini still essentially dominated religious and educational affairs in Italy. To maintain control over every facet of the economy he developed a system of national "corporations" or "syndicates," each representative of a particular industry or profession and all required to work together with the government for the best interests of the state. In theory, businessmen were still free agents but, in practice, Mussolini's "corporate state" meant the elimination of free-enterprise capitalism and the establishment of a state-controlled economy, or state-capitalism.

### The Fascist Economy

Mussolini declared that it was his desire to rebuild Italy and to increase her economic self-sufficiency (autarchy), and he made some hopeful beginnings in this direction. Swamp drainage and land reclamations programs were undertaken and agricultural techniques were improved, resulting in some dramatic increases in Italian grain production. Hydroelectric power plants were built to help compensate for coal shortages. Government subsidies were granted to industries, railroads, and shipping concerns. Public-works projects were initiated to stimulate the economy and increase employment. Unfortunately these laudable initial efforts were constantly thwarted by serious problems. First, Italy had little capital to undertake such ambitious projects because of her lack of productivity and her bad international credit position. Furthermore, she was woefully lacking, especially, in the natural resources necessary for industralization. Also, her birthrate was increasing rapidly under state encouragement. Finally, her Fascist government seemed more genuinely interested in preparing for war and costly foreign adventures than in earnest internal reconstruction. It is interesting to wonder what Mussolini might have accomplished in economic reform if he had not been so absorbed in foreign affairs.

### Foreign Affairs

From the beginning, however, both his Fascist philosophy and his overbearing ego drove him more to plans of rebuilding the glory and prestige of ancient Rome than to rebuilding Italian trade. During the twenties Mussolini demonstrated his imperialist appetites by threatening the Greek island of Corfu, by annexing the port of Fiume, and by taking control of Albania. In 1935 to 1936 he undertook his most ambitious act of aggression: the conquest of Ethiopia. Forty years earlier the Ethiopians had inflicted a humiliating defeat on another Italian invasion army and it seemed as though they might do it again, but finally modern artillery, tanks, and bombing planes prevailed over the antique defenses of the Africans and they were forced to surrender. Their Emperor, Haile Selassie, appealed personally to the League of Nations for assistance, and just as in the case of Manchuria, the League was deeply sympathetic, talked a great deal, applied some minor economic sanctions against Italy, but took no effective action to force her withdrawal. Collective security had received another critical blow and militant aggression another strong encouragement. Between 1936 and 1939 Mussolini intervened in the Spanish Civil War, assisting Franco's Fascist forces and testing his weapons on the Spanish Republicans. Also in 1936, Italy formed an alliance with the rising power of Nazi Germany, thereby creating a Fascist power bloc called the Rome-Berlin Axis which dominated European affairs and the attentions of the world to the eve of World War II.

### Germany

Although Germany should not be made to bear the major share of the blame for the First World War, she certainly was most directly responsible for World War II and its grim consequences. Within twenty short years after she had left Versailles, a beaten and humiliated nation, she emerged once again an aggressive military power threatening the peace of Europe and the world. What course of events had brought about his new "German problem"?

#### Causes of the New "German Problem": Versailles

The first factor was the deep German bitterness over the felt indignities of the Treaty of Versailles itself. Germans fiercely resented the "war guilt" clause, the huge reparations demands, their great territorial losses, forced disarmament and demilitarization, and many other provisions of the Treaty. Their resentment intensified during hard times and was directed generally against the Western powers and against their own Weimar government for accepting the situation.

**Economic Factors.**   Economic problems also plagued the Germans during the interwar years; they blamed the Treaty (among many other things) and especially war reparations. The fact was that reparations added hardly at all to Germany's financial difficulties since she ended up paying only a small part of them. Her most serious and continuing problem was inflation. It began during the war and persisted through the twenties and into the thirties. At its peak, in 1923, one dollar which had been worth four German marks before the war was now worth about four trillion marks. The German middle class was financially destroyed during these years. Its confidence in its republican government was shattered, but it was too class-conscious to turn to working-class parties, so it became a ready listener to the supremacist talk of emerging rightist groups like the Nazis. Germany was further weakened in the early twenties by the French takeover of its coal-rich Saar basin and its heavily industrialized Ruhr valley. Then in 1929 the Great Crash occurred, bringing to an abrupt end a five-year period of recovery and sending Germany once again into the depths of depression. Business collapsed; six million people—or two-fifths of the labor force—was unemployed; as elsewhere, fear and discontent spread, and extremist groups on both the left and the right commenced again to exploit the disaffection.

**Political Factors.**   Along with her economic troubles Germany also had serious political problems during the interwar year. In 1919, a duly authorized National Assembly met in the provincial city of Weimar, removed from the Prussian, military traditions of Berlin, and drew up a new, thoroughly democratic constitution for the country. It set up a Federal German Republic based on universal suffrage with an elected president, an elected bicameral legislature (*Reichstag* and *Reichsrat*), a chancellor or prime minister, and a cabinet responsible both to the president and the *Reichstag*. It also included a long list of civil rights guarantees.

From the democratic point of view this seemed to be a fine start for a new, more liberal Germany. But things did not go well for the Weimar Republic. To begin with, the Western democracies, which should have encouraged it, gave it little moral or material support. The German people themselves were unused to democracy, many of them looking upon it as an inherently weak, inefficient system linked somehow to the unpopular "Allied" powers and Versailles. The people blamed the Weimar government when it failed to cope with the nation's economic difficulties in the early twenties and the early thirties. And they gave it too little credit during the recovery period of the latter twenties when it led Germany into the League, moved France out of the Saar and Ruhr valleys, and restored German prestige with the signing of the conciliatory Locarno Pacts.

The Weimar Republic produced no real social change and no strong leaders who could unify her centrist parties and give her the kind of political stability she needed. Nor were her leaders ever able to deal decisively with political extremist groups. A provisional government had to call in the army to put down the leftist, "Spartacist rising" in 1919. In 1920, the rightest "Kapp Putsch" in Berlin was defeated but mainly by

Berlin workers rather than by government forces. In 1923, another rightist "Beer Hall Putsch" took place in Munich. This rising was sparked by a group called the National Socialist German Worker's Party and was led by a former general, Eric von Ludendorff, and a former corporal, Adolf Hitler. The rising was broken up and the leaders jailed but they were soon freed to begin agitating again.

### Adolf Hitler

The Munich Beer Hall Putsch is of course, important primarily because it marked the first public appearance of Adolf Hitler on the stage of history. Hitler was born in Austria of a lower middle-class family. He aspired to be a painter but apparently lacked esthetic feeling. He drifted from Austria to Bavaria where he joined the German army just before the outbreak of World War I. During the war he served with some distinction and was made corporal before his discharge. He left the service, a lonely frustrated spirit, embittered by personal failure and German defeat, seeking a channel for his starved ego and ambition. He found this channel in the leadership of the National Socialist (Nazi) Party. After the abortive Putsch he spent a few months in relatively comfortable confinement where he passed the time very profitably writing a book which was to become the "Bible" of the Nazi movement—*Mein Kampf (My Struggle)*. Few read it through and many of those who did dismissed it as the ravings of a pitiful egomaniac. Besides a mass of autobiographical detail, it contains Hitler's rough blueprint for world conquest and a comprehensive, if unsystematic, exposition of the Nazi philosophy.

### Naziism

Naziism was the Germanic form of Fascism. Its main themes, just as in Italian Fascism, were glorification of the state, the leader, the party, war, and conquest. But Hitler added some new concepts, or myths, to the original Italian model. The most important of these were the myths of the "super-man" and the "super-race." These ideas had been developed out of the prewar philosophies of such thinkers as Hegel, Nietzche, and Austen Chamberlain. They held that the "Aryan," "Nordic," "Germanic" peoples (Volk) were superior to all other races or ethnic groups and were destined to rule the world under the leadership of the Nazi Party and its Fuehrer (father-leader) Adolf Hitler. All other peoples were fit only to serve the "master-race," or to be exterminated by it to make more living space (lebensraum) for the chosen ones. According to Nazi theory, the most despicable and dangerous of the "inferior" peoples were the Jews. They became the chief domestic "whipping-boys" for the Party and for many ordinary German citizens who followed the Party lead in trying to reestablish their shattered self-confidence by blaming everyone but themselves for Germany's postwar breakdown. Other Nazi-German scapegoats were international bankers, the Communists, the decadent democracies and, of course, the whole Paris Peace System. Hitler maintained that Germany was encircled by foreign, inferior peoples who would destroy her if she did not strike first.

### The Rise of Naziism

During Germany's relatively prosperous, settled period of the latter twenties, the Nazis and other extremist groups went into temporary eclipse. But after the crash of 1929, they began to gain strength once more by taking advantage of a deteriorating economy and a confused, fear-ridden people. Hitler uncovered his genius for emotional oratory and demagogic rabble-rousing. Through propagandistic appeals, martial parades and spectacles, and the strong-arm tactics of his Brown Shirts or storm-troopers (the SA), Hitler had, by 1932, built the Nazis into the largest single party in the *Reichstag*. The venerable, but increasingly senile President von Hindenburg was compelled to declare Hitler Chancellor of Germany in 1933, even though the Nazis were never able to obtain more than forty-four per cent of the vote despite their coercive tactics. As Chancellor, Hitler moved quickly to seize absolute control of the government. He apparently ordered the burning of the *Reichstag* building to create an incident, blamed the fire on the Communists, and used the ensuing panic to suspend all civil rights and to have himself made "temporary" dictator with the power to change the Constitution.

### The Third Reich

Hitler not only changed the Weimar Constitution, he abandoned it completely and created in its place a "New Order" for Germany and a new political system which he called the "Third Reich." It was a highly centralized, totalitarian state with all power in the dictator, or Fuehrer, who was, of course, Hitler. After July of 1933 only the Nazi Party was permitted to exist in Germany and it continued to enforce its will through the elite SS corps and later through the dreaded State Police, or Gestapo. Citizens could vote at first but only for Party candidates. The law was whatever Hitler decreed, or allowed the rubber-stamp *Reichstag* to pass, and it was carried out by Party controlled Ministries and an efficient, totally regimented bureaucracy. Political cases were tried in a system of People's Courts where many thousands of people were arbitrarily sentenced to prison, labor camps, and death on little more than personal accusation. Civil rights were permanently eliminated, all political opposition to the regime was crushed and many religious and ethnic minorities were ruthlessly persecuted. The Jews, of course, bore the brunt of this savage attack. Legislation such as the infamous Nuremberg Laws of

**Figure 23-1.**  Hitler reviewing Brown Shirts, 1935.

1935 deprived them of jobs and citizenship and forbade them intermarriage with gentiles. They were stripped of property, beaten, sterilized, and suffered mass deaths in concentration camps and gas chambers. By the end of the war six million Jews had lost their lives in this incredible Nazi madness.

### The Nazi Economic System

The economic system of the Third Reich could best be described as "state capitalism." The government permitted the forms of private ownership but maintained close supervision and control over every aspect of the economy. The great industrialists who had planned to manipulate Hitler for their own purposes soon discovered that he had out-maneuvered them and was instead using them to help him build his Third Reich. Like Mussolini, Hitler was not interested in economic affairs as such. He was primarily interested in making the German economy strong and self-sufficient (autarchistic) so that it would be capable of producing and supporting a new, modern military machine that could restore the nation to its rightful place in the world.

The entire economy was mobilized to that end. The government fixed production goals and prices. Dr. Robert Ley's Labor Front controlled all labor organizations, imposed compulsory arbitration, forbade strikes, and fixed wages and hours. Great public works projects were undertaken by labor battalions to rebuild Germany and ease unemployment. Intensive programs of swamp drainage, reforestation, housing, road construction (beginning of the autobahns), and the building of fortifications, like the Siegfred Line, were successfully carried out in a very few years. Aggressive German traders once again began to fan out around the globe, capturing markets and spreading Nazi political propaganda. In 1935, Hitler virtually eliminated unemployment and dramatically revitalized industry by ordering universal military conscription and rearmament. Having laid a firm base for the economic recovery and military rejuvenation of the state, he could now turn his attentions to the chief Fascist goal—glorification of the state through foreign affairs.

### Foreign Affairs

Each defiant, aggressive action taken by Hitler during the thirties sharply increased international tensions and marked a series of tragic steps on the road to World War II. In 1933, shortly after taking power, he preemptorily withdrew Germany from the League of Nations, thus dealing that organization and its principle of collective security another hard blow. Two years later he further demonstrated his disdain for the Paris Peace system by abrogating the Treaty of Versailles and beginning to rearm Germany in direct violation of the Treaty. No serious international objections were raised and, in 1936, Hitler gambled again by ordering his still relatively weak forces to reoccupy and remilitarize the Rhineland area. Britain and France might have stopped him on this crucial occasion and ended his career but France would not act without Britain and Britain would not act at all. Once again the vacillating democracies and collective security had failed and bold aggressiveness had won. Hitler's confidence and prestige soared.

Fresh from their victories in the Rhineland and Ethiopia, Hitler and Mussolini joined forces to aid the Fascist cause in the Spanish Civil War (1936–1939), and in 1936 formed the Rome-Berlin Axis to seal their friendship. This alliance was extended to include Japan by the Anti-Comintern pact of 1937, directed against Russia. With all of this support behind him and a growing certitude that the Western democracies would never risk war to check his ambitions, he defied the Versailles treaty ban against Anschluss and annexed Germanic Austria to the Third Reich in 1938. Russia urged Britain and France to take a stand with her against this invasion of Austria but Britain remained indifferent and neither Russia nor France was willing to move alone.

**Munich.** Each triumph whetted Hitler's appetite for more, and shortly after the Austrian annexation, he demanded the German-populated western border areas of Czechoslovakia, called the Sudetenland. The Czechs, under their courageous President Benes, rejected the German ultimatum and began to mobilize their small army. But their resistance was worn down by the subversive, fifth-column activity of the Czech Nazi Party of Conrad Henlein and by the failure of the British and French to unite with them and the Russians to oppose Hitler's demands. The Czechs decided they could not fight alone. The British and the French again decided they could not risk a war to save a piece of foreign territory. In September of 1938, Neville Chamberlain, prime minister of Britain and Edouard Daladier, premier of France met with the Nazi dictator at Munich and agreed to let him have the Sudetenland in return for his promise to make no more territorial demands in Europe. This cynical Munich Pact symbolized the final breakdown of collective security and the final shameful act in the policy of "appeasement."

**The Non-Aggression Pact.** Greeted by many as a hero upon his return to England, Chamberlain stated his firm belief that the Pact meant "peace for our time." Only six months later in March of 1939, Hitler sent his troops in to occupy the rest of Czechoslovakia! Britain and France were now shocked into wakefulness and began furiously rearming and seeking to bind up their alliances. But it was too late as far as Russia was concerned. Disgusted with the Munich appeasement and suspicious of British-French motives, she sought to protect herself and gain time to

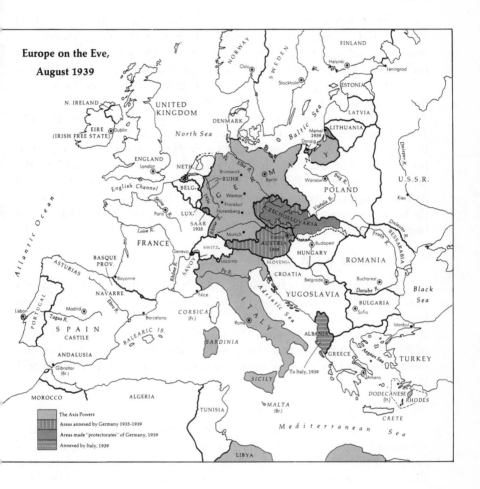

Figure 23-2.

build up her defenses by signing her own cynical non-aggression pact with Germany, in August, 1939. The signatory powers pledged themselves not to attack one another for at least ten years. The Soviet Union was to be given a free hand in Finland, Estonia, Latvia, Bessarabia, and eastern Poland. Germany was granted freedom of action in Lithuania and western Poland.

**The Polish Crisis.** Temporarily secured against Russian attack in the east, and thoroughly persuaded that the craven, decadent democracies would not act against him under any circumstances in the west, Hitler now turned his full attention to the conquest of Poland. He had begun his diplomatic campaign of provocation against Poland in early 1939, making territorial demands of her which she could not possibly accept. At the same time he was proceeding with a military build-up along Poland's western frontier. On September 1, eight days after the signing of the non-aggression pact, and without a declaration of war, he unleashed his modern war machine in a "blitzkreig" (lightning) attack on the heroic but woefully weak Poles. Finally, recognizing the inevitable, and living up to their treaty commitments with Poland, Britain and France declared war against Germany on September 3, 1939. World War II had begun for Europe!

### Causes of World War II

In retrospect, we can see that the "peace" after the First World War was chimeric, little more than an armistice, or an interlude between hostilities. Marshall Foch said after Versailles in 1919: "This is not peace. It is an armistice for 20 years." World War I had, in fact, created more problems than it solved, and one way of viewing the events of the twenties and thirties is to see them as a series of causative factors leading to World War II.

#### Versailles

One major cause of World War II was the inequitable Paris Peace Settlement that terminated World War I. The real, or imagined, injustices of the treaties created serious problems and continuing bitterness among many peoples of the world—victors, vanquished, and neutrals alike.

#### Economic Instability

Also, as we have seen, the First World War precipitated widespread economic and social dislocation whose effects were felt throughout the twenties, climaxing in the crash of 1929 and the disastrous depression of the thirties. Most countries were wracked by trade and tariff wars, autarchy, inflation, unemployment, and the interlocked problems of war debts and war reparations. This economic instability produced an atmosphere highly charged with anxiety, suspicion, fear, and belligerence, perfectly conducive to further world conflict.

### Militant Nationalism

Probably the primary cause of World War II, however, was the spirit of blind, narrow nationalism that continued to be at least as prevalent during the interwar years as it had been in the pre-1914 period. Despite the inspired efforts of a few to lead the way to peace through world government and internationalism, most peoples still clung desperately to their own local or national allegiances, while lashing out at the competitive allegiances of others. But it was not until after the terrible economic breakdown of 1929 that these nationalist antagonisms began seriously to erupt again in a militant form. Japan, Italy, and Germany, in the name of national honor and necessity, then launched into that series of military aggressions that ultimately led to World War II.

### Disunified "Allies"

Aside from a miraculous moral conversion of mankind, the one development that might have averted world conflict was the unification and preparation of the non-aggressor nations in the face of the Axis threat. But, as we know, this kind of "collective security" was never achieved either through the League of Nations, or through regional alliances. Still drained, cynical, or "gun shy" as a result of World War I, most countries were unwilling to risk their own immediate security in defense of a distant people, with the uncertain hope that this sacrifice would finally check aggression and preserve long-range peace. Neither the United States nor Britain would act at all and neither France nor Russia would act unilaterally. Consequently, the Axis powers were given time to build their strength and were encouraged by lack of opposition to continue their aggressions. Hitler and the Axis alliance probably could have been stopped in 1936 by the unified action of Britain and France. By 1939, it was almost too late. Appeasement and the failure of collective security not only helped cause the war but very nearly lost it for the non-aggressor nations.

## World War II

So, twenty short years after Versailles the world found itself again divided tragically into two camps: on the one side the so-called Axis, or Anti-Comintern powers, Germany, Italy and Japan; and on the other side those nations that were forced into opposition by Axis aggressions, beginning with China, France, and the British Commonwealth. Between 1939 and 1942 the Axis was constantly and successfully on the offensive, thrusting out from its European power center in Germany to the English Channel, the Volga, and North Africa; and from its Asian power center in Japan to the verges of India, Australia, and Alaska. In 1942, it seemed that the totalitarian powers might, in fact, be well on the way to world conquest as Hitler had promised. But in that year the strength of the "late entries"—the Soviet Union and the United States—began to be felt and the tide of war shifted in favor of the "Grand Alliance" (as Winston Churchill called it) made up of Britain, America, Russia, China, and the "free" fighters and "resistance" forces of the subject nations. Between 1943 and 1945, the allies took the offensive and began to drive the Axis inexorably inward, from the high-tide line of its furthest advance, back upon its original bases in Germany and Japan. To help simplify a very complex story let us examine the events in the European and Asian theatres of operation separately even though these events, of course, were taking place concurrently and were interrelated parts of the same great global conflict.

### The War in Europe

**Blitzkreig in the East.**   The conflict in Europe began officially with the Anglo-French declaration of war against Germany for her violation of Polish territories, but neither the British nor the French were actually capable of giving military aid to Poland in 1939. The previous decade of appeasement and determined avoidance of war had left them without a ready offensive capability—and Poland, like Czechoslovakia, could not stand for very long without their aid.

Polish courage and an excellent cavalry force were insufficient against the new war machine that Hitler had built out of the shambles of Versailles. The Poles were helpless before this first great mechanized "blitzkreig" in the history of warfare. The Panzer (armored) divisions of Hitler's Wehrmacht (fighting forces) devastated Poland by land while his Luftwaffe (air force) demoralized her from the skies. At the same time, with relatively little fanfare or resistance, Stalin's Red Army moved in and occupied the eastern half of Poland which had been designated in the Non-Aggression Pact as a Russian sphere of influence. Within a month it was all over. Once again Poland had fallen victim to a display of power politics at least as brutal as the Russo-German Partitions that had brought about her dismemberment in the late 1700s.

**The "False War."**   During the winter of 1939 to 1940 Europe and the world nervously awaited new aggressions on the part of the dictators. Stalin did not disappoint these expectations. Under the shield of the

Non-Aggression Pact he began (much like Alexander I after Tilsit) to develop a series of buffer territories along his western frontier. He incorporated Moldavia, Latvia, Lithuania, and Esthonia, as well as east Poland, into his new Soviet Empire; and after a few months of unexpectedly stubborn Finnish resistance (The Winter War) he further expanded Russian territories at Finland's expense. During these same winter months Hitler and Germany remained quiescent. The Fuehrer made no new demands in Europe and many people were ready to believe that Poland had fully satisfied him and that peace could now be restored. They sometimes referred lightly to the months between September, 1939, and April, 1940, as Hitler's "Sitzkreig" or the period of the "False War."

**Blitzkreig in the West.** Unfortunately the wishful thinkers proved to be wrong once again. Hitler was building supplies and planning new and greater triumphs for German arms, to begin in the warmer weather of spring. In April, he launched the first of a series of devastating blitzkreig attacks that would not end until he had most of Europe in thrall. Denmark, then Norway, were overpowered within a few days in April; Holland and Belgium were overrun in the early days of May; and on May 12, 1940, the first German panzer units rolled across the Belgian frontier into France.

**France.** The French, at least, should have been prepared to meet the German onslaught in 1940. They had been fearful, almost psychotic, about Germany since 1871 when she first emerged as a powerful, competitor nation; and since Versailles they had been constantly and apprehensively readying themselves for the possible reemergence of this German power. The trouble was that the psychology of most French leaders was retrospective and defensive. They ignored the perceptive warnings of a few officers like Charles de Gaulle and chose to believe that any new conflict with Germany would be essentially static, linear, and defensive in the same pattern as warfare along the Western Front during the First World War. With their huge conscript army, well supplied with traditional weaponry, standing behind the amazing concrete and metal bulwark of the Maginot Line, the French were magnificently prepared to fight World War I again.

But they were no more ready than Poland, Norway, or Holland to fight Hitler's new kind of fluid, "total war." Nazi armored columns swept out of Belgium around the open northern end of the "impregnable" Maginot Line and swiftly fanned out southward across the interior of France. The Luftwaffe thundered over the Line dropping paratroopers behind it and mass-bombing civilian populations as well as military targets. Already weakened internally by appeasement, complacency, and the work of fascist "Fifth Column" agents, French resistance quickly crumbled before the devastating thrust of the Nazi war machine. Within six weeks Hitler had accomplished what the Kaiser had not been able to do in four years. He gleefully accepted the French surrender on June 22, 1940, in the same railroad car where the Germans had been forced to surrender in 1918. By the terms of the peace treaty France was divided into two parts—a northern, German-occupied sector centered in Paris, and a southern "unoccupied" sector with its capital at Vichy. Vichy France and its president, Marshal Pétain (the 84-year-old former hero of Verdun), remained virtual puppets of Hitler until the liberation.

**Britain.** Outside of neutral Sweden, Switzerland, Spain, and Ireland, the only nation in western Europe still free of Hitler's control by mid-summer, 1940, was Great Britain—the Fuehrer now turned his full attentions to her. Infuriated by her rejection of his peace overtures, Hitler determined to crush her totally. He could see no serious obstacles in the way, with the possible exception of British stubbornness and the British fleet, and he believed that both of these could be broken by air power. He knew that the British regular army was small and woefully ill-equipped despite the desperate post-Munich efforts at rearmament. The core of this army had miraculously escaped entrapment by the Wehrmacht at Dunkirk on the Channel coast in early June. Some 350,000 men had been saved by the British navy (and a motley collection of fishing boats, tugs, and merchant vessels) but they had left most of their precious equipment behind. Hitler also knew that the ratio of British Royal Air Force (RAF) strength in relation to that of the German Luftwaffe was roughly one to four. With these odds in mind, he ordered his Air Marshal, Herman Goering, to unleash an all-out air attack upon England either to force a quick surrender or soften her up for invasion. The most intense period of the air war, which ensued between August and December of 1940, has been called the "Battle of Britain."

During these months Britain took everything that German air power could deliver but refused to break or even consider capitulation. What supported the nation during its "ordeal by fire"? What factors enabled it to survive one of the most concentrated attacks on a civilian population in the history of warfare? We do not know all the answers but certainly one of them must be the indomitable spirit of the British people themselves. The harder they were hit the more stubborn and resistant they became. Hitler could never understand this British spirit nor could he understand the man who emerged as the chief organizer and symbol of it—Winston Churchill. This eloquent, cigar-smoking, bulldog of a man must also be given major credit for Britain's survival. From the time he became prime minister, in April of 1940, he galvanized the nation into action, inspired it with his ringing speeches, and re-enforced its determination to resist Nazi aggression. In the darkest hours of the Battle of Britain he said: "We shall defend our island whatever the cost may be. We shall fight on the beaches . . . on the landing grounds . . . in the fields and streets. . . . We shall never surrender!" He also bolstered British resolve with the hope of increased American aid and ultimate American entry into the war.

The most crucial military factor in explaining England's triumphant resistance during the Battle of Britain was clearly the Royal Air Force. Thanks to a few hundred courageous pilots, some excellent pursuit planes like the Spitfire, and a newly developed "early-warning" radar system, the RAF, despite its much smaller numbers, was able to inflict such heavy losses on the Luftwaffe that Hitler was forced to sharply reduce heavy bombing raids and to postpone indefinitely his plans for the invasion of Britain. "Never in the field of human conflict," said Churchill, "was so much owed by so many to so few."

Not as dramatic perhaps, but equally important in keeping Britain alive was the work of the navy and the merchant marine. The role of the navy, as in previous English conflicts with continental powers, was to defend England from possible sea attack or invasion and to protect her vital trade lanes. Germany's aim, as in World War I, was to cut off or check the main flow of goods (and later troops) across the Atlantic between America and Britain. The resultant sea war was at its height between 1940 and 1944 and has been called the Battle of the Atlantic. In this period the allies lost more than 20,000 ships, half of them British; 70 percent of them sunk by deadly German U-boats. In 1942 alone, 8000 allied ships were sent to the bottom. But after that nadir, American naval aid began to become effective and American industry began to build merchant ships faster than Axis aircraft and submarines could sink them. By 1944, the Allies had essentially won the Battle of the Atlantic.

**Russia.** Meanwhile, thwarted by Britain in the west, Hitler had turned his legions eastward and had swept over the Balkans in late 1940 and early 1941. By the summer of 1941 his huge war machine lay triumphant, and idling, along the frontier of the Soviet Union. On June 22, without any declaration of war, Hitler ordered it across that frontier. The decision to invade Russia turned out to be Hitler's climactic blunder (just as it had been Napoleon's) but for him it was probably an inevitable decision. His egomania and his yearning to do what even the great Napoleon had been unable to do drove him to ignore the opinions of many of his generals. Also, his system required continued war and conquest and the despised Soviet Union was the only nation left on the Continent that could offer employment for his Werhmacht as well as vast potential supplies of raw materials and laborers to sustain his empire.

He predicted an easy six-week war, and for awhile it seemed that his prediction might be accurate. Russian resistance melted before his speeding Panzer divisions. In fact, many peasants in the border provinces at first greeted the Germans as liberators. By October, the German armies had pushed close to Leningrad and Moscow and deep into the Ukraine. Although the fierce Russian winter stopped them there, and a stiffened Soviet military effort in the summer campaigns of 1942 prevented the taking of Leningrad and Moscow, the southern prong of the Nazi offensive reached the Caucasus and the city of Stalingrad on the Volga River. At Stalingrad perhaps the most crucial battle of the war took place. In a desperate heroic stand (September, 1942 to January, 1943) the Red Army defeated the Wehrmacht for the first time, then proceeded to launch the first of a series of amazing counter-offensives which drove the Nazi forces completely out of Russia by 1944 and back into Germany itself by 1945.

**The United States.** During the latter half of the thirties, as war tensions mounted in Europe and Asia, most Americans continued to cling tenaciously to the policy of isolationism. They were determined not to be dragged into foreign conflicts as they had been in 1917. Until September of 1939 they remained generally opposed, in the area of foreign affairs, to leaders like President Roosevelt who advocated sending aid to the democracies and placing a "quarantine" on aggressor nations. When war finally came, however, the majority came to support the idea of giving all possible material aid to the allies short of actual military involvement. As a result, an increasing volume of "lend-lease" foodstuffs and hardware began to flow across the Atlantic to Britain. So, even before actual United States entry into the war, it had become what Roosevelt called "the arsenal of democracy." Our close tie with Britain and our "non-neutrality" were further emphasized when Roosevelt and Churchill met in August of 1941 off Newfoundland and issued the "Atlantic Charter," pledging the establishment of a better world "after the final destruction of Nazi tryranny."

The event that finally propelled America into the conflict was the Japanese attack on Pearl Harbor, on December 7, 1942, six months after the forced entry of Russia. Two new powers were now pitted against the Axis, although it was many months before their strength was felt. However the speed and efficiency of the American mobilization, once it began, was even more incredible than it had been in World War I.

Within two years the once moribund, consumer-oriented economy of the United States was producing twice the volume of military hardware and consumer goods as all of the Axis powers combined. It continued adequately to supply the needs of Americans while still supporting the desperate needs of allies like China, Britain, and Russia. Ten percent of Soviet military equipment used to drive the Germans out of Russia came from the United States. The American merchant fleet grew from one million tons in 1941 to nineteen million tons in 1943, despite the fact that in the disastrous year of 1942 the Axis was sinking allied vessels faster than they could be built. By 1943, the American navy had emerged from the ruin of Pearl Harbor as the largest and best-equipped in the world. The American air force expanded, between 1941 and 1945, from a few hundred outdated planes to a strike force of 300,000 modern aircraft. And totally, by the end of the war, the United States had trained and equipped an armed force of some fifteen million persons.

The first, crucial, strategic decision that American leaders had to make after Pearl Harbor was whether to concentrate their initial military effort in Europe or in Asia. The decision to focus on Europe was dictated both by the immediate plight of European allies, Britain and Russia, and by the weakened capability of the Pacific fleet after Pearl Harbor. The second major question was where and when to begin the attack on Hitler's "Festung Europa" (European Fortress). Stalin urged the speedy opening of a "second front" in northern Europe to relieve some of the pressure along Russia's "first front." But the Western leaders decided to make their first experimental strike at the less formidable southern periphery of Axis power in North Africa.

**North Africa.** Here—as everywhere, in the summer of 1942—Fascism was in the ascendant. Hitler, through his Vichy satellite, controlled Morocco and Algeria. Mussolini controlled Tunis and Libya, and their combined armies, commanded by the brilliant Field Marshal, Erwin Rommel ("the Desert Fox"), were threatening to drive the British out of Egypt. In October of 1942, however, the tide of battle in North Africa began to shift. The British Eighth army of General Montgomery defeated Rommel at El Alamein, less than one hundred miles from Cairo, then launched a counter-offensive thrusting him back upon Tunisia. In November of 1942 an Anglo-American invasion army under the command of General Dwight D. Eisenhower landed in French Morocco and Algeria, forced their quick surrender, and drove on eastward into Tunisia trapping the retreating enemy between themselves and Montgomery and the coast. By early May, the Allies had triumphantly terminated their first great combined operation of the war. They had defeated Rommel's proud "Afrika Korps" and had inflicted heavy losses in the process (250,000 captured or killed). They had opened the Mediterranean once again to allied shipping and had made the North African coast available as a potential base of operations against what Churchill called "the soft, underbelly of Europe." Also, this victory, along with Stalingrad, gave a much-needed boost to the sagging morale of anti-Axis peoples everywhere.

In January, while the North African campaign was underway, Roosevelt and Churchill met in Casablanca and had made several important decisions that affected the future course of the war. They determined that when the conflict ended they would accept only "unconditional surrender" from the defeated Axis powers, so that future peace would not be compromised by preconditions. They also laid the groundwork for a Free French Government in exile, centered in Algeria and London with the controversial General Charles de Gaulle at its head. Most significantly, however, they began to discuss plans for the ultimate invasion of northern Europe and for the more immediate invasion of Sicily and Italy.

**Sicily.**   In fact, the plan to invade Sicily went into effect in the summer of 1943, only a few weeks after the victory in Tunisia. Profiting from the experience of the recent invasion and the shorter, protected supply lines from North Africa, the armies of Generals Patton and Montgomery moved steadily around opposite sides of the island and despite stiff German resistance, succeeded in taking it within a month (July).

**Italy.**   Even before the main Allied invasion of Italy in September, Mussolini's Fascist regime had fallen and Mussolini himself had been carried north by the Germans to form a rallying point for any party faithful that might still be left. There were few. Most Italians seemed content with the passing of the Fascist order. A military commander, Marshal Badoglio, was requested by King Victor Emmanuel to form a new government. He did so, and immediately agreed to the unconditional surrender of Italy to the Allies. He also encouraged his people to oppose the Germans as intruders. In July and August, Italy was in chaos and the German forces in Italy were shaken. If the Allies had invaded during that period their task might have been easier. But by September the German army had reorganized itself and when the Allied forces under General Mark Clark landed on the beaches of Salerno and Anzio they were met with some of the fiercest opposition of the war. Through the rainy winter and spring of 1944 they pushed doggedly northward along both sides of the Appennines, forced to fight the resourceful Wehrmacht every foot of the way. Rome and central Italy were not liberated until the summer of 1944 and northern Italy remained in German hands until the spring of 1945. The prolongation of this Italian campaign, however, cannot be blamed solely on the stubbornnesss of German resistance. As early as 1943 the focus of Allied attentions, and logistics, had begun to shift from the Mediterranean area to the North Atlantic and the Pacific.

**Wartime Conferences.** During the latter months of 1943 Allied leaders held several war-planning conferences similar to the earlier meeting in Casablanca. At Quebec, Canada, in August, Roosevelt and Churchill considered plans for a cross-channel invasion of northern Europe ("Operation Overlord"). They also discussed with Chinese foreign minister, T. V. Soong, stepped-up, coordinated action against Japan in the Asian theatre. At Cairo, Egypt, in November, Roosevelt and Churchill met with Chiang Kai-shek himself and agreed on increased aid for China and the postwar return of all Japanese-seized territories in China. The foreign ministers of the United States, Britain, and Russia came together in Moscow in October, to lay the groundwork for a meeting of their respective heads-of-state—Roosevelt, Churchill, and Stalin. This first "Big Three" summit conference took place the next month in Teheran, Iran, and, among other global questions, dealt with the possibility of opening Stalin's long awaited "second front" in northwestern Europe.

**Preparations for "D-Day."** Allied leaders had talked of a Channel invasion ever since America's entry into the war but felt unprepared for such a perilous undertaking until the spring of 1944. By that time Germany could not concentrate her major strength in defense of her "Atlantic Wall" because she was already heavily engaged, as we have seen, on the Russian and Italian fronts. Furthermore, she had been hurt by months of day and night Allied aerial bombardments aimed at urban and industrial centers as well as military targets, such as airfields, naval bases, and coastal fortifications. Many German cities were much more heavily bombed and damaged than London had ever been during the Battle of Britain. The Allies had learned some lessons in "total war" which Hitler had helped to teach them. Also they had learned to cope with the German U-boat menace. With the use of improved submarine detection and destruction devices, air protection, destroyer convoys, and search teams, the British and American navies had cleared the Atlantic sea lanes so effectively as to permit an ever-increasing flow of men and materials from the United States to England in the early months of 1944. Britain became a huge military base and warehouse, ultimately containing over 1.5 million men, over 160 airfields, and millions of tons of supplies.

**The Battle for France.** Hitler knew, of course, that an attack was coming but he did not know when or where it would come and was compelled to stretch a thin line of defenses along the whole north

Atlantic coast from France through Belgium and Holland. "Decision Day" (D-Day) finally came on June 6, 1944. The supreme Allied commander, General Eisenhower, ordered the initial attack across the Channel against a narrow strip of French coast in Normandy. This greatest seaborne invasion in history was also one of the most successful. On the first day, 130,000 troops were landed, and the German shoreline defenses were breached. Within a month, some 4000 ships and 11,000 planes had landed almost one million men on the French coast with the total loss of 9000 men. Despite heavier German resistance inland, the Allied armies broke through in late July, reached the Seine River, and liberated Paris in August, and by October had driven the last German divisions out of France.

**The Battle for Germany.**   Many persons predicted that the war would be over by Christmas, but behind their own original frontier of the Rhine and the Seigfried Line (built in the thirties to parallel the Maginot Line) the debilitated Wehrmacht stiffened and held. An Allied effort to sweep around the northern end of the line through Holland was checked at Arnhem with heavy losses on both sides. Then in December, Hitler launched his last desperate offensive of the war out of the Ardennes region; he aimed to drive a wedge through the Allied armies and split them. The successful counter-attacks of Montgomery from the north and Patton from the south were called the Battle of the Bulge (January, 1945) and resulted in further irredeemable German losses. While the Allies were defeating Germany in the Ardennes, Russia was battering down the German defenses in Warsaw and Budapest. Victory over the Third Reich seemed imminent, though victory over Japan was not. Under these circumstances, Roosevelt, Churchill, and Stalin held their third, and last, wartime conference in February, at Yalta in the Russian Crimea. Here the Western leaders, besides rededicating themselves to the quick and unconditional surrender of Germany, granted Stalin certain postwar territorial concessions in Poland and the Far East in return for his promise to enter the war against Japan within ninety days after the end of the European conflict. Also they agreed that Germany should be divided into three occupation zones after the war and that an international meeting should be held in April in San Francisco to set up a permanent United Nations Organization to keep the peace after the war.

**Victory in Europe.**   During March and April as the Allied armies drove eastward from the Rhine and the Russians rolled westward out of Poland and Hungary, the German fighting spirit began to crumble rapidly. By the time the two armies had come together at the Elbe in central Germany (on April 25) there were only isolated pockets of resistance left. The most important one of these was Berlin itself. Here in a concrete bunker in the grounds of the Chancellory, Hitler had

**Figure 23-3.** Conference at Yalta. (left to right) Churchill, Roosevelt, Stalin. U.S. Army photograph.

gathered his few remaining minions around him and demanded that they, and all Germans, should give up their lives rather than surrender to the hated enemy. As Soviet tanks rumbled through the devastated streets of the city, The Fuehrer and his wife, Eva Braun, committed suicide on April 30. Others either followed suit or hastily fled the burning ruins of Hitler's "Thousand-Year Reich." Mussolini had been killed by Italian partisans just a few days before the German army in Italy surrendered (April 29). On May 8, 1945, Germany surrendered unconditionally to the allies and an uneasy peace settled once more on Europe. Unfortunately the war in Asia continued.

### The War in Asia

Japanese militancy and expansionism precipitated World War II in Asia just as German and Italian aggressions did in Europe. The Japanese partially justified their aggressions on the grounds of economic necessity and the need for living space. But political power and domination in Asia were at least equally important motivations among the military clique that had taken control of Japan in the thirties. As we have seen, these leaders had a clear-cut vision of a Japanese dominated Asia, to be euphemistically called the "Southeast Asia Co-Prosperity Sphere." They had begun to implement this plan with the takeover of Manchuria in 1931 and the invasion of China in 1937. Also in 1937 they had bolstered their strength by joining their fascist fellow-aggres-

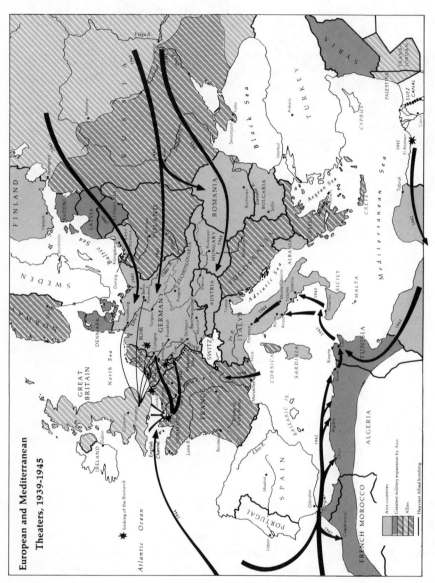

European and Mediterranean
Theaters, 1939–1945

**Figure 23-4.**

sors, Germany and Italy, in the Anti-Comintern Pact. But their ambitions for further expansion were still blocked by the presence of the Western powers in southeast Asia. Even though the outbreak of war in Europe in 1939 might have eliminated Britain, France, and Holland as effective barriers to this expansion, one large obstacle still remained —the United States.

**Pearl Harbor.** Driven by their desperate need for the raw materials (especially oil, metals, and rubber) of Southeast Asia, and inflated by fanatical chauvinism and previous military success, the leaders of Japan decided on a great gamble. They would attempt to destroy or cripple American naval power in the Far East, thus clearing the way for the fulfillment of their imperial goals. They chose to believe, as did Hitler and Mussolini, that soft, decadent America would not prove to be a formidable adversary. On December 7, 1941, while Japanese envoys were in Washington discussing ways of improving relations with the United States, the Japanese government launched its devastating, carrier-based air attack on Pearl Harbor, the center of American naval operations in the Pacific. Apparently the attack came as a complete surprise to both the government of the United States and its commanders in Hawaii. Few planes were able to get off the ground to provide air protection for the unprepared "sitting ducks" in the harbor. Almost half the Pacific fleet was permanently or temporarily put out of action within one hour.

In short-range terms the attack was clearly a triumph for Japan and a serious blow to the United States. But it succeeded in doing what previous years of Axis depredations had been unable to do. It finally awakened the American people from an isolationistic complacency that had helped to make possible the tragedies of Manchuria, Ethiopia, Czechoslovakia, and Pearl Harbor. It finally and unequivocally aligned the full resources of the United States against the Axis powers. On December 8, America declared war on Japan, followed by Britain and the Dominions, China, the European governments in exile, and the central American republics, Three days later Germany and Italy declared war on the United States. By January, 1942, a total of twenty-six governments had pledged to support the principles of the Atlantic Charter and to stand united against the aggressor nations for the duration of the conflict.

**Blitzkreig in Asia.** The height of Japanese ascendancy in Asia came during the first six months after Pearl Harbor, while the Pacific fleet was being rebuilt and before American mobilization could become effective. The speed, scope, and success of Japanese expansion in this period was incredible, even to many Japanese, and certainly frightening to the Allies. They had taken the islands of Wake, Guam, and Hong Kong by the end of December. Vichy French Indo-China and Thailand surrendered to them without a fight. In the months of December and January they pushed through the supposedly impenetrable jungles of the Malay Peninsula and forced the capitulation by February 15 of the supposedly impregnable, and very strategic, British Crown Colony of Singapore. Between January and March, they overran most of the islands in the Dutch East Indies and were threateningly close to Australia and New Zealand. Despite the stubborn resistance of outmanned American forces under Generals MacArthur and Wainwright at Bataan and Corregidor, all of the Philippines passed into their hands between January and May. Thrusting into Burma, they defeated a British-Indian army under General Alexander and an American-Chinese army under General Stilwell and cut the so-called Burma Road which had been the only route for the transport of vital Allied supplies to Chiang Kai-shek in China. By the middle of May they held all of Burma and were poised on the frontier of India. In June, they occupied Attu and Kiska in the Aleutian Islands, pointing toward Alaska.

**The New Order.** Whether the Japanese could or would have expanded this huge new empire further, whether they could or would have been able to hold their New Order together with wisdom and benevolence rather than force, we will never know. We do know that in the short period she had control of these vast new resources and populations she did not use them well. Arrogance, exploitation, corruption, and inefficiency often marred Japanese colonial administration. Nor did the Japanese masses themselves profit much from their new role as "masters of Asia."

**The Allies Fight Back.** We do not know how she would have managed her empire in the long run because there was to be no long run for the Co-Prosperity Sphere. In mid-1942, when Japan's power seemed unassailable, two events occurred that marked the turning of the tide of war in Asia, just as Stalingrad had marked it in Europe. In May, an American naval victory in the Coral Sea checked the Nipponese advance southward, and in June, at Midway, another triumph for the refurbished American fleet halted the Japanese eastward advance. After these setbacks Japan never again mounted a sustained offensive against the Allies, and the war resolved itself into a series of grim and bloody island-hopping joint operations, carried out primarily by United States naval and military forces. Admiral Chester Nimitz was commander-in-chief of all American forces in the Pacific. Admiral (Bull) Halsey was in charge of naval operations, and General Douglas MacArthur was army chief. Each successful insular compaign moved the Allies closer to the Japanese home islands: The first, as well as the longest and most costly was Guadalcanal in the Solomons (August, 1942–February, 1943); it was followed by the Battle of the Bismarck Sea (March, 1943); Tarawa

(November, 1943); Saipan (June, 1944); Guam (August, 1944); Iwo Jima (February–March, 1945); Okinawa (April–June, 1945).

In October, 1944, the greatest naval battle in history was joined between the main bodies of the American and Japanese fleets in Leyte Gulf in the Philippines. It resulted in a resounding American victory, the virtual end of Japanese naval power, and the successful beginning of United States reoccupation of the Philippines. General MacArthur presided over the final drive to take Manila between January and March of 1945. At about the same time British armies had moved into Burma from India and had reopened the Burma Road, enabling larger amounts of supplies to reach the Nationalist Chinese in Chunking. It was hoped that Chiang would finally open a major offensive against the Japanese, but both he and Mao were conserving their forces for a long anticipated struggle against one another after the Japanese withdrawal.

**The Allies Close in.**   A few carrier-based light bombing attacks had been made on Japan earlier in the war simply for their psychological effect. But the capture of Okinawa and Iwo Jima just a few hundred miles south of Japan permitted the intensification of constant land-based, heavy bomber strikes at the home islands. These raids were devastating; they were aimed against Japan's concentrated industrial areas and her densely populated paper and wood cities. Loss of life, surprisingly, was not great but by early 1945, 5 million people were homeless, supply systems were disrupted, food was scarce, and morale rapidly declining. Still, the nation showed no signs of breaking or yielding.

**The Bomb.**   When President Roosevelt died in April he left his successor, Harry Truman, with the heavy responsibility of ending the war and bringing peace to a war-weary world. He also left Truman with the awesome secret of the atomic bomb, which a group of American scientists had been laboring to perfect since 1940, under the code name "Manhattan Project." In July, 1945, the first test bomb was successfully exploded in the New Mexico desert and President Truman now had to decide whether or not to use it to foreshorten the Asian war. His military advisers indicated that it might cost 1 million American lives to storm the Japanese home islands with traditional weapons. In the light of this projected casualty report the President decided that the atomic weapon would have to be used.

**Victory in Asia.**   In July, the members of the Potsdam Conference issued an ultimatum for the immediate surrender or "complete and utter destruction" of Japan. Leaflets were dropped over the islands and unofficial contacts were made with the Japanese government expressing the same warning as the Potsdam declaration. When, by

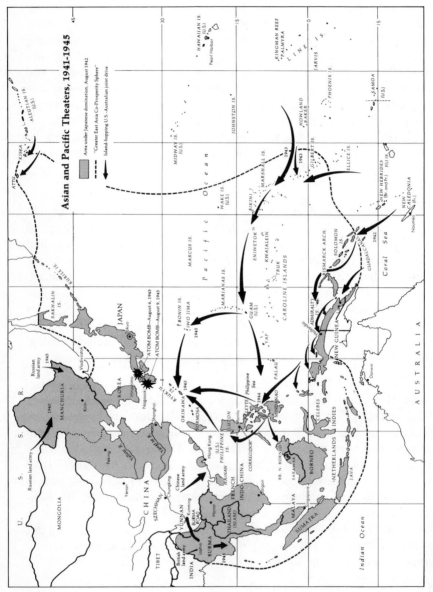

**Figure 23-5.**

August 6, no peace overtures had been received, a bomb was released over the unfortunate city of Hiroshima. In the elemental explosion that followed 70,000 to 80,000 lives were lost and the city was leveled. On August 8, Russia entered the war against Japan, fulfilling her promise at Yalta and, not incidentally, capitalizing on Allied territorial concessions made to her at Yalta. Still no capitulation came from Tokyo, and on August 9 a second bomb was loosed on the naval base of Nagasaki, destroying it and killing some 50,000 persons. Finally bowing to grim reality, the Japanese government accepted the Potsdam ultimatum on August 10. On September 2, 1945, aboard the battleship Missouri in Tokyo Bay, the formal surrender document was signed, ending World War II six years to the day from which it began.

### The Peace Treaties

No systematic set of peace treaties, like the Paris Peace System, has ever been drawn up between all the Allied powers and all the Axis powers. Immediate and continuing Soviet-American cold war differences have blocked such a development. The United States did not sign an official treaty with Japan until 1951 and Russia has still not done so. Pacts with Italy, Finland, Hungary, Rumania, and Bulgaria were ratified by 1947, but none was concluded with Austria until the termination of Allied occupation of that country in 1955. And, because of her East-West cold war split, no treaty has yet been signed by the Allies with Germany.

### Summary

The causes of World War II go back at least as far as World War I. They summarize the melancholy history of the interwar years: the failure of the Paris peace settlement, worldwide economic and social instability, the militant nationalism of the totalitarian powers, and the inability of the democracies to unite against totalitarian aggression. The war itself has been called a "total war" because it was directed against civilians as well as soldiers, minds as well as bodies, and also because its destructive force was so enormous. It has been estimated that some 50 million people lost their lives during the course of the conflict and that almost two-thirds of these were civilians. Thus the total loss of human life was twice as great as that in World War I. In monetary terms, World War II cost over three trillion dollars, or ten times the price of World War I. The ultimate material argument against any future war may well lie within these grim statistics. Certainly they contain many keys to an understanding of the immediate postwar world.

# Cold War, Culture, and Change

The Second World War brought even more terrible devastation and dislocation to Europe than World War I. In 1945 much of the continent lay in ruins again, seemingly a grim and final fulfillment of Oswald Spengler's prophecy concerning the *Decline of the West* (published during World War I). But this time Asia and Africa were also deeply affected, not only by the destructive force of the conflict, but by the fact that Europe's weakness enabled them finally to slip the bonds of colonialism and begin to pursue their own destinies.

The war also destroyed the old European balance of power and brought about the emergence of the United States and the Soviet Union as the two dominant world "superpowers." The ideological rivalry between them led, in turn, to the formation of two conflicting power blocs and a consequent three decades of tension, which we have called the "Cold War." Russia dominated the "Communist Bloc" nations of Eastern Europe and China, while the United States led the "Anti-Communist Bloc," made up of most Western European and Latin American countries as well as Turkey and Greece.

There were many peoples who were not concerned with the ideologies of the Cold War struggle, or who wanted simply to remain neutral, such as Yugoslavia, India, and most of the newly independent, underdeveloped nations of Asia, Africa, and the Middle East. During the fifties these uncommitted, "third world" nations began to organize themselves and to come together to discuss their own special problems. They met first at Bandung, Indonesia, in 1955, then again at Belgrade, Yugoslavia, in 1961, at Jakarta in 1970 and in Algiers in 1973. Since the sixties, there have also been several purely Pan-African and Pan-Arabian conferences. In all of these meetings of the Afro-Asian leaders have emphasized their desire to see the end of imperialism, to have the powers recognize their political independence and their right to follow their own course to maturity. These "have-not" nations yearn for improved standards of living, and welcome economic assistance from the "have" nations but resent aid programs with political strings attached.

Another important product of the war years was the United Nations Organization, which grew out of the wartime hopes and conferences of Allied leaders. At Yalta, in January of 1945, Roosevelt, Churchill, and Stalin agreed upon a meeting of the nations united against the Axis, to be held the following April in San Francisco. Tragically, President Roosevelt died April 12 and did not live to see the accomplishment of two great goals he had labored for—the end of a world war and the beginning of a new, world government that he hoped would preserve the peace. But the San Francisco Conference took place as scheduled and produced the Charter for an international organization to be called the "United Nations."

The Charter created a structure similar to that of the ill-fated League of Nations. The central body, or General Assembly, is made up of representatives of all member nations. There were 50 members in April, 1945, and over 120 by 1970. The Assembly functions primarily as a policy making, discussion group. The Security Council is a kind of powerful executive committee of the United Nations, invested with the major responsibility of maintaining world peace and order. It consists of five permanent members (the United States, the Soviet Union, Britain, France, and China) and six rotating members, elected by the Assembly for two-year terms. The Economic and Social Council works to promote higher living standards and basic human rights for all member nations, while the Trusteeship Council was set up to administer the affairs of colonial peoples. The chief legal and judicial organ of the United Nations is the International Court of Justice, which sits at the Hague in Holland rather than at the general United Nations headquarters in New York. Taking care of the administrative business of the entire organization is the Secretariat, and its very important chief, the Secretary-General.

Whatever the ultimate dreams of the founders and supporters of the United Nations, their immediate hope was that it would serve, at least, as a center for the promotion of world understanding and the idea of collective security. They hoped that the member nations, as they talked together and worked together on economic and social assistance programs, would also learn to act together politically to check global aggression and preserve the peace. The fact that the world body has seldom, if ever, acted with unity or effectiveness in a political crisis is due not to any particular defect in its organization but primarily to the refusal of member nations to yield any degree of their national sovereignty to the common interest. This narrow nationalism is reflected in the veto power of the five permanent members on the Security Council. It is also reflected in the ineffective enforcement system of the United Nations, in the frequent financial problems it suffers, and in the formation of power blocs within the body paralleling those in the outside world. One of the burning issues of our postwar period is whether the "one world" concept, represented ideally in the United Nations, can prevail over the long-entrenched tradition of "many warring worlds."

## The Americas

### The United States

**The Complacent Fifties.** The United States came out of World War II as the greatest power in the world—and her people were aware of that fact and reveled in it. Demobilization was carried out amazingly quickly (perhaps too quickly) and smoothly. Factory and farm continued to pour out goods to meet the enormous pent-up demand of "home-front" citizens and veterans hungry for consumer items. The economy boomed and a larger percentage of Americans began to know affluence than had ever known it before. The generation that had passed through the depression of the thirties and the war of the early forties was more than ready to accept the prosperity, comfort, and stability of the late forties and the fifties. They liked the material things they were finally able to afford. They felt good about the system that had provided these things and which had made America the first nation in the world. They knew there were some imperfections in the system but they did not worry about them. The mood of Americans in the first postwar decade was clearly conformist rather than reformist.

**The Security Conscious Fifties.**   They quietly, and rather guiltily, come to terms with the new Keynesian economic approach, which derived from the English economist John Keynes and had been incorporated into the New Deal programs of Roosevelt in the thirties. The New Deal tendencies toward big government regulationism, deficit spending, social welfare, higher taxes, and a mounting national debt had come to mean economic security. They reelected Truman in an upset victory over Thomas E. Dewey in 1948, partially because he perpetuated these policies in his Fair Deal program, and partially because he was a comfortable man with a common touch. In the fifties, they twice elected General Eisenhower over the scintillating Adlai Stevenson probably because "Ike" was a warm kind of "father figure." He symbolized for them wartime victory, conformity, and security, and despite his chance Republicanism, he deviated little from the ideals of New Deal economic liberalism.

**The United States as a World Leader.**   Truman and Eisenhower also perfectly represented the views of a majority of the American people in the area of foreign affairs. During the war the nation had decisively swung away from its traditional policy of isolationism, and had enthusiastically accepted its role as a world leader. It joined the United Nations, which it had also helped to create. But when it became clear that the United Nations could not cope with the postwar belligerence of Communist Russia, the United States assumed leadership of what came to be called the Anti-Communist Bloc. The principles of international cooperation and collective security, which had been anathema to her between the wars, became the guiding lights of her postwar foreign policy.

**Military Alliances.**   She played the major role in establishing various regional military alliances aimed at checking Communist aggression globally. In an effort to shore up Pan-American unity she reconstituted the Organization of American States in 1948. In 1949, the Truman Administration initiated the most effective of these military alliances, the North Atlantic Treaty Organization (NATO), made up of the United States and the Anti-Communist Bloc nations of Europe. In 1954, the Eisenhower administration helped fashion the less effective Southeast Asia Treaty Organization (SEATO), including, besides the United States, Australia, New Zealand, the Philippines, Thailand, Britain, and France. And, in 1958, Eisenhower put together the relatively ineffective Central Treaty Organization (CENTO) consisting of the Middle Eastern nations—Turkey, Iran, and Pakistan.

**Economic Aid Programs.**　Postwar American participation in world affairs did not stop with military alliances. It also took the form of extensive foreign aid programs. The Truman Doctrine of 1946 bolstered the economies and defenses of Communist-threatened Greece and Turkey and, in a sense, marked the beginning of Western Cold War resistance. The Marshall Plan (European Recovery Program) of 1948 was the most ambitious and successful foreign aid project in history. It proffered economic support to any needy European nation that would agree to help itself. By the middle fifties, seventeen billion dollars had been spent to rebuild Western European economies and undercut the growing power of indigenous Communist party groups. The Eisenhower Doctrine of 1957 extended aid to any Middle Eastern country that indicated a determination to resist the mounting Soviet pressures there. In 1960, President Kennedy launched two foreign aid projects—the Alliance for Progress and the Peace Corps. The Alliance for Progress was cast in the traditional mold but sought to appease Latin American peoples who were resentful that the United States had neglected them in favor of more distant friends and, even, former enemies. The Peace Corps, however, was an innovative experiment in combining assistance with popular diplomacy. Ordinary Americans with special skills were recruited to go abroad to teach these skills at the "grass-roots" level in the underdeveloped countries of the world.

**Since the Fifties.**　By the late 1950s important changes were beginning to take place in America and elsewhere. We do not know all the reasons for the changes but we can guess at some of them: a new generation questioning the values of the parent generation; the parent generation, bored with affluence, questioning its own values; broader horizons and rising expectations due to the spread of affluence and knowledge; Soviet and Cold War shocks to Western ideological complacency. Whatever the reasons, the period since the fifties has been a time of tremendously accelerated change: a time of self-examination rather than self-satisfaction or self-indulgence—a time of mounting discontent and dissatisfaction with "things as they are." In the United States and, to some degree, in most nations that have enjoyed industrial prosperity, there has been a reaction against the materialism, standardization, and dehumanization of the industrial "affluent society."

*Attacks on "The System."*    We do not know how deep the disaffection is nor how long it will last. We do know that it was first expressed by youthful student groups at Berkeley and New York (or Paris and Tokyo) and that it has since spread to other age groups and interest groups. The new movement has sometimes challenged "The System" as a whole and all of its fundamental values. Or, it has attacked particular societal defects, such as environmental spoilation, urban congestion and squalor, economic and civil rights inequities, racial inequality, educational backwardness, and war. It has also lashed out at national leadership ("The Establishment") and its alleged corruption of government and law.

*"The System" Responds.*    Despite widespread public resistance or apathy, and many failures, this new reformist spirit has had many positive effects on American (and world) society since the fifties. It helped produce the forward-looking and challenging leadership of John F. Kennedy who said in his inaugural address (1961): "Do not ask what your country can do for you. Ask, rather what you can do for your country." During Kennedy's "New Frontier" administration the Peace Corps was created, the "man-on-the-moon" program launched, and the first nuclear test-ban signed. Also, partially as a result of reformist pressures, the "Great Society" administrations of Lyndon B. Johnson (1963–1968) established the first federal Department of Housing and Urban Development; pushed through the most comprehensive civil rights and voting rights safeguards in our history; and allocated billions of dollars for educational reform, for medical assistance to the aged, and for "all-out war on poverty."

*Cold War and Vietnam.*    These administrative programs failed to appease many critics of "The System," and the disaffection spread, expressing itself in various ways, from riots, rallies, boycotts, and sit-ins to "free sex," drug use, and mysticism. In the early sixties, this protest generally focused on economic and racial inequities and civil rights questions, with lesser emphasis on war. But after 1964 a sharp shift occurred. President Johnson's hopeful antipoverty and civil rights enactments, on the one hand, and his marked intensification of the Vietnamese War, on the other, swung the heavy weight of protest in the latter sixties against the Cold War in general and against the Vietnam War in particular. Reacting to the increasingly violent antiwar sentiment (and to the widening Sino-Soviet split), President Richard M. Nixon, between 1969 and 1973, took several important actions which it was hoped would ease world tensions and finally wind down the Cold War. In February of 1972 he

**Figure 24-1.** 1965 march on Washington.

made an unprecedented, goodwill tour to Red China. In May of the same
year he signed an agreement with the Soviet Union limiting the nuclear
arms buildup between the two countries. And in January, 1973, he effected
a formal cease-fire in Vietnam and ordered the withdrawal of all American
combat troops from that country, thus ending over a decade of costly,
divisive strife for the United States. It is interesting to wonder whether
recent events such as these will be seen by future historians as marking
a terminal stage of the Cold War and the beginning of a more stable era
for the United States and the world, or, simply as the beginning of a new
phase of the conflict.

One thing seemed certain about the United States in the postwar
period. Whatever it did (right or wrong) had a marked impact on the
rest of the world. It has been the pacesetter or bellwether for peoples
from Rio and Paris to Istanbul and Saigon. As one European writer put it
"America is our model, for better or worse. What happens there, we find,
comes here later."

### Canada

**Postwar Condition.** Canada entered the war against the Axis immediately after Britain, and contributed valiantly to the Allied cause
throughout the European theatre. Although her losses in manpower were

considerable in relation to her population, she profited economically from the war in the same way as the United States. Her secure farms and factories expanded to meet increased wartime demands, and her economy has generally remained healthy through the postwar decades. Other than special Commonwealth trade relations, her ties with Britain are now purely sentimental. Whether she likes it or not, she is today more clearly in the American orbit than in the British and that is why she is discussed in this "Postwar" chapter under the The Americas rather than the British Commonwealth. Her economy is locked in many ways into that of the United States and her cultural patterns become increasingly American—which is to say "modern" or "industrial"—as the years go by. Her political system is still federal, like that of the United States but parliamentary like Britain's. Like both, she is becoming rapidly a social welfare state. Since the war, her foreign policy has closely paralleled that of the United States but has been less frenetically anti-Communist and very carefully independent.

**Problems.**  Her problems remain basically the same as they were prior to the war. She has vast territories (larger than the United States) and rich resources but too few people (20 million) and too little capital with which to exploit them. She could encourage more immigration and capital from south of the border but she fears being engulfed. She wants to be independently Canadian and not an American satellite. Of course, many residents in congested urban areas like New York or Los Angeles might consider the limited population and the wide open spaces of Canada not a problem, but a blessing. Canada's only serious sociopolitical problem today would seem to be the small but determined group of French-Canadian nationals who have been agitating for years to split Quebec from Canada and make it a separate French nation. Charles de Gaulle offended the Canadian government deeply when, on a visit to Canada in the sixties, he seemed to give encouragement to this separatist faction.

### Latin America

**Postwar Conditions.**  All Latin American countries ultimately severed relations with the Axis powers during World War II, but only about half of them did so before 1943 and several of them did not act until 1945. Few of them actually participated militarily in the conflict, so the war changed them little. Their economies remained desperately weak. Most of them still had no industry and a specialized one-crop agricultural system which left them totally at the mercy of nature and the world market. Only a small minority, like Mexico, Chile, and Uruguay, have made any appreciable economic or industrial progress. The wealthy, landholding, aristocratic few dominate and exploit the abysmally poor masses who often live in animal squalor. To add to their difficulties, population growth in the Latin Americas during the postwar years has been accelerating faster than in any other area of the globe. Average life expectancy is presently about forty years.

**Economies.** They suffer from chronic and critical economic need and, in the forties and fifties, began to express sharp resentment that the United States was neglecting their wants in favor of more distant peoples in Europe and Asia. Responding to this justified criticism, President Kennedy created the Alliance for Progress, in 1961, as a kind of Marshall Plan for our southern neighbors. Billions of dollars in aid have been funneled into Central and South America since that time with discouragingly little effect. Some of it is siphoned off for personal use by the avaricious ruling classes while the rest of it seems too little to meet the fast rising needs of the masses. Greed and need seem to be running ahead of supply in Latin America.

**Politics.** Latin American governments are still generally oppressive tyrannies, controlled by unenlightened, military juntas or strong-man dictators like the former "Papa Doc" Duvalier of Haiti, or Juan Batista of Cuba. Changes of government occur frequently, and usually by revolution or military *coup*, seldom through democratic elections. Less than half a dozen countries have enjoyed continuously elective governments during the post-war period. Mexico is one of these rare states. And Chile was another until 1973, when the legitimately elected administration of Marxist Salvador Allende, was toppled in a violent military coup.

**Foreign Affairs.** During the Cold War, the Latin American nations have been considered to be within the Anti-Communist Bloc and members of the initially Anti-Communist Organization of American States. However, in recent years, as bloc allegiances have been loosening, many of these states are becoming more independent and neutralist. A few, like Chile, Guyana, and Cuba, have actually experimented with Marxism but of these, only Cuba has posed a threat to Western Hemisphere security. In 1959, black-bearded Fidel Castro with a hardy guerrilla army seized power from dictator Batista and set up his own Communist dictatorship in Cuba. He soon began to receive Soviet arms and to make himself the center for potential Communist expansion throughout the Americas. Castro used a clumsy, abortive, CIA-backed attack against Cuba (the Bay of Pigs, 1961) as an excuse to request more military support from Russia. Soviet leader Nikita Khrushchev saw this as a rare opportunity to breach pan-American solidarity and strike a decisive blow for "his side" in the Cold War. He began a missile build-up in Cuba only ninety miles away

**Figure 24-2.** Castro, 1959.

from the Florida coast. Viewing this action as a vital threat to American security, President Kennedy risked possible war with the Soviet Union when, in October, 1962, he proclaimed an aerial and naval blockade against all offensive weapons being shipped into the island. To the great relief of an anxious world, Khrushchev backed off and a face-saving compromise was struck between the two powers ending one of the most critical United States–Soviet encounters of the Cold War. Disgusted with Russian "weakness," Castro tried a brief romance with Red China which proved unsatisfactory to both. He has perhaps failed as a global "wheeler-dealer" but he, and other leaders, have been very important in stirring up a rising tide of popular discontent among the long-suffering masses of Latin America. Also, justifiably or not, his beard, his garb, and his avowed revolutionary principles became rallying symbols in the sixties for disenchanted, aspiring young rebels everywhere.

### Europe

#### The Soviet Union and Eastern Europe
The Soviet Union emerged from World War II as one of the two great powers. She claimed the largest army in the world and an empire more extensive even than that of Czarist Russia in 1914. Her empire, with

its dependencies, stretched from the Kuriles, north Sakhalin, and North Korea in Asia to central Germany in Europe.

**East Europe Under Stalin.** As her Red Armies rolled westward across Europe in the latter months of the war they left behind them Communist, puppet governments in each occupied nation. After the war, Stalin refused to permit free democratic elections in these countries, as he had pledged at Yalta, and he exploited and stripped them to help rebuild the Soviet economy. Between 1944 and 1948, he made Poland, Hungary, Albania, Rumania, Bulgaria, East Germany, and Czechoslovakia "satellite" nations of the USSR. He dropped an "Iron Curtain" of security around them isolating them from the West, and, until his death, he completely dominated this East European "Communist Bloc." Only a few areas of eastern Europe evaded his grasp. Due to a combination of Western support and determined nationalist opposition, Finland, Austria, West Berlin, Yugoslavia, and Greece were able to remain unincorporated and independent of Russian control. Particularly significant were the resistance of West Berlin and Yugoslavia.

After the war the only Communist leader who resisted Soviet domination was Josip Broz Tito of Yugoslavia. With a small but effective guerrilla army behind him, Tito dared to defy Stalin and set up an independent, national Communist regime, thus establishing a dangerous precedent for the future. Enraged by this "heresy," Stalin expelled Tito from the Party in 1948 but was never able to break his power in Yugoslavia nor discourage him from developing friendly relations with the West. Yugoslavia was perhaps the first of the "uncommitted" nations.

**The Berlin Crisis.** The other thorn in Stalin's side was the western part of the city of Berlin which was in the middle of the Soviet occupation zone of East Germany and supplied by autobahn (freeway) from West Germany. By the Potsdam Agreement, it had been left under the joint control of the Western Allies—Britain, France, and the United States. But Stalin was never happy about this bustling Western "showcase" in his backyard, and in 1948 he used it as the stage for his first serious challenge to Western resolve in Europe. He set up a blockade around West Berlin to starve it out, and left the Allies, seemingly, with only two alternatives: either to give up Berlin or strike at the Soviet blockade and risk war. He believed they would not want to risk war over Berlin any more than they had wanted to risk it over Czechoslovakia in 1938. Fortunately they did not have to make that unhappy choice. They relieved the city by airlifting materials in, and finally forced Stalin to call off the blockade. The Berlin Crisis itself had ended, but it had several important consequences.

*Results of Berlin.* Perhaps, most important, it indicated to Stalin that the democracies would stand firm against aggression as they had not done in the thirties. It also brought about a formalization of the division of Germany. West Germany became the separate and independent Federal Republic of Germany in May of 1949 and East Germany became the separate, but still *de*pendent, Democratic Republic of Germany five months later. The failure of the United Nations to act in the Berlin crisis and the threat of future Cold War clashes in Europe gave birth to the North Atlantic Treaty Organization in the West and its Soviet counterpart in the East—the Warsaw Pact alliance. Stalin also tried to strengthen his Eastern bloc nations by establishing a Communist economic aid program, or Comecon, to counterbalance the Marshall Plan. Cold War rivalry was further intensified after 1949 when Russia began to develop nuclear armaments. By the early fifties Stalin had, with more or less success, endeavored to extend Russian influence and the Communist creed into most corners of the globe. Exploiting economic malaise, popular discontent, and native nationalist movements, he pursued his Cold War agitations not only directly, as in Eastern Europe, but indirectly, in such areas as Western Europe, the Middle East (Afghanistan and Iran), Indochina, and China itself.

**Soviet Postwar Economy.** World War II had not only brought great power to the Soviet Union but it had brought great destruction as well. Some twenty million of her people had died, some twenty-five million were made homeless, as the war devastated her land. Agricultural and industrial production had been cut by one-quarter to one-half since 1940. So Stalin's major domestic concern in the postwar period was to rebuild shattered Russia physically and economically. This time the Soviet people had two advantages they had not had in the twenties and thirties. First, they did not have to build "from scratch" because there were thriving farms and factories east of the Urals which had escaped the pounding of the Wehrmacht and Luftwaffe. Second, they brought with them to this vast new reconstruction project all the experience they had gained working under pressure during the earlier Five Year periods. Once again, with fantastic discipline and crusading zeal, they carried through two new, gargantuan Five Year Plans between 1945 and 1955. The emphasis was still on heavy machine industry and armaments rather than on consumer goods but some progress was made in solving the drastic housing shortage, and increasing food production. Within one decade, output in most industries shot up as much as fifty to one hundred percent.

**Soviet Postwar Politics.** Politically, the war stimulated in the Russian people a strong nationalist sentiment and a certain reverence for the Soviet system and for "the organizer of victory," Josef Stalin. When Stalin told the people that they had won the war unaided, that Slavic, Great Russian culture was superior to all others and that most important inventions (like the steam engine and the airplane) had originated in Russia, they were ready to believe him. When he told them that constant labor, self-sacrifice, and unquestioning obedience to the state would ultimately create a workers' paradise and protect Russia from capitalist encirclement, they generally accepted his word. When he closed off Russia from the West and began an intensive campaign to smother all opposition and force complete conformity—in science and the arts as well as in politics and economics—to the Stalinist "Party line," a majority of the people apparently went along with him. When he died in 1953, a sick, psychotic man, he was certainly feared by many but sincerely mourned by most Russians as the personification of their new national greatness.

**The Soviet World Since Stalin.** Stalin's death had deep effects both inside and outside the Soviet Union. It resulted in a power struggle similar to that which had taken place after the death of Lenin, only this time there were more than two potential contenders. The notorious Lavrenti Beria, head of the Soviet secret police, made the first bid, but was quickly dispatched by zealous competitors. Next Georgi Malenkov, heir-apparent to Stalin, took power for a few months but "resigned" in 1954, confessing to "serious inadequacies." Then Premier Nicolai Bulganin and First Party Secretary, Nikita Khrushchev shared leadership until 1956, when Khrushchev made his dramatic and successful solo move for supremacy. At the Twentieth Party Congress in 1956 he delivered a speech in which he boldly and mercilessly attacked the towering image of Stalin and his "cult of personality" and declared him to be, not a godlike leader, but a power-hungry, vicious monster. This speech not only helped make Khrushchev the focus of a new leadership but it shook the very foundations of the Soviet-Communist system around the world. It brought confusion and doubt to the minds of many of the Party faithful and opened up a serious Stalin-Khrushchev schism, which still exists. The round, human, ebullient Khrushchev held power until October of 1964 when he was forced into retirement by a new "collective leadership" headed by First Party Secretary Leonid Brezhnev, Premier Alexei Kosygin, and President Nicolai Podgorny. These men seem to be a new breed of "managers" and specialists—still authoritarian, but more pragmatic and less political and doctrinaire.

**Current Domestic Trends.** Since the death of Stalin there have been many subtle changes in Soviet domestic affairs. The central government still works through the Five Year Plans to achieve ambitious production goals and it still strives to surpass the production levels of capitalist countries. But since the sixties, under the new "Market Socialism" of Liberman, there has been a degree of decentralization and more attention has been paid to local management, the profit motive, and customer

demand. Consumer goods and housing have been increasingly emphasized over heavy industry. Supermarkets, night clubs, and highrise apart-
ment buildings are beginning to appear. In the social and intellectual
sphere a bit more freedom and criticism is permitted. The secret police
are not so much in evidence. There has been some liberalization in education and Soviet youth has begun to express itself in a kind of pale
reflection of the youth rebellion in the Western world. Also, despite
continued censorship, a critical intelligentsia has reemerged again in the
Soviet Union and is particularly well represented by its novelists, like
Pasternak (*Dr. Zhivago*) and Solzhenitsyn (*A Day in the Life of Ivan
Denisovitch*), or its poets, like Yevtushenko and Sinyavsky. Best known
to the West, and unfortunately most closely tied into the Cold War competition, have been Russia's recent great achievements in nuclear physics
and space flights (for example, Sputnik, in 1957).

**Current Soviet Foreign Policies.** Russia's leaders since 1953 have
seemed to pursue the same Cold War goals as Stalin: namely, to eliminate
non-Communist systems and to extend Soviet power and Communist ide-
ology everywhere in the world. Their stated methods for achieving these
goals, however, have changed. They appear to believe that full-scale war
and violent world revolution are too dangerous, and are also unnecessary
to the accomplishment of their ends. They declare that Soviet-Communist
victory can be won by economic means, ideological warfare, and constant
small brush-fire wars. They have called this approach "peaceful coexistence," and it has helped, at least indirectly, to moderate East-West Cold
War tensions by sowing seeds of disunity within the Communist camp
itself.

**Communist Bloc Schism.** One of the most important international
realities since Stalin's death has been the slow dissolution of the two great
power blocs. There are many factors that may account for the growing
slippage in the Communist bloc. (We will examine the Anti-Communist
bloc later.) The death of Stalin in itself removed a long-existent iron hand
from the political controls and perhaps created an impression of new
freedom. Certainly Khrushchev's "de-Stalinization" program caused much
questioning and scepticism about the whole Soviet system. But probably
the most critical factor was simply the mounting resentment of Communist bloc nations against Soviet exploitation. Generally, the Soviet Union
took more from her satellite nations than she gave them and maintained
control by the use of secret police and the Red Army.

### Eastern Europe
In June, 1953, the first crack in her Eastern European bloc occurred.
The workers of East Germany revolted against their miserable economic

conditions and had to be put down, finally, by Russian armored divisions. But during the remainder of the fifties East Germany's depressed citizenry defected in such large numbers to the West (200,000 per year) that Khrushchev, in 1961, was forced to build a grim wall between East and West Berlin to check the flow of fleeing emigrants through that major escape zone. East Germany is still the most closely guarded of Russia's Eastern "allies." In Poland, during the summer and fall of 1956 a series of strikes and demonstrations caused by bad working conditions and food shortages, brought the quick promise of Russian aid and greater autonomy for Poland. In 1956 also, the Hungarian people rose in frustrated fury and lashed out at their Soviet-dominated governors, driving them, and the Soviet occupation force, out of Budapest. But the Russians called in armored reinforcements and after bitter fighting (over 50,000 Hungarians lost their lives) they were able to crush the rising.

In 1961, little Albania declared her independence from the Soviet bloc and realigned herself with Red China. Rumania began to ease out from under Soviet dominance in the mid-sixties, first opening up trade relations with Western countries, then dropping her military commitments within the Warsaw Peace Alliance. Then, in 1968, an emerging Czechoslovakian independence movement was stifled by Soviet trickery and the implied threat of force. Yugoslavia has continued to walk her sovereign, uncommitted way despite the determined efforts of Khrushchev to woo her back in the early sixties. It does not speak well for the lure of Soviet Communism that during the postwar period no nation has been brought into its orbit, or held in it, without the use, or threat, of force. Despite the attempts of the Soviet Union to keep them relatively weak, unified, and dependent, the Eastern European states since the sixties have begun to achieve some degree of economic progress and political independence. The Soviet-Chinese schism and the rising prosperity and trade ambitions of Western Europe have helped to stimulate this progress and to shake the imposed unity of the "Eastern bloc."

**Soviet Success in the Third World.** Although Russia has continued to agitate in each global pocket of discontent and poverty and to encourage each nationalist movement everywhere, she has made few Cold War gains since the fifties. The people of Latin America, Africa, the Middle East, and Asia have found that her brand of Communist imperialism has no more charm than the traditional Western brand. She has gone nowhere in the Americas and Africa. She is an uneasy guest in Egypt, the Middle East, and India. And she has generally been replaced by China in the Far East. If the Communist victory in China in 1949 was Russia's greatest postwar triumph, then the widening Sino-Soviet rift since Stalin's death must be counted as Russia's greatest postwar defeat.

## Western Europe

### Postwar Debilitation

In 1945, Western Europe was almost as thoroughly shattered by the war and by the exploitive German occupation as Eastern Europe. The Second World War seemed to have completed the destructive work which the First World War had begun. Once again the Western European nations, which had dominated the world for so long, had suffered terrible physical losses in human life and material damage. Large parts of Britain, France, the Netherlands, Denmark, Norway, Germany, and Italy had been ravaged by land or by air. Their economies had again been vitally disrupted and their finances drained. Even the neutral nations, Sweden, Switzerland, Spain, Portugal, and the Irish Republic had been negatively affected by the war. Prisoner-of-war stockades and Nazi concentration camps yawned open to reveal the extent of modern man's inhumanity to man. Thousands of displaced persons wandered hopelessly across the Continent searching for food, work, lost families, and homes. Feeding on this misery, leftist political groups emerged in many countries fomenting discontent and urging overthrow of the established order. In fact, within a few months after the war, indigenous Communist factions had become the largest single political parties in both France and Italy and were rapidly gaining ground elsewhere. In 1945, then, Europe once again stood seemingly exhausted and helpless, on the verge of economic collapse and social anarchy or revolution.

### American Assistance

This time, however, the United States did not back away from the crisis of the European community. It assumed the role of responsible world leadership, as it had not done in 1919, and began vigorously to rechannel its vast energies from Anti-Fascist "hot war" to the reconstruction of Europe and Anti-Communist "cold war." As we have seen, this effort resulted in the formation of an American dominated, Anti-Communist European military alliance, called the North Atlantic Treaty Organization, and the development of crucial American economic aid programs, like the Truman and Marshall Plans and the Berlin Airlift. By the end of the forties, these projects had played an important part in stimulating economic recovery and checking the expansion of Communism in Western Europe. In fact, by the mid-fifties, production in most Western European countries was greater than it had been in 1939.

### European Recovery

America assistance was not, of course, the only factor that helped to halt the "decline of the West" and bring about the beginnings of a kind of "new Renaissance" for Europe. The native dynamism of the European peoples began to reassert itself. Responding to the desperate needs of the time and to the challenge of Soviet-American dominance, Western European nations commenced to help themselves up.

### Britain

**Political Development.** Britain voted Conservative Winston Churchill and his wartime coalition government out of office in 1945 and gave to Clement Attlee's Labour Party the first clear electoral majority in its fifty-year history. Backed by this popular mandate, Attlee proceeded to launch a socialistically inclined austerity program designed to salvage the crippled British economy. Public health and social welfare operations were expanded. The Bank of England and many industrial facilities were nationalized, wage and price controls established, the pound devalued, taxes increased, and large loans floated with the United States and the Commonwealth nations. Motivated partly by economic necessity and partly by moral conviction, the Labour government also began the final harrowing process of liquidating Britain's huge, overseas empire. The Commonwealths of Canada, Australia, New Zealand, and South Africa were, of course, already completely independent. But between 1945 and 1950, Britain gave up her remaining Middle Eastern mandates in Transjordan and Palestine and her imperial claims to India, Ceylon, and Burma in south Asia.

These severe measures, plus American and Commonwealth financial aid, stimulated British economic revival by the 1950s. But they had also made the Labour government unpopular, and in 1951 Churchill and the Conservatives were voted back into office. After Churchill's retirement in 1955 the Conservatives remained in power until 1964, under prime ministers Sir Anthony Eden, Harold Macmillan, and Sir Alec Douglas-Home. They eliminated some of the more unpopular domestic features of the Labour program but retained some nationalization and almost the entire health and social welfare system, which had become a cherished part of the British way of life. Although Churchill refused to "preside over the further liquidation of the British Empire," his successors did, and during the fifties and sixties Britain surrendered most of the rest of her holdings in Asia and Africa. Her humiliating, forced backdown at Suez in 1956 was one of the few exceptions in a generally gracious and dignified withdrawl from her centuries-old position as a great world power.

**Economic Development.** Economically, Britain was moving ahead in the late fifties, but not as rapidly as several nations on the Continent that had formed in 1957 an organization called the European Economic

Community (EEC) or the Common Market. It was made up of six states (France, West Germany, Italy, Belgium, the Netherlands, and Luxemburg) and it proved to be so effective that Britain initiated a rival European Free Trade Association (EFTA) made up of seven European nations (Britain, Norway, Sweden, Denmark, Austria, Switzerland, and Portugal). But in 1961, fearing a disruptive trade war between the two groups and desirous of bolstering its own economy, Britain sought membership in the flourishing Common Market despite objections from her fellow members of the EFTA and the Commonwealth. President de Gaulle of France, however, blocked British entrance into the EEC throughout the sixties, basically because he felt Britain would challenge French hegemony within that continental organization.

In the latter half of the sixties, a slowdown in the economy and a serious fiscal crisis forced the Labour government of Harold Wilson (1964–1970) to institute another austerity program, another devaluation of the pound, and another fruitless effort to enter the Common Market. Wilson's stringent measures helped to check the economic slippage but once again resulted in much public discontent, frequent demonstrations and strikes, and the election of Edward Heath's Conservative Party to office in 1970. By this time de Gaulle had abdicated power in France and the new French government was willing to open discussions that finally led to the admission of Britain to the Common Market in 1973. For the first time in her modern history she seemed to be locking her national interests into those of the European community instead of an overseas empire. The effects of this new orientation remain to be seen, but 1973 might mark the beginning of a new phase in British history.

### France

**The Fourth Republic.** A provisional government under the leadership of Free French hero, General Charles de Gaulle, ruled liberated France from 1944 to 1946. In 1946, a new constitution was drawn up and approved by the people establishing a Fourth French Republic similar in many ways to the weak Third Republic that had collapsed so ignominiously in 1940. It also featured a dominating but fractionated multiparty legislature and powerless presidency. The imperious de Gaulle turned his back on this weak structure and retired with disgust from public life. The Fourth Republic lasted for only twelve years and was plagued, as de Gaulle had foreseen, with many of the same problems as its unfortunate predecessor. Political parties proliferated but not even the largest of them—the Communist, Socialist, and Catholic MRP parties—were large enough to gain a parliamentary majority. Consequently governments were made up of highly volatile coalitions, often to the right of center. No less than twenty-six governments rose and fell between 1946 and 1958.

**French Recovery.** Yet despite this continuing political instability, expensive colonial wars, serious inflation, chronic budgetary and balance-of-payments deficits, strikes, and general public cynicism, French reconstruction and economic expansion during the fifties were amazingly rapid and successful. Of course, American Marshall Plan aid paved the way for this revival, but even before its introduction, enlightened French leaders like Jean Monnet and Robert Schuman began to think in terms of long-range planning and inter-European cooperation as methods for bringing about their own recovery and salvation. In 1949, they helped plant the first seed of a potential European political union with the creation of the Council of Europe, made up of most Western continental nations plus the United Kingdom, Greece, and Turkey. Fully aware of the incredible barriers in the way of ultimate European political union, they began to concentrate instead on plans for more easily and quickly realizable economic cooperation.

**Economic Cooperation.** The first fruit of their effort was the European Coal and Steel Community (ECSC) formed in 1952 and including, besides France, West Germany, Italy, Belgium, the Netherlands, and Luxemburg. So successful was this organization in its special function of integrating and improving coal and steel production and distribution that its six member nations agreed, by the Treaty of Rome in 1957, to form a broader trade and customs union called the Europeon Economic Community (EEC) or Common Market. As already noted, Britain followed suit two years later with the initiation of a separate seven-nation union called the European Free Trade Association (EFTA). These two groups, which came to be known respectively as the "Inner Six" and the "Outer Seven," lowered tariffs and improved trade conditions dramatically among their own member nations but began to create new economic problems between themselves and with other countries outside the two blocs. France and Europe are now in the process of trying to work out these conflicts. The merging of all European nations (Eastern as well as Western) in one great Continental Common Market is, of course, the most logical solution, and the entrance of Britain, Ireland, and Denmark into the European Economic Community in 1973 points the way to that solution. Whatever final form these economic cooperatives may take, they have already been notably effective in promoting European unity and progress.

**Dissolution of Empire.** One of the most debilitating and disruptive problems of France during the immediate postwar decades was the dissolution of her empire. Her demise as an imperial world power, unlike that of Britain, was generally graceless, costly, and violent. She was drained and frustrated by her long struggle (1946–1954) to hold on to Indochina against the nationalist forces of Ho Chi Minh. That bloody conflict was only brought to an end by the determination of one of the ablest premiers of the Fourth Republic, Pierre Mendès-France. In 1956, he averted serious colonial wars in French-controlled Tunisia and Morocco by granting these areas independence. This firm action alienated French nationalists and lost him the premiership, so that his abilities were not available to cope with the climactic Algerian rising that erupted in that some year. Many Frenchmen, still suffering from the humiliations of World War II and Indochina, determined to make their stand for French imperial pride in Algeria. Four ensuing French governments failed to act either to grant Algerian independence or to crush the rising tide of Algerian nationalism and, in 1958, the army in Algeria mutinied and threatened to overthrow the government in Paris.

**De Gaulle and the Fifth Republic.** This severe crisis brought Charles de Gaulle out of retirement and back to power on his own terms. He reestablished order and issued a new constitution, overwhelmingly approved by the people, which provided for a very strong president, elected by popular vote and relatively independent of the legislature. De Gaulle was, of course, the first president, holding office from 1958 to 1968. By 1962, the Gaulists had won an absolute majority in the National Assembly and had finally brought the deadly Algerian war to an end and granted that country her independence—along with all the other French colonies in Africa. Now, politically secure and freed from colonial problems, "le Grand Charles" proceeded to rebuild French power and prestige. During the sixties he brought to France the greatest prosperity and the strongest, most efficient and stable government she had known in the twentieth century. He also made France a nuclear power, built up her military forces, gave her dominance in the European Economic Community, and opened up relations with Russia and China.

**Western Bloc Schism.** However, Charles de Gaulle was first and foremost a French nationalist, and in the course of his arbitrary, self-righteous and highly independent drive to restore France, he frequently trampled on both the nationalist and internationalist sentiments of others. His actions were as decisive in beginning the breakup of the American-dominated Western bloc as were Tito's in shaking the unity of the Soviet-dominated Eastern bloc. For example, he constantly challenged American hegemony in NATO. He insisted on developing his own atomic weaponry and rejected the nuclear test ban treaty signed by the United States, Russia, and Britain in 1963. And by his veto of Britain's entry into the Common Market in 1963 he not only slowed the progress of that international body but also alienated many Britons. By the latter sixties there was a growing resentment within France itself against de Gaulle's high-handed, autocratic policies and against many, still deeply entrenched educational and class inequities in French society. In 1968, a serious outbreak of student strikes and riots in protest against "the System" convinced the aging and bitter de Gaulle to lay down once more the burdens of public life.

**Georges Pompidou.** He was replaced in the presidency by his former premier, Georges Pompidou who is less colorful but also less arrogant than de Gaulle. Pompidou has generally followed the successful domestic policies of his predecessor and has witnessed the continued growth of French prosperity within the Common Market. In foreign affairs he has remained independent but is less narrowly nationalistic and more inclined to international cooperation than de Gaulle. Improved relations with Germany and the United States, and the recent admission of Britain, Ireland, and Denmark to the EEC illustrate the point.

### West Germany

**Economic Recovery.** West Germany's postwar recovery has been more remarkable, perhaps, than that of any other country in Europe. Physically and economically shattered by the war, politically divided, and militarily occupied by the victorious allies, she reemerged within a decade as one of the most stable, productive nations on the Continent. Obviously Allied aid, and particularly the American Marshall Plan, played an important role in stimulating her recovery, but the industry of her people and the resourcefulness of her leaders must receive the final credit. After the Berlin Crisis of 1948, the East-West division of Germany was formalized with the creation of the Western German Federal Republic and the Eastern Democratic Republic.

**Political Development.** In 1949, a West German constitution was drawn up, and approved by the people, providing for a federal, parliamentary system featuring two elective legislative bodies called the *Bundestag* and the *Bundesrat,* and a prime minister, or Chancellor, responsible to the broadly representative and powerful *Bundestag.* The first postwar Chancellor, Conrad Adenauer, and his dominant Christian Democratic Union party gave West Germany firm and skillful leadership through the fifties and early sixties. In 1961, however, the party lost its majority in the *Bundestag* and both Adenauer and his successors, Ludwig Erhard and Kurt Keisinger, had to govern in coalition with the small Free Democratic party. Finally, in 1971, the Christian Democrats were ousted from power by their perennial opposition, the Social Democrats, led by the popular ex-mayor of West Berlin, Willy Brandt.

**West German Achievements.** Irrespective of the party in power, the West German people have made phenomenal progress during the past three decades. Despite the continued existence of some authoritarian Neo-Nazi sentiment, the majority seems to have abandoned the absolutist, militaristic tendencies of the past and to have accepted representative, democratic institutions as they were never able to do during the Weimar period. They also seem to have become more internationalistic in their thinking, supporting German membership in the United Nations, the Council of Europe, NATO, and the Common Market. And, of course, within the Common Market, they have again become one of the most industrially productive and prosperous peoples in the world. In 1973, their gross national product ranked third behind that of the United States and the Soviet Union, and their standard of living (according to per capita GNP) was inferior only to those of the United States, Sweden, and Denmark. They have generally enjoyed full employment during the postwar decades in spite of the constant influx of East German refugees. In fact, the only major, war-connected problem still facing the West German people in the early seventies was the problem of East Germany and the refusal of the Soviet Union and its East German satellite government to seriously discuss German reunification. Although Brandt's administration has succeeded recently in moderately improving its relationship with the Soviet Union, East and West Germany still do not even recognize one another diplomatically and the chances of reunification between them seem as unlikely today as they did in 1949.

### Italy

**Economic Recovery.** American aid and the Common Market system even succeeded in reviving war-wasted Italy and her traditionally moribund economy. By the 1960s she had developed thriving automobile, movie, and apparel industries and had become one of the major, "smart" style and tourist centers in Europe. Unfortunately, the prosperity of the industrialized northern and central areas did not extend to the chronically depressed regions of southern Italy and Sicily, nor wipe out unemployment, nor adequately raise the living standards of many expectant groups within Italian society. As a partial consequence of "too much" or "too little," economically booming postwar Italy has been plagued by social malaise and discontent, the highest rate of labor strikes in the world, the most unstable government, and the largest Communist party in Western Europe.

**Political Development.** Immediately after the war she abolished her antiquated monarchy, created a new, republican, parliamentary system, and elected to office by a clear majority the Christian Democratic party of Alcide de Gasperi. But in the twenty years between 1953 and 1973, neither de Gasperi nor any of his many successors were again able to command a majority. Governments have been created by centrist coalitions and by crisis, rising and falling with dangerous frequency. In spite of her bright new prosperity, Italy today would seem to be in need of some thoroughgoing economic, social, and political reforms.

### Other Nations of Western Europe

**Scandinavia and the Low Countries.** Most of the other Western continental nations of Europe have profited in the same way (though not necessarily to the same degree) as France, West Germany, and Italy from the combination of American aid and participation in the EEC or the EFTA. The peoples of Scandinavia, Belgium, and the Netherlands have experienced steadily rising prosperity, increased social security benefits, and stable democratic government within the framework of their traditional, constitutional monarchies. The Danes and the Swedes, in fact, enjoy the highest standard of living in Europe. Ironically, they also have the highest suicide rate in the world. The Belgians and the Dutch, like the British, have been drawn more closely into the European community since the painful loss of their rich overseas holdings in the Congo and Indonesia. All of these countries belong to the United Nations, and all except Sweden and Finland belong to NATO.

**Austria, Ireland, and Switzerland.** After the war, Austria was saved from incorporation in the Soviet bloc only by determined Allied intervention. She was saved from complete economic collapse by American aid and has since made a remarkable recovery as a member of EFTA. She is a member of the United Nations but cannot join NATO because she was pledged to neutrality by the Peace Treaty of 1954. Switzerland, that vulnerable little hub of international diplomacy and banking in the center of Europe, has chosen to continue her traditional policy of neutrality in the postwar world. To preserve this neutrality, she belongs neither to NATO nor to the United Nations. She is, however, a member of EFTA and has built herself since the war into one of the most prosperous industrial states on the Continent, while managing to maintain one of the most efficient and democratic political systems in Europe. Like Switzerland, the Irish Republic is a small, neutralist democracy but there the similarity ends. Ireland is as politically turbulent and poor as Switzerland is stable and prosperous. Perhaps her recent entry into the Common Market will strengthen her economy, but it is difficult to foresee what miracle will finally settle her incessant strife with England or the interminable Catholic-Protestant and ethnic class conflict with the Irish of Ulster.

**Spain and Portugal.**   Along with Ireland, the least prosperous nations in Europe are Spain and Portugal. Both countries are poor in natural resources and both countries have been controlled by suppressive dictatorships. The Fascist dictator Francisco Franco had ruled Spain since his victory in the Spanish Civil War in 1939. He has brought order but little reform or progress to his people. His régime has been ostracized by many countries, consequently Spain was not admitted to the United Nations till 1955 and has still not been admitted to NATO or to either of the European trading communities. The alleged Cold War need for United States air bases in Spain began to bring money and tourism into the once-isolated land and by the sixties the Spanish people were enjoying a minor economic revival. Franco has decreed that when he retires or dies there will be a restoration of the Bourbon monarchy. Portugal, like Spain, remained depressed and backward but well-ordered and peaceful under the long dictatorship (1932–1968) of the mild-mannered but iron-willed ex-economics professor, Antonio Salazar. Unlike Spain, however she was admitted to NATO and EFTA as well as to the United Nations. Portugal and Spain have been the only European nations to hold on to their African colonial possessions into the seventies. The Spanish holdings are small but Portugal still stubbornly controls the huge territories of Angola and Mozambique. Marcelo Caetano took over for the ailing Salazar in 1968 but up to this time (1973) has no notable changes in either the domestic or foreign policies of his small country.

**Summary.**   The devastation that World War II brought to the individual nations of Europe and the loss of their global empires forced them to turn to economic cooperation for survival. This economic cooperation worked so well that within two decades between 1950 and 1970 their collective GNP growth rate had surpassed even that of the United States (for example, 7.1 for West Germany compared to 3.5 for the United States in 1965) and their share of the world's gold supply, roughly within that same period, had increased from about 10 to 45 percent while the American supply had dropped from 70 to 40 percent. A burning question of the seventies will be whether this profitable cooperation is a temporary phenomenon, which will break down before reemerging nationalisms, or whether economic cooperation may ultimately become actual political union, as Robert Schuman anticipated. If such an evolution should take place, a prototype institution has already been set up to accommodate it in Strasbourg. It is called the Council of Europe, and hopefully, one day it will include representatives of all the states of a truly united Europe.

### Asia

#### China

**Civil War.** World War II brought only a temporary and uneasy truce in the Civil War between the Nationalist forces of Chiang Kai-shek and the Communist cadres of Mao Tse-tung. In fact, the conflict with Japan had not yet officially ended when Soviet invasion armies in Manchuria handed over to Mao huge caches of surrendered Japanese arms to be used against the Nationalists. Chiang was dismayed by this transaction but he, in turn, had spent the last years of the war building up his own armies and his own stores of military equipment from supplies sent by the United States for use against Japan. He never used them against the Japanese but instead turned them northward, in 1945, in an attack designed to finally wipe out the Communist threat to his regime. Ignoring the requests of American envoy George Marshall to establish a new united front with the Communists and to restore peace to China, Chiang continued to drive relentlessly into Maoist North China. Within a year, his ravaging armies had occupied much territory but had failed to destroy, or even seriously hurt, the shrewdly deployed forces of Mao. And in 1947, Mao launched a brilliantly successful counter-offensive against the now discredited and spent Nationalists. By 1949, the Red Armies of General Lin Piao had thoroughly defeated the Nationalists and had driven hundreds of thousands of them to seek refuge on the large offshore island of Taiwan, or Formosa. Chiang and his followers have remained "holed up" on that island kingdom since 1949, protected by the American fleet and nourishing themselves on the belief that they will one day return to mainland China and re-establish themselves as the only true government of the Chinese people.

**Political Development.** Setting up his capital in Peiping, Mao immediately declared the creation of a new Communist People's Republic of China, based on the three principles of "class struggle," "party rule," and "democratic centralism." A political structure was developed, similar to that of the Soviet Union, with a large National People's Congress that chooses a Premier, or Chairman, and an administrative State Council. Also, as in the Soviet Union, the real power center in the state is not in this formal government apparatus at all but is in the Communist party organization itself, and more specifically, in the hands of party Chairman Mao Tse-tung and the members of his Politburo. Chairman

Mao quickly and forcefully established absolute, centralized controls over both the party and the people. Millions of politically dissident "enemies of the people" were liquidated, imprisoned, or placed in labor camps during the first years of the regime. Education was opened to the masses of the Chinese people for the first time in their history, but it featured perhaps the most thorough mass regimentation and indoctrination the world has ever seen. Each citizen is constantly exposed to the Marxist gospel as interpreted by Chairman Mao. A kind of Confucian syle compendium of Maoist-Marxian wisdom, called the "Little Red Book," is required reading throughout China. People who have deviated from the Communist faith, or party line, are expected to confess all in public "self-criticism" sessions. The arts and sciences are confined to what will serve the state, to what is called "socialist realism." Initiative and creativity are discouraged and traditional religious faiths are smothered. "Thought control" and a "religious" faith in the new system are apparently the aims of China's leaders, and however restrictive Mao's "Red Revolution" has been in terms of individual freedom, it seems to have succeeded in affecting a dedication and unity among the Chinese people which has never existed before and which Chiang's "Nationalist Revolution" certainly did not achieve.

**Economic Development.**   Communist collectivism has also effected great changes in the economic sphere. With initial Soviet aid and following the Soviet pattern, sweeping programs of land confiscation and redistribution were carried out and state farms and collectives set up. Businesses and banks were nationalized and a Five Year Plan was instituted in 1953 to accelerate both agricultural and industrial production. The moderate success of the first plan encouraged the government to undertake a much more ambitious and radical second plan, in 1958, which they hoped would bring about a "Great Leap Forward" for the Chinese economy. Massive communes were organized where thousands of people lived and worked together like ants in a colony, feverishly trying to increase production on the land and in the factories. During the first year of the "Great Leap" some dramatic progress was made but then came a terrible breakdown in the plan as more and more workers began to react against the frenetic pace and the regimented dehumanization of communalism. As production plummeted and famine threatened, the government backed off and returned, in the sixties, to more realistic socioeconomic approaches and goals ("Walking on Two Legs") but still within the framework of the collectivist Five Year Plans. By the seventies, China had not yet come close to the production levels of the Western powers and Japan, but she had raised the standards of living of her 800 million people to a degree that would have been considered impossible in 1949. Thanks to the diligence of Chinese farmers and agronomists, agricultural production in relation to population has risen sufficiently that the average citizen now enjoys a dependable, above subsistence food supply for the first time in his history. Chinese industry, technology, and science have made even more dramatic advances, especially in the areas of machine production and military hardware. By 1964, despite Russia's refusal to help, China had developed her first nuclear bomb and, by 1971, had orbited her first satellite.

**Domestic Problems.**   Probably the large majority of China's people are content with Mao's system because, despite its suppression, it has given them much. Many however have reacted against it. Hundreds of thousands have left China since 1949. Some who stayed took advantage of Mao's one "liberal" period, in 1957, when he declared his willingness to "let 100 flowers bloom, 100 schools of thought contend." They bloomed but were quickly clipped in Mao's "Rectification Campaign" of 1958. The "100 schools," however, began to contend again after the failure of the Great Leap Forward, and in the sixties occurred the strange phenomenon called the "Great Proletarian Cultural Revolution." This was a factional clash between the radical "Red Guard" groups led by Mao, which favored quick, dramatic change as represented in the Great Leap Forward, and the more moderate groups in the army and bureaucracy, who favored evolutionary change directed by experts and specialists. Many died before Mao could check the fanatical fury of the young Red Guards (perhaps a Chinese manifestation of the worldwide youth rebellion). But factionalism did not die and we believe that today a silent maneuvering for power continues in anticipation of the aging Mao's Death.

**Foreign Policies.**   The foreign policies of Red China, like those of Red Russia, have been guided through the sixties by at least two prime, interconnected motives: first, to reestablish herself as a great world power, perhaps the great world power, in the old image of the "Middle Kingdom" or the "Great Within"; second, to destroy all non-Communist systems everywhere and replace them with Maoist-Marxist systems. Considering these goals, it is not surprising that she has been one of the most aggressive and expansive nations in the Cold War world. Mao has always preached "self-determination" for minority peoples. But after his accession to power in 1949 he proceeded in quick order to absorb the minorities in Manchuria, Inner Mongolia, and the western mountain provinces such as Sinkiang. In 1950, he sent 100,000 troops into Tibet, occupied it, and forced the Dalai Lama to seek refuge in India. In 1954, 1962, and 1967 he caused clashes and continued tensions with India itself by seizing small territories along India's northern frontier. He has championed and tried to exploit the cause of almost every nationalist movement in every underdeveloped area of the world, as in Indochina, the Congo, and Cuba.

**Changes in Foreign Policy.**   During most of the Cold War period China's major antagonist has been the United States, not only because the United States was the leading force in the Anti-Communist bloc but because, more specifically, she prevented China's takeover of Korea, Nationalist Formosa, and the offshore islands, and, possible dominance in Southeast Asia. Prior to the mid-fifties Russia was China's major ally but after the death of Stalin this accord began to deteriorate because of Russia's enunciation of the policy of "peaceful coexistence" with the West and because of her cutting back on aid to China and her refusal to share her nuclear knowledge. As Russo-American relations improved over-all in the sixties, Sino-Russian relations worsened over conflicting territorial claims, and border clashes occurred along the huge frontier from Sinkiang to Manchuria. Also, as Sino-Russian relations worsened, Sino-American relations improved. The Sino-Soviet rift has been a crucial factor in drawing both Russia and China closer to accommodation with the West and leading to a possible détente in the Cold War. In 1972, President Nixon made his amazing goodwill visit to China and in that same year China was finally admitted to the United Nations and given a seat on the Security Council, as Nationalist China resigned in protest. In 1949, China was a backward, chaotic ruin. Today, she is a fast-advancing, unified power, and, potentially, the greatest power in the world. The world trusts she will use this potential in increasingly constructive and peaceful ways.

### Japan

**American Occupation.**   Between 1945 and 1952, Japan was formally controlled by an international Allied Council but, in fact, it was the United States military establishment under the strong command of General Douglas MacArthur, Supreme Commander of Allied Powers (SCAP) which truly governed Japan, and governed it amazingly well. For a combination of reasons this was one of the most successful occupations in modern history. To begin with, Japan had been thoroughly crushed. Her population was decimated, her economy shattered, and her leaders were either dead or discredited. Also her peoples were adaptable and accustomed to obedience and military rule. MacArthur was a very sure and capable military ruler who immediately launched a positive program of relief and reform. Japan was quickly demobilized and a new constitution was drawn up in 1947, built on a Japanese

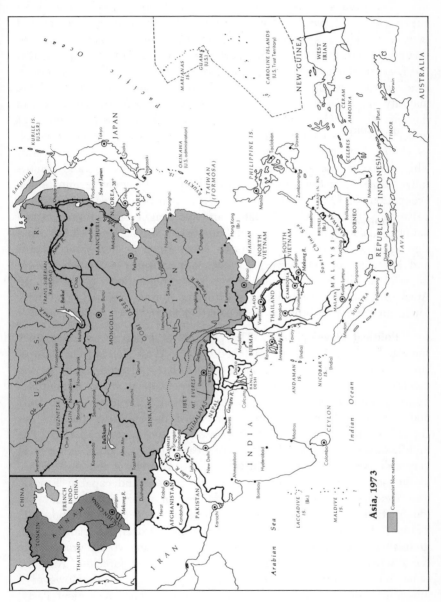

Asia, 1973

Communist bloc nations

**Figure 24-3.**

framework but incorporating many American and British democratic parliamentary elements.

**New Japanese Government.**    This constitution basically created the government of Japan as it exists today. The Emperor still reigns but is now merely a symbolic, ceremonial figurehead without power or divinity. There is a bicameral, parliamentary legislative branch called the Diet, similar to the British House of Commons and House of Lords. The members of the executive branch, or Cabinet, are leaders of the majority party in the Diet and are responsible only to the Diet and the electorate. There is an independent Judiciary with powers of judicial review, a comprehensive Bill of Rights, and an Article 9, which precludes Japanese rearmament or participation in an offensive war. This system was so effective in helping to stabilize, pacify, and democratize Japan that the United States felt it could safely terminate the occupation. In 1951, at San Francisco, a formal peace treaty was signed between Japan, the United States, and forty-eight other former Allied nations. Cold War disagreements prevented Russia and China from signing. The treaty restored Japan's sovereignty in her home islands and her right of self-defense but officially stripped away her former imperial holdings and required moderate reparations payments. In April of 1952, the United States signed a mutual Security Pact with Japan and formally brought its occupation to an end.

**Political Developments.**    The progress of Japan in all areas since the war has been incredible, matched only by West Germany in Europe. In the political sphere the Japanese seem to have adopted "alien" parliamentary democracy as their own and have made it work. A multiple-party system has not led to unstable, coalition governments as in Italy and France. In fact, one party has received the majority vote and has controlled the government during most of the postwar period. The middle-of-the-road Liberal-Democratic Party has produced a series of very able prime ministers, from the revered Yoshida of the early fifties, to the popular Sato of the sixties, to the current and capable Tanaka. The Democratic Socialists on the left remain weak because they are too fractionated and caught in a struggle between the more moderate Trade Union Council, or Sohyo, and the more extreme Socialist Youth groups. The Communists with their very militant youth groups like the Zengakuren are loud but too extreme for most Japanese. And the same may be said for the extremist groups on the right. However a moderate rightist party called the Komeito or Clean Government Party, backed by the popular Buddhist, Soka Gakkai, has been gaining ground rapidly in recent years. These extremisms on both the left and the right, plus the seemingly universal "youth revolt," have certainly affected contemporary Japan. In fact, one of her most serious political problems today, as in most democratic countries, is how to control blind extremism while at the same time fulfilling genuine needs and preserving essential democratic freedoms. Thus far Japan has not reverted to her authoritarian, militaristic tradition.

**Economic Triumph.**   Japan's most phenomenal progress, however, has been economic. After the Communist takeover of China in 1949 and the opening of the Korean War in 1950, the United States began to view Japan as a potential ally and consequently to aid in her economic reconstruction. Programs in land reform, mechanization, and scientific farming increased domestic rice and food production and lessened Japanese dependence on foreign food imports. Japanese capitalists (the Zaibatsu), industrialists, and workers were given new economic aid and incentives and responded to them so magnificently that by 1951 they had restored production in most areas to optimum prewar levels. By 1970, Japan had not only once again become the "Workshop of Asia" but one of the top four or five economic powers in the world, competing for world trade markets on an equal basis with the United States, West Germany, and Russia.

**Social Change.**   This political and economic progress has led to dramatic changes in Japanese social patterns. Japan has become a thoroughly modernized ("Westernized"), industrialized urban society. Her urban population today surpasses her rural population. Tokyo, with its more than 10 million people, is the largest city in the world. Movies, television, pop music and art, musical reviews, night clubs, and baseball have become part of the Japanese way of life. Traditional dress, customs, and social, familial relationships have not disappeared but are being undercut by, or at least asked to share the stage with, the newer cultural patterns and practices.

**Foreign Affairs.**   The combination of devastating defeat in World War II, American postwar occupation, and the treaty stipulations against remilitarization and aggression, have helped to make Japanese postwar foreign policy generally inoffensive and pacific. She officially rejoined the family of nations again through the Peace Treaty and the Security Pact of 1952, and by assuming United Nations membership in 1956. Her diplomatic and trade relations with most countries have been amicable and productive. During the Cold War her moderate governments (though not all of her people) assumed a cautious pro-American, anti-Sino-Soviet stance, but since the "thaw" of the seventies they have eagerly followed the American lead in attempting to improve relationships with their two giant Communist neighbors.

### India and Pakistan

**Independence and Civil War.**   Among the most important of the emerging Third World nations in the postwar period were India and

Pakistan. During the interwar years the Indian nationalist movement, led by Gandhi, Nehru, and the Congress Party, gained force and by the end of World War II it would not be denied. Britain was in no condition to fight it further, and the new Labour government of Attlee was in no mood to deny it. So in 1947, independence was finally granted, but not to a united India. Because of the deep Hindu-Moslem split in the subcontinent, two independent nations were created instead of one. A northwestern and a northeastern section of the subcontinent together became Moslem "Pakistan," while the largest part of the land mass (containing two-thirds of the population) became Hindu "India." No sooner had the settlement been made than a terrible civil war broke out between migrant Hindu and Moslem factions, and before the conflict had run its course more than a million persons died, including Gandhi and Ali Jinnak the Moslem leader. An uneasy peace between the two countries was broken several times in the fifties and sixties and was breached most recently in 1971 when India intervened to help the East Pakistanis achieve independence from West Pakistan and create the new state of Bangladesh.

**Political Developments.** While Pakistan developed an authoritarian, presidential system, controlled generally by military dictators, India created a British-style parliamentary democracy with a cabinet and prime minister responsible to its bicameral legislative body. The liberal National Congress Party, led successively by Nehru, Shastri, and Indira Gandhi, has dominated the Indian multiple-party system from the beginning. Though its power has not yet been seriously challenged on the national level it has faced some sharp attacks from the radical, Communist left and the reactionary Jan Sangh and Swatantra parties of the right. Economically India has followed a moderate, middle way, called "democratic collectivism" or "democratic socialism" featuring close regulation, but not total ownership, of the means of production and distribution.

**Problems.** At this stage, democratic collectivism does not seem to have been as successful in India as Communist collectivism has been in China. Despite the fact that both industrial and agricultral production have risen during the period of independence they have hardly been able to keep pace with the frighteningly rapid growth of the Indian population. Both the Indian birth and death rates are among the highest in the world. So, also, are the levels of poverty, beggary, illiteracy, resistance to change, and narrow localism. India is perhaps the central "test case" in the contemporary world, which may show whether or not democratic collectivism is a strong enough medicine to cure the chronic ailments of a truly massive, depressed, and backward society. India's domestic difficulties are further complicated by her foreign affairs problems. China and Pakistan have been a constant threat on her northern frontier, diverting both her attentions and her funds from domestic concerns to defense needs. Also, she has sought to follow a neutralist policy of nonalignment in the Cold War between the superpowers, but, because of these external threats and critical internal needs she has been forced to seek aid from both sides and has had to struggle constantly to remain clear of ideological commitments to one or the other. If the Cold War should peter out, then India's role as a third world peacemaker would become, happily, less difficult and less necessary.

### Other Nations of Asia

In 1940, almost all of the "lesser" peoples of Asia were still under the domination of one of the imperial powers. Japan held Korea and Formosa; the United States controlled the Philippines; and various European powers held sway over the rest. But the events of World War II so weakened the powers and so stimulated Asian nationalist movements that within a short decade after the war most of the colonial peoples had succeeded in winning their political independence.

**Ceylon, Burma, Malaysia.** Britain not only granted independence to India and Pakistan but also to Ceylon and Burma in 1948. After finally crushing a strong, native Chinese, Communist insurgency in Malaysia, Britain, in the late fifties, also extended independence to the peoples of the Malay Peninsula and Singapore and to the peoples of Sarawak and Sabah in North Borneo. In 1963, all of these countries except Singapore united in the Federation of Malaysia. Singapore, heavily Chinese in population, and dissatisfied with the new political arrangements that allegedly gave too much power to Malay Moslems and Buddhists, held back from the Federation and in 1965 became an independent nation. Both Indonesia and the Philippines claimed the area of North Borneo and, since its annexation, the relations with the Federation have been deteriorating.

**Thailand.** Along with Burma and Malaya, the other areas that constitute the Southeast Asian mainland are Thailand and Indochina. Thailand (formerly Siam) was the only region of Asia never colonized or exploited by the powers, since she served as a kind of buffer between British Burma and French Indochina. She is also the only lesser Asian nation that put up no resistance to Japanese wartime occupation. In fact, she used Japanese cooperation during the war to seize territories in Burma and Indochina. As a result, today, although she is one of the most prosperous and stable of the smaller Asian states, she is also one of the least popular among her neighbors.

**Indochina.** After the war, France struggled desperately to hold on to her Indochinese provinces of Vietnam, Cambodia, and Laos but the

determined nationalist resistance movement of Communist leader Ho
Chi Minh finally brought French defeat at Dien Bien Phu in 1954. By
the Geneva Accord of that same year France agreed to withdraw from
Indochina and to recognize the separate independence and sovereignty
of the three kingdoms. Vietnam was to be temporarily divided into
northern and southern sections until national elections could be held
to determine whether the Vietnamese people preferred the Communist
government of the north or the anti-Communist government of the
south. These elections never took place because basically neither side
trusted the other or was willing to let its fate be decided by electoral
chance. Instead, in 1959, civil war broke out in South Vietnam between
the misdirected government forces of Ngo Dinh Diem and a new, Com-
munist-aligned National Liberation Front called the Viet Cong. Communist North Vietnam, backed by the Soviet Union and Red China,
began to aid the Viet Cong. The United States, fearful of further Communist expansion after Mao's victory in China, and the Berlin and
Korean crises, commenced to send increasing amounts of aid to Diem,
and to the self-seeking array of leaders who succeeded Diem after his
assassination in 1963. Laos and Cambodia were inevitably drawn into
this "Communist—anti-Communist" conflict. All three nations of Indochina not only became the tragic victims of civil war but also inadvertent participants and pawns in the global Cold War between the
powers.

In 1968, when the Indochinese war was at its peak, the United
States had more than 500,000 men in Vietnam and was bombing North
Vietnam with more destructive force than she had used against Germany
in World War II. This awesome show of strength did not succeed in
breaking North Vietnamese resistance but it did turn American and
world opinion more and more sharply against the war. Reacting to
antiwar presures and mounting casualty reports, the embattled governments initiated a long series of peace talks in Paris which accomplished
nothing until the relations between China and the United States started
to improve in the early seventies. Shortly after President Nixon's visit
to Peking, special envoys were sent to Paris by both the American and
North Vietnamese governments and definite progress began to be made
in the peace talks. In 1973, a cease-fire was declared, prisoners of war
were released, and the United States withdrew its last forces from Vietnam. Unfortunately the cease fire has been frequently violated and strife
continues in Cambodia and Laos. But the United States has pledged
that when peace is fully restored she will help to rebuild the devastated
lands of Indochina.

**Indonesia.**   Following World War II, the Dutch fought with the
same determination as the French in Indochina to reestablish themselves in their rich island empire of Indonesia. But they, like the French,

**Figure 24-4.**   Sp. 4 J. E. Relaford keeps watch beside a stream in the mountains southwest of Phu Bai while other members of of his company fill their canteens.

were faced by a strong nationalist, resistance movement which, under its leader, Sukharno, declared independence for Java and Sumatra immediately after the Japanese withdrawal in 1945. The Dutch could not crush this nationalist movement, but the severity of their efforts to do so brought United Nations intervention and forced them first to grant Indonesia commonwealth status within the Empire and finally complete independence in 1950. The new Republic of Indonesia at first looked like a responsible, Western style, parliamentary democracy, but President Sukharno gradually gathered all power into his own hands by playing off against one another the three major interest groups in the country: the army, the Communist Party (PKI), and the Moslem factions. Allegedly because of clashes among these groups, he felt compelled in 1957 to declare martial law, to suspend parliament, and to establish his own absolute, personal control over a system that he called a "guided democracy." He nationalized the shaky economy with no positive effects. He not only claimed neutrality and nonalignment in the Cold War, but prided himself on being a foremost figure among the leaders of the Third World nations, hosting two of their conferences in the fifties.

Despite his avowed neutrality, he began increasingly to oppose Western policies and to draw closer to Communist positions in both foreign and domestic affairs. This tendency he referred to as "active independence." Through the early sixties the powerful army and the predominantly Moslem population gradually became disenchanted with Sukharno's charm, his lavish personal spending, and his pro-Communist leanings. In 1966, an army commander, Suharto, fearing the mounting power of the PKI over the President and the army, seized power from Sukharno and triggered a bloody civil war in Indonesia between the Moslem and Communist elements in the population. Sukharno died in confinement and Suharto has ruled the country as a military strong man since his *coup*. He has made few domestic changes but his foreign policies have been markedly pro-Western.

**The Philippines.**   By the Tydings-McDuffie Act of 1934, the United States guaranteed independence to the Philippines within ten years and began to prepare her people for self-government. World War II and the Japanese occupation disrupted this timetable but in 1946, true to its word, the American government liberated the Philippines and instituted an aid program designed to prop up her chronically weak economy and her experimental, democratic institutions. Unfortunately, neither American aid nor an occasional reform administration, like that of President Ramon Magsaysay (1953–1957), has yet been able to develop a truly viable economy or a stable political system. Because of alleged critical conditions in the country, President Ferdinand Marcos (1965–   ) declared a state of martial law in 1972 and indicated his intention to retain power until a new parliamentary constitution would be drawn up and certain reforms carried out. Only time will tell whether Marcos's actions will mean a genuine extension of democracy or a turn in the direction of authoritarianism. In the Cold War the Philippines aligned herself with the United States against the Communist nations, but her only real postwar clash has been with Malaysia over control of Sabah.

**Manchuria, Formosa, and Korea.**   In 1945, Japan was forced to surrender not only the territories she had conquered during the war but also most of her prewar empire. Manchuria and Formosa, which she had held since 1895, were returned to China. Korea, which she had annexed in 1905, was declared an independent state but was to be "temporarily" divided along the thirty-eighth parallel into two occupation zones. Soviet forces occupied the northern, industrial zone while American troops took control of the more populous, agricultural, southern zone. In North Korea, the Soviets constructed a Communist government modeled on their own system and, in South Korea, the United States created the framework for an American-style, presidential democracy. From the first then, the unfortunate people of Korea were locked into the Cold War struggle between these superpowers and, when the powers withdrew in 1948, they left behind them two separate and antagonistic sister states increasingly in conflict with one another.

**The Korean War.**   Apparently fearing the growing unity and strength of the southern Republic of Korea under its new president, Syngman Rhee, the Communist Democratic Republic launched an attack against its sister state in 1950. The United States, determined to "contain" Communist expansion (as it had not contained Fascist expansion in the thirties), convinced the Security Council to order a United Nations police action against the North Korean aggressors. A largely American, United Nations army, led by General Douglas MacArthur, quickly took the offensive and within a few weeks drove the invaders back deep into their own territory. Seemingly on the verge of defeat, the North Koreans were saved by massive reinforcements of Red Chinese "volunteers" sweeping down out of Manchuria. MacArthur now urged direct action against China itself but President Truman, conscious of the possible consequences of a full-scale war with China and perhaps Russia, ordered the continuation of "limited war" and the conflict settled into a grim stalemate along the thirty-eighth parallel. After interminable peace talks an armistice was finally signed at Pusan in 1953.

**Since the War.** During the fifties and sixties, relations remained strained between North and South Korea just as relations have been strained between their respective allies, China and the United States. There have been frequent border clashes and incidents, such as the Pueblo affair in 1968, involving the North Korean capture of an American gunboat. Both Syngman Rhee and his successor, Park Chung-hi have maintained close defensive alliances with the United States and have sent troops to aid in South Vietnam. Similarly, North Korean leader, Kim Il Sung has negotiated defensive pacts with Red China. Since the beginning of the Cold War thaw, however, relations between the two Koreas have noticeably improved and there has even been some talk of a possible future reunification.

### Europe in Asia

**Siberia, Hong Kong, Macao.** Of the once vast holdings of Europe in Asia there are left today only Soviet Siberia, parts of which are coveted by China; British Hong Kong and Brunei; Portuguese Macao, which exists primarily on the sufferance of China; some scattered Pacific islands; and the Commonwealth nations of Australia and New Zealand.

**Australia and New Zealand.** The position of these latter two nations is particularly interesting. One outstanding fact about them is their relative geographic isolation, tucked away as they are in the southernmost corner of the South Pacific and surrounded by ocean. This isolation helps to explain why they were among the last areas touched upon by European explorers and why few Asian peoples, until recently, paid them much attention. But in the past century, as the world has grown smaller, its population larger, land hunger greater, and transportation easier, the "wide open spaces" of Australia and New Zealand have been eyed with increasing interest by jaded, crowded Europeans and Americans, but also by larger numbers of depressed and crowed Asians. The Japanese, of course, almost turned their yearning into reality in 1942. Only American naval power thwarted them. It is almost a certainty that the current Chinese government, in its drive for more living space, has not limited its thinking to Russian Siberia. And the Marxian prohibition against imperial expansion does not seem to apply to Marxists. Certainly it would not apply to Maoist, Asian Marxists who covet European-held territory in Asia. The Australians and New Zealanders have always been aware of the delicacy of their position in relation to their Asian neighbors and they have developed some of the strongest immigration regulations in the world to try to avoid ethnic inundation. But in the future it may well be that neither these regulations nor declining Anglo-American naval strength will withstand the rising force of Asian economic and population pressures.

**Postwar Conditions.**    Certainly there has been much to envy in the postwar life of Australia and New Zealand. Their governments have remained stable and democratic. Their economies have been generally sound and expansive. They have developed one of the most complete social welfare programs in the world, without suffering exorbitant taxes or loss of freedom. Like Canada and India, they still maintain a formal tie with the British Empire Commonwealth, which carries with it no real political obligations but which has provided some very real economic benefits over the years. These benefits may diminish, however, if Britain moves closer into the orbit of the European Economic Community.

## The Middle East

### Independence and Problems
Five of the nine nations of the Middle East were already politically independent before World War II: Afghanistan, Iran, Turkey, Iraq, and Saudi Arabia. Syria and Lebanon were freed by France in 1945; Jordan, by Britain in 1946; and Israel (Palestine) declared her own independence in 1948. Unfortunately for the people in most of these states, independence has led neither to economic security nor to political stability and freedom. Israel, Lebanon, and Turkey are the only three who have developed modern, productive economies capable of lifting the standard of living of the masses above subsistence level. They are also the only three who have established any sort of representative government, and even Turkey's system has sometimes been shaky and army dominated. All the other states have authoritarian political systems, essentially either military monarchies or military dictatorships, frequently changing and inevitably maintained by force. Shah Reza Pahlevi of Iran and King Hussein of Jordan have demonstrated some reformist tendencies, but few of the arbitrary rulers of Iraq, Afghanistan, Syria, or the Arab states have shown any real concern for the needs of their people. Instead they have gen-

erally been concerned with self-aggrandizement, self-enrichment, oil rights and profits, internecine power struggles, and plotting the destruction of the hated Jewish state of Israel.

### Israel
Israel was created out of the British Arabic Mandate of Palestine. Between 1945 and 1948, despite Arab and British resistance, Palestine was flooded with a tide of Jewish refugees seeking a new homeland where they could put the memories of Hitler's Europe behind them. They were finally moving to fulfill the once-shattered Zionist dream of an independent Jewish nation. But the Arabs looked upon the influx as an invasion of their lands and began to take action to repel it. The British custodians, caught in the middle, first tried unsuccessfully to stem the tide and then called upon the United Nations to adjudicate the conflict. Before the United Nations could act, however, the Jewish leadership declared the creation of the sovereign state of Israel. Having repelled a first Arab effort to dislodge them in 1948, the Israelis proceeded with amazing skill and energy, while under constant threat of Arab attack, to construct the most progressive, prosperous, and democratic state in the Middle East.

### Africa
Perhaps even more remarkable than the postwar independence movements in Asia and the Middle East has been the rapid, and relatively smooth, postwar decolonization of the huge, multicolonied continent of Africa. In 1945, out of a total of more than 40 African states, only three were independent of European political controls. By 1970 approximately 35 had gained independence.

### Egypt
The first African nation to slip the bonds of colonialism was Egypt, in 1952. In 1952 the weak irresponsible monarchy of King Farouk was overthrown in a military coup, led by General Mohammed Naguib and Colonel Abdel Gamal Nasser. In 1954, Nasser emerged as virtual president-dictator of the new Republic of Egypt (called, after 1958, the United Arab Republic) and began to socialize and nationalize the Egyptian economy. He sought aid in his rebuilding program from both the United States and Russia and attempted to remain neutral in their Cold War conflict. But when the United States refused to finance his pet Aswan Dam project he turned more and more toward Russia for both economic and military assistance. In 1956, his effort to nationalize the Suez Canal led to a brief war with Britain, France, and Israel in which Egypt was saved only by the intercession of the two superpowers and the United Nations.

**Nasser's Policies.** Although Nasser, in the long run, did little to improve the economic or social condition of his people he did much to restore their pride, and the pride of the Arabic peoples in general. Like Tito, Nehru, and Sukharno, he also saw himself as a champion of the third world nations against the great powers. Under his leadership, Egypt became a dominant force among the Arabic nations of the Middle East and North Africa. He stimulated Arabic nationalism and he attempted to develop a Pan-Arab union. Thus far, however, Pan-Arabism has not gone beyond a few wordy conferences and the abortive Egyptian-Syrian "United Arab Republic" of 1958. Even the common hatred for Israel, which Nasser and most Arab leaders have exploited to the fullest, has failed to bring the widely divergent Arab states together. In fact, the constantly disruptive activities of the anti-Israel, Palestine guerrillas and the failures of Arab arms against Israel in 1948 and 1956 and in the humiliating "Six Day War" of 1967, and the "Yom Kippur War" of 1973, have probably done more to weaken Arab unity than to strengthen it. Nasser's death in 1970 did nothing to improve Egypt's position or to bring the Arab states closer together. His successor, Anwar Sadat, inherited Nasser's problems and goals but not the master's charisma or prestige. As long as his all-consuming aim continues to be the build-up of military force for the destruction of Israel, he can neither do without the worrisome presence of anti-Israeli Russia nor can he seek assistance again from pro-Israeli America. Worst of all, he cannot attend to the pressing domestic problems of the Egyptian people.

### African Independence

In the spirit of the postwar period, and following the example of Egypt, most of the remaining African nations sought, and gained, their independence in the fifties and the sixties: Italian Libya in 1952; French Tunisia and Morocco and the British Sudan in 1956; and French Algeria in 1962 after five years of grim colonial war. South of the Sahara most of French West Africa, French Equatorial Africa, British East and West Africa, and the Congo were given independence between 1960 and 1966. The only areas still in European hands in 1970 were the Spanish colony of the Sahara; the Portuguese colonies of Guinea, Cabinda, Angola, and Mozambique; and the independent southern African countries of Rhodesia and the Union of South Africa, where the large white ruling minorities strive to maintain a "safe" distance between themselves and the black majority through the imposition of a strict segregation plan called "apartheid."

### Conclusions

These few European islands seem reasonably secure today but, with the tide of Black African nationalism still running so strong across the

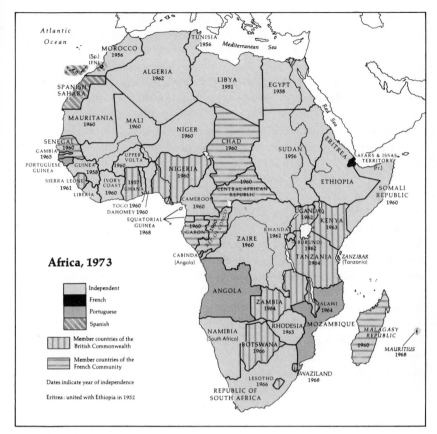

Africa, 1973

Independent
French
Portuguese
Spanish

Member countries of the
British Commonwealth

Member countries of the
French Community

Dates indicate year of independence

Eritrea: united with Ethiopia in 1952

**Figure 24-5.**

continent, it would be difficult indeed to predict what their life expectancy might be. It seems a strong probability, however, that by the end of this century there will be no European colonies left either in Africa or Asia.

Having given the underdeveloped nations their political independence it is to be hoped that the more advanced nations will now help them to help themselves to achieve genuine political stability and some degree of economic independence and security. Failing this, the world can anticipate a continuation and intensification of international conflict.

## A Summary of the Twentieth Century

### Age of Conflict

The twentieth century has been called an "Age of Conflict." A review of the historical record will indicate the accuracy of that description. The century opened with the startling Japanese victory over Russia in 1905, marking the emergence of Japan as a new and powerful Westernized nation-state and the decline of European Russia. The Chinese Revolution of 1911 further illustrated the new ferment in Asia, as well as the passage of the old order in China. A few years later the old order in Europe also came crashing down in the debacle of World War I and the great upheaval of the Russian Bolshevik Revolution of 1917. The reverberations from these events were felt throughout the world, and not the least, in Europe's overseas empire. Afer a short decade of splendid isolation and prosperity the mighty American economic machine also broke down, causing a crash and depression that lasted throughout the thirties and ultimately affected almost every nation across the globe.

Out of the ensuing social and political chaos emerged the belligerent forces of German and Italian Fascism and Japanese militarism. In 1937, Japan invaded China and in 1939 Nazi Germany invaded Poland, precipitating the second terrible World War in 20 years. The first atomic bombs were developed and dropped on Japan, large areas of Europe and Asia were shattered, and man began to consider how close he was to achieving a total destructive capacity. At the end of the war the former great powers of Europe were broken (along with the traditional balance-of-power concept) and they were compelled to release their colonial holdings. The United States and the Soviet Union emerged as the two most powerful nations in the world and immediately proceeded to initiate an ideological conflict with one another that has been called the Cold War. Clearly, the twentieth century has earned its title as an "Age of Conflict."

### Age of Change

This century has also been called, with equal justification, an "Age of Crisis and Change." Of course all ages experience change, but what makes the twentieth century distinctive is the volume and speed of change. Old patterns have been broken, and new ones formed, with numbing rapidity. Cultural patterns are dispersed worldwide within a few years or even a few months. For example, nationalism and industralism spread out of the Western world and across Asia and Africa within a half-century. In 1945, there were perhaps only a dozen nations in Asia and Africa that were independent—twenty-five years later almost all of them were. Rome's dominance in the ancient Mediterranean had lasted over 500 years—American and Russian postwar dominance lasted for less than thirty.

The spread of modern nationalism, industrialism, science, technology, and medicine has helped to create the mounting worldwide crisis of overpopulation. And in its turn, the population "explosion" has been largely responsible for many other contemporary problems, such as environmental spoliation, food and water shortages, extreme urban congestion, and a dangerous aggravation of both individual and social tensions. Other twentieth-century phenomena related to the rise of "mass-man" are educational and cultural democratization and the decline of "elitism"; the development of collectivistic tendencies in most societies, whether Communist, Fascist, or democratic; and the growth of standardization and conformity in dress, customs, and ideologies.

### The Sciences

While the "practical" men of affairs were attempting to lead the world through this century of turbulence and change, and while the world's masses were being buffeted by a dizzying succession of wars, depressions, and revolutions, many men of thought, science, and the arts were also busy helping to create the century's rapid flow of events. In fact, the men of science, in particular, must be given a giant share of both credit and responsibility for the pace of change in modern times. Building upon the data and hypotheses of their illustrious predecessors of earlier centuries, and using dramatically improved instruments and techniques, modern scientists have virtually initiated an "intellectual-scientific" revolution which would seem to be at least as consequential as the "economic-industrial," the "political-nationalist," or the "social-collectivist" revolutions of the modern periods.

**Astronomy.** Astronomers have seen 10 billion light years into the macrocosmic universe and have calculated the existence of 10 billion galaxies. Even though observers like Moulton, Jeans, and Gamow have not been able to give us any conclusive theories about universal beginnings and endings, they have been able to tell us much about the nature of the cosmos and to provide information that has made the incredible postwar moon landings possible and phylogenic immortality conceivable.

**Physics and Astrophysics.** The science of physics has been concerned with probing the nature and relation of matter, motion, and energy; and the instruments of physics and math are used today as frequently as telescopes to unlock the secrets of the heavens. These astronomical probings with the methods of physics have led to the development of a hybrid science called astrophysics. Earlier Newtonian physics of the Enlightenment period had postulated a typically ordered, mechanistic universe whose "natural laws" could ultimately be discovered by reason. Matter, motion, and energy were parts of the same universal machine but were essentially separate phenomena. The work of such physicists as Rutherford, Clerk-Maxwell, Roentgen, Planck, and Einstein in the late nineteenth and early twentieth centuries pointed out some inadequacies in the Newtonian system. In his Theory of Relativity published in 1915, Albert Einstein united the concepts of mass, motion, and energy, along with time, as a "fourth dimension," and at the time of his death was working toward a universal formula that would incorporate all phenomena. Max Planck's Quantum Theory proposed that the ultimate "material unit" could never be observed but only studied in its effects and was, in fact, a subatomic "wave particle" or "package of energy" (a quantum). The Uncertainty Principle of Werner Heisenberg declares that it is impossible to check simultaneously the precise velocity and the location of "a quantum" or subatomic particle, not because of observer inadequacy but because of the nature of the particle itself. The proof of its actual existence lies in its harnessing and use in revolutionary technological devices such as atomic generators, or, atomic bombs. All of these new theories present us with the view of a universe much more complex, and much less comprehensible and predictable than the universe of our ancestors.

**Chemistry and Biochemistry.**   Chemistry has developed no new theories to match those in physics but it has continued to search out and classify new elements and combinations of elements, to the total of some 120 today. Its most important work is done, however, in the practical fields of commerce and medicine. Chemists are constantly at work trying to produce improved synthetic products like rubber, plastics, textiles, and fertilizers and pesticides that have helped to revolutionize agriculture. Unfortunately, neither their very valuable work in agronomy or in chemical birth control has sufficiently affected most of the backward countries, and people continue to die because of overpopulation. When chemists deal with the chemical compounds and processes of plant and animal organisms they are called biochemists and, in conjunction with doctors and biologists, they have developed a wide variety of tremendously useful drugs and medicines, such as the antihistamines and the antibiotic sulfas, Fleming's penicillin and Salk and Sabin's polio vaccine. Unfortunately, however, extensive research has thus far failed to find a way to successfully combat virus infection and cancer.

**Biology.**   In the 100 years since Darwin's publication of the famous *Origin of Species,* his theory of biological evolution has been so thoroughly tested and validated that, for many persons, the "theory" has become "law." Certainly it has become one of the most commonly accepted and affective ideas in modern history. The theory, of course, explains how one species may perish and another survive through the process of "natural selection" and "survival of the fittest" but it does not explain how a new species is originally created. In the pursuit of an answer to that question the science of genetics was born. Men like Mendel, Weismann, and de Vries intensively studied genetic development in both plants and animals and discovered how traits were transferred through combinations of chromosomes in the genes of special germ cells. Further research since World War II has uncovered basic constituents of the germ cell called amino, nucleic, and deoxyribonucleic acids which, the biologists tell us, are the basic building blocks of life, and probably reproducible by man. Man already uses artificial insemination and has been able to make exact duplications of simple life forms (cloning). He may be rapidly approaching the day when he will be able artificially to create and shape human life. If so, he stands on the threshold of the most fantastically important development since the beginning of life itself.

**Technology.** Science and industry together have also produced in this century an amazing and dizzying revolution in the area of technology and automation. Machines have become more dominant each year, taking over vast new areas of human work and "thought." Machines can register, store, transfer, and reproduce information in greater volume and with greater rapidity and efficiency than humans. Machines have transformed both human transportation and communication. Within a single century, man has moved from the horse and buggy to 100-mile-per-hour autos and trains, and from boxkite aircraft to supersonic flight and space ships. In that same century he has moved from primitive crystal set to television and orbiting communications satellites, carrying words and pictures instantaneously across ten thousand miles. These great technological advances and a thousand others have certainly given the average man relief from drudging labor, and some recreational freedom for the first time in history. The manner in which he uses this new leisure time will fundamentally affect the quality of his life in the future.

**Psychology.** Probably the most dynamic of the social, or behavioral, sciences in this century has been psychology. In 1900 Ivan Pavlov helped lay the foundation for a new behaviorist school of psychology with his canine experiments on "conditioned reflexes." But certainly one of the most influential thinkers of the modern period was Sigmund Freud, who around the turn of the century developed a strikingly new approach to the study of the human mind, called psychoanalysis. He believed that besides the conscious, rational, regulative area of the brain there was another, unknown, subterranean level, which he called the subconscious mind or libido, containing urges or emotions stored and suppressed since infancy. He declared that the emotional content of this unconscious mind is primarily sexual and that when it breaks through the conscious layer it causes the individual to act irrationally and antisocially. Freud used free-association hypnotism and dream analysis to get to the deeply buried subconscious root of his patient's problems. Most psychologists have accepted Freud's notion of the existence of the subconscious and the importance of suppressed emotions but many, even of his own students, have disagreed with some of his techniques and his central emphasis on sexual motivation. One of Freud's chief disciples, Carl Jung, placed his emphasis on the collective, social content of the subconscious and the urge for approval and prestige. Another student, Alfred Adler, underlined the importance of the drive for superiority and self-assertion.

In recent decades there has been considerable reaction by Gestaltists, Radical Therapists, and others against certain Freudian principles and practices, but the basic insights of Freud seem likely to remain as important and germinal in the field of psychology as those of Darwin in biology and Newton and Einstein in the physical sciences.

### Philosophy

Twentieth-century philosophy has followed the lead of society and science in its adherence to the theme of relativism and scepticism. The empirical pragmatists, such as John Dewey in the United States and Bertrand Russell in England held that values are relative and that "what works is good"; that ideas and institutions are not ends but only instruments or means for the purpose of improving human life. Henri Bergson's view, popular between the wars, held that life was a constantly flowing force (élan vital) which cannot be grasped by man's intellect at all but only by his "intuition." The most publicized postwar schools of thought are really "antiphilosophical," rooted in the thinking of Neitzsche and Kierkegaarde. The Existentialists like Sartre and Camus, say that the only thing we can be sure of in life is individual existence and that the only value is the freedom to make choices and to accept responsibility for those choices. The universe, itself, is completely alien and irrational; man cannot know it and should not try. The so-called Logical Empiricism of Wittgenstein and Carnap declares that philosophy is meaningless because it asks questions that cannot be answered. Both groups deny the validity of value systems and essentially take the view that "anything goes."

### Religion

Perhaps because of the general feeling of rootlessness and insecurity, many people have turned back to a religious faith in both the Eastern and Western worlds. Some have returned to rigid orthodoxy and fundamentalism; some to established "status religions"; many to "secular faiths" like Communism or Fascism; reacting against the system, increasing numbers in the West have looked to Eastern mysticism, cultivism, and even witchcraft. Some have followed Paul Tillich in his belief that the traditional, personal God "is dead," that God *is* being, or ultimate reality, not a *part* of being. At any rate, religion like most other areas of life, is in a state of flux and uncertainty.

### The Arts

The arts sometimes anticipate and sometimes simply reflect the conditions of a society, but always they abstract and intensify those conditions that affect the individual artist most. It is clear that what has most affected the Western artist from 1914 to 1973 has been pessimism, ugliness, emptiness, and decay. He has tended to become more subjective, symbolic, abstract, and less objective descriptive, and representational. He looks into himself, and inner feeling becomes more important than external communication. In style and method he has generally discarded traditional patterns and given himself over to free-flowing experimentation. Eastern, Communist art, on the other hand, has either remained traditionalist or has been confined in the strait jacket of "socialist realism."

### Literature

Clearly Western literature reflects all of the previously mentioned characteristics. James Joyce's *Ulysses* beautifully illustrates the stylistic breaking of patterns, and experimentation. He uses a so-called "stream of consciousness" technique, paying no attention to traditional grammatical form but simply putting down his thought in any order they occur. Emotional feeling rather than rational communication is the object. Exposure of the inner man is all-important in this literary "voyage through the psyche." In the works of T. S. Eliot, Marcel Proust, Albert Camus, and Jean-Paul Sartre the felt emptiness and absurdity of the contemporary world and the alienation of man are dominant themes. F. Scott Fitzgerald reflected perfectly in his life and works the vacuous search for "fun" and escape in the American twenties. Eugene O'Neill, Tennessee Williams, Arthur Miller, and Edward Albee paint tragic portraits of the sickness and crassness of society and the terror of failure and of loneliness in the modern world. Even contemporary Russian authors like Pasternak and Solzhenitsyn or Yevtushenko and Sinyavsky write of Soviet man's inhumanity to man, and of hopelessness and sterility within the collectivist societies.

### Painting and Sculpture

The painter and the sculptor followed the same general approach as the writer. Working in their own media they experimented with the subjective expression of their own souls. They abstracted and dissected nature and reproduced her through the prism of their inner eye. Dali's surrealism and Pablo Picasso's abstract paintings tell a clear story of disgust and rage against the cruelties and stupidities of life as they saw it. It is difficult to know what Jackson Pollock and the recent representatives of Pop Art are trying to say—perhaps nothing. They may be carrying out a great public hoax, or they may simply be cynically reflecting some of the tawdry, automated confusion of our time.

### Architecture

In architecture, the tendency in the works of such men, as Sullivan, Wright, Fuller, and Gropius has been to make "form follow function," to believe that harmony, simplicity, good design, and the construction materials themselves will create beauty with no need for superficial adornment. Their towering steel and glass skyscrapers, geodes, domes, and gracefully functional residential structures are excellent representations of the twentieth century building arts.

## Music

In music, we are witnessing the same breakdown of old classical forms and the same subjectivist experimental approach as in the visual arts. The innovative, but still romantic, impressionism of Claude Debussy in the early nineteen hundreds becomes distortion, atonality, and even cacophony in some of the music of Bartok, Honegger, Stravinsky, and Schoenburg later in the century. Schoenburg even developed a special twelve-tone scale to mark a clean break with western musical tradition.

Popular music, both recorded and "live," more than almost any other art form, illustrates the faddishness and the dizzying pace of change in our twentieth-century mass society. It also illustrates the rapid global dispersion of modern cultural patterns. Jazz, the Blues, Swing, Rock, and many other musical styles have spread across the world and have, with increasing regularity, succeeded one another in the popular fancy. Of the thousands of musical practitioners who have appeared briefly in the public spotlight, only a handful will be remembered beyond tomorrow as genuine creators and artists—George Gershwin, Kurt Weil, W. C. Handy, Louis Armstrong, perhaps Glen Miller, Benny Goodman, and the Beatles. But the voracious appetite of contemporary man for change and novelty allows the artist and his work less and less time for a reflective hearing.

The cinema and television, as popular art forms, have had an incredible impact on twentieth-century society. They have played a major role in shaping modern man's styles, manners, and thinking. Their output has been vast and, at its best, ennobling and inspirational. Unfortunately, too often the output has been shoddy, shallow, and escapist, tending to produce a body of inert observers, perhaps superficially sophisticated and knowledgeable, but with a weakened capacity for dealing with the realities of life beyond the fantasy world of the "screen" or the "tube." For many people movies and television have become more desirable and absorbing than their own lives. The media, the image, the word have become the reality, as Marshall McLuhan has said. The answer, of course, is not to eliminate movies and television, but to try to improve their content so that their unparalleled educative and esthetic potential can be realized. Beyond that, we must strive to improve the quality of real life, to make it "competetive" with the life of fantasy.

## Epilogue

In one sense every age in history is equally important because history, like life, is a connected whole, a continuous flow. Every event issues from, and is effected by, the events and the times that have pre-

**Figure 24-6.** Regency Hyatt House, San Francisco. Photo by Steve Lux (Light Unlimited).

ceded it, and will affect the ages that follow it. Yet, in another sense, certain ages and events are more crucial than others because they mark "new beginnings" or "turning points" in history.

Certainly all lists of "great events" would logically have to begin with the creation of the universe itself. Next in importance, from the human point of view at least, would be the creation of the earth; the evolution of life-forms on the earth; the appearance of man himself. The uniqueness and the importance of man lay in the special quality of his reasoning power which enabled him to see himself apart from nature and to consciously use or manipulate his natural environment. Although prehistoric man remained a simple food gatherer and hunter like other animals, he did develop the first distinctly human tools, art, and social patterns.

The next great turning point came between 5000 and 10,000 years ago, when man started to convert his primitive cultures into more advanced civilizations by trying actively to control his environment rather than simply using it. He learned to partially control food supply by domesticating animals and cultivating the land. He developed more complex economic and political organizations, which enabled him to harness river waters, build cities, make war, and retain his social security as he drifted further away from nature. He discovered, or invented, gods to help him "control" everything, and later worked out idea systems or philosophies to help him better understand the universe and his increasingly uncertain place in it.

The fifteenth-century "Renaissance" in Europe marked the beginning of another great generative period in human history when man took several giant steps forward in his knowledge of the world and his ability to control his environment. These steps were, in fact, so consequential that they may justly be termed "revolutions." Man's development of a new "scientific method" of thought, for example, launched a dramatic intellectual or scientific revolution. His voyages of exploration and discovery resulted in a veritable geographical revolution and a shrinking of the globe. His groping for more stability and order produced a kind of political revolution which we have called "nationalism." And all of these forces together helped to generate fundamental economic revolutions in technology, commerce, and industry.

These sweeping revolutions had changed the face of the earth and had brought civilization, by the last quarter of the 20th century, to perhaps the most critical stage since its inception. They had given man a more complete control over his environment than he had ever known, but at the same time had given him the power to totally destroy this environment. They had tremendously increased his knowledge of the physical and economic world, but had not taught him enough about himself and his relationship with other humans and with nature. Today man seems to have reached a most crucial historical crossroad. If he can rediscover his place in nature and learn to live more harmoniously with his fellow man, he can move into a new "Golden Age." If his survival instrument—his mind—fails him, and he cannot make the necessary adjustments, then it seems likely that human civilization as we know it will be destroyed—either quickly by some lethal device like the bomb or gradually through environmental spoliation, nervous prostration, and societal breakdown. Man himself will decide whether the strife and turbulence of the twentieth century will prove to be the death throes of human civilization or the birth pains of a new and more hopeful age.

# Index